THE · WORLD · OF
Plácido Domingo

THE · WORLD · OF
Plácido Domingo

Daniel Snowman

McGRAW-HILL BOOK COMPANY

NEW YORK   ST. LOUIS   SAN FRANCISCO
TORONTO   HAMBURG   MEXICO

First published in England 1985 by The Bodley Head
9 Bow Street, Covent Garden, London WC2E 7AL
First U.S. publication 1985 by McGraw-Hill Book Company

1 2 3 4 5 6 7 8 9 D O C D O C 8 7 6 5

ISBN 0-07-059527-5

Library of Congress Cataloging in Publication Data

Snowman, Daniel.
The world of Placido Domingo.
1. Domingo, Plácido, 1941–   . 2. Singers—Biography.
I. Title.
ML420.D63S6 1985   782.1'092'4 [B]   84-29990
ISBN 0-07-059527-5

CONTENTS

ILLUSTRATIONS

(Thanks are due to the owners of copyright photographic material whose names are listed below in parentheses.)

Central Park, New York, June 1981: Domingo acknowledges the applause of some 250,000 people at the Met's free, open-air *Tosca* (J. Heffernan)

Sherrill Milnes, Renata Scotto and Domingo in Central Park, New York, June 1981, after the rehearsal of *Tosca* (Barbara Lorber)

Domingo in the CBS recording studio, August 1982. Left to right: Lee Holdridge, Rosemary Okun, Milton Okun, recording engineer Mike Ross, Plácido Domingo (CBS News, 'Sixty Minutes')

Domingo as Don Carlo over the murdered body of his friend Rodrigo (Louis Quilico) at the Metropolitan Opera, New York, March 1983 (J. Heffernan)

Kiri Te Kanawa and Domingo (in his ACT III cloak) rehearsing *Manon Lescaut* at Covent Garden, April 1983 (Catherine Ashmore)

Domingo, Sir John Tooley and the Queen Mother at the first night of *Manon Lescaut* at Covent Garden, May 1983 (Christina Burton)

Marilyn Zschau arrives on the scene to rescue Domingo from hanging. A rehearsal of *La Fanciulla del West*, Madrid, June 1983 (Clive Barda)

Domingo's father and mother, the Queen and King of Spain, Marta and Plácido Domingo during the interval of *La Fanciulla del West*, Madrid, June 1983 (Gyenes, Madrid)

Domingo in his Don José costume talking to the youngsters assembled in the Cinema Merced in Ronda, July 1983 (Marta Domingo)

Domingo off-duty in Ronda during the filming of *Carmen* (Marta Domingo)

Domingo rehearsing the Orchestre National de France, Paris, October 1983, prior to *Le Grand Echiquier* (Marta Domingo)

Curtain call after *Die Fledermaus* at Covent Garden, 31 December 1983. Left to right: Kiri Te Kanawa, Hermann Prey, Domingo, Benjamin Luxon (Zoe Dominic)

Domingo in Vienna on his 43rd birthday, with his sons Alvaro *(left)* and Placi *(right)*, and Austrian football star Hans Krankl (Axel Zeininger)

After the first night of *Carmen in Vienna*, January 1984. The photo includes Ruggero Raimondi and Franco Zeffirelli (top left), Lorin Maazel (top middle), Faith Esham (top, second from right, in blonde wig), Domingo and Ages Baltsa (centre, front) (Axel Zeininger)

THE · WORLD · OF
Plácido Domingo

INTRODUCTION

I was taken to my first opera, *Rigoletto* at the Cambridge Theatre, London, by my father when I was eight. After the first scene he leaned towards me and asked benignly if I had had enough and would I prefer to go home? I replied roundly that I most certainly did not want to go home; why, they had not even reached most of the bits I knew from his record collection! I insisted on staying to the end of the performance and of course enjoyed every minute. From that night I was irretrievably hooked.

In 1972, twenty-five opera-saturated years after my first *Rigoletto*, I happened to be in Los Angeles at the time of the annual visit of the New York City Opera. Among the performances for which I booked was one of *Carmen* in which the tenor was to be the young Plácido Domingo, already by reputation, and by the evidence of his early recordings, one of the most stunningly endowed of the younger generation of singers. The performance of *Carmen* was good, if under-rehearsed, but Domingo's portrayal of Don José was over-whelming and for me opened up an entirely new era of opera. Here was a man with a voice of gold, tall and handsome, and—wonder of wonders—capable of acting as well. He could sing as elegantly as Carlo Bergonzi or Luciano Pavarotti, was as sensitive to musical meaning as Nicolai Gedda, sounded and looked as heroic as Franco Corelli, and acted with voice and body with the passionate conviction (and none of the mannerisms) of Jon Vickers. There was no mistaking the intense commitment of this performer. He was never out of character even when momentarily out of the musical or

1

dramatic spotlight, yet nothing in his acting or his singing appeared to be forced. He seemed to ride with the score, swim with the musical-dramatic tide, gain and project strength from his inner understanding of the forces of which he was part. Never before had I heard such lyrical singing allied to such dramatic intensity—hitherto, indeed, I had tended to consider these qualities mutually exclusive. Yet Domingo effected a marriage of the operatic arts with such consummate skill and apparent ease.

Over the ensuing years I came to hear and see Domingo perform a good many times, most often in London but also in various cities of Europe and the USA, in over a score of different operatic roles. The consistent all-round quality of his performances, the regular displays of vocal, musical and dramatic art of the highest level, are in my experience unmatched and the promise of that first *Carmen* has been fulfilled on more or less every subsequent occasion on which I have seen him perform. As he approaches his mid-forties, Domingo has already given 1,700 performances (well over twice as many as Callas in her entire career), has sung altogether some eighty different operatic roles (compared with the sixty-odd of Caruso and Gigli, and Pavarotti's thirty), and has already recorded—twice or even three times in several cases—around fifty of them. On top of all this Domingo nowadays appears frequently on television in all the countries in which he performs, singing or conversing in any of five languages, and he has also found time to develop subsidiary careers as a conductor and as a singer of middle-of-the-road 'pop' music.

In addition to his wide-ranging talents as an artist, Domingo seems to be a man genuinely at one with himself, a member of that lucky band whose capacities, needs and outlets appear to feed eagerly upon each other. He seems to know when to expend and when to conserve his energies, is intensely competitive yet generous to a fault with colleagues. His patience and good humour at rehearsals are a by-word in the opera houses of the world, yet so is the intensity of his performances once on stage. A man of immense personal charm with a magnetic impact upon women, yet he is a deeply and genuinely committed husband and father. A bundle of contradictions? Possibly. Yet in many ways Domingo seems successfully to have integrated artistic and personal qualities that in most remain either unachieved or at best awkwardly at odds.

What makes Domingo tick? What impels him to work so hard, to perform so frequently, to record as much as he does? And what sort of price has he paid, physically, mentally and psychologically, for his dazzling array of achievements? Questions such as these are not susceptible to simple answers. Or, rather, the obvious answers—that Domingo likes his work and enjoys communicating his pleasure to others—can scarcely tell the whole story. Any serious attempt to tackle the question of what motivates a figure like Plácido Domingo must involve some consideration not only of Domingo's own conscious and possibly subconscious motives but also of the wider world within which he operates—the way opera houses and recording companies conduct their business, the role of the modern media of mass communication and transportation, and so on. We are all products of the interaction of our talents, inner drives and external circumstances, and the pages that follow will inevitably weave in and out of these three dimensions.

Much of the book describes Domingo at work and will, I hope, give some idea of the flavour of his professional life—the alternating intensity and *longueurs*, the constant artistic refining, the moments of humour and relaxation. We see him rehearsing and performing opera in Italy, Austria, Spain, Britain and the United States, follow him into the recording studio and watch him working on his 'pop' albums. We see him preparing for a television show, wearied by an almost insupportably hectic schedule yet bracing himself to do his best once the cameras and microphones are switched on. We catch him in the opera house during the countdown as performance time approaches, signing autographs or dining with friends afterwards, relaxing at home with his wife and sons. Above all, we obtain a privileged view of a great artist at the height of his powers as he devotes hour after hour, day after day, to the painstaking process of working on a new role or production or polishing a familiar one, gradually building it up until it is ready to be unveiled before the public. People who see and hear the finished product of outstanding artistic endeavour often have little idea of the effort that has preceded it, the days and weeks of stage and musical working and re-working that are

3

necessary prerequisites to a successful operatic production. If Domingo is perceived (correctly but inadequately) as living a high-powered, glamorous, jet-set existence, these pages also reveal him as a patient, practical craftsman devoted to his art, most of whose work takes place outside the public spotlight. A compulsive performer striving to receive the plaudits of the crowds everywhere he goes? Perhaps. But also an intensely serious artist who never stints in his dedication to the art he serves and loves. Both sides of this complex personality can be observed in the way Domingo paces himself through the constant barrage of challenges and opportunities he sets for himself.

In addition to watching Domingo at work I have also tried to place him in a broader context. Domingo's varied career in fact provides a useful launching pad for some consideration of, for instance: the role of the electronic media in helping to make a traditionally élite art like opera more popularly accessible; the pros and cons of recordings *vis-à-vis* live performances; the demands on the superstar in the jet age; and the question of how far opera is a 'museum' art and what it has to say to our own age. On these and similarly large questions the observation of the work of a single artist can scarcely be expected to provide definitive answers, but Domingo's career has been so multi-faceted and his achievements so far-reaching that he is at once a shining exception and the absolute paradigm. By watching him at work we may learn not only what makes the man himself tick but also something about the wider world of opera and entertainment in which he is so stellar a figure.

This book is in no way 'authorized'. Plácido has, of course, known from the outset that I was working on it and has kindly helped me to have access to his recording sessions, rehearsals and the like whenever I have requested it. His wife Marta and other members of the Domingo family, and also his secretary Paul Garner, have all been unfailingly courteous and friendly, regularly extending help and hospitality as I have bobbed up uninvited at places where they have been temporarily encamped. All this has represented a considerable act of faith on their part as Plácido has had no editorial rights in this book and did not see any of the text until a very late stage. There are, I know, several sections or at least opinions in the book about which he has reservations. But he has scrupulously respected my author's integrity and it is to Plácido as both artist and friend that my first and overwhelming debt of acknowledgement is due.

Among the countless others who helped me as I compiled the various pieces of the jig-saw and attempted to put them together, I would like to express special thanks to the following, all of whom will doubtless recognize the extent to which their help and influence have been incorporated into the text, and none of whom is responsible for any errors of fact or judgement it may contain: Roger Alier, Daniel Barenboim, Jennifer Batchelor, Alan Blyth, Mr and Mrs Emerson Buckley, Julian Budden, Humphrey Burton, Riccardo Chailly, Teresa Cole, James Conlon, Ileana Cotrubas, Susan Daniel, Joe Dash, Denny Dayviss, Sergio Escobar, Faith Esham, Lee Holdridge, Joan Ingpen, Madeleine Kasket, Lothar Knessl, Richard Laver, Norman Lebrecht, Robert T. Levine, Mary-Jo Little, Barbara Lorber, Lorin Maazel, Bill McClure, Cornell MacNeil, Gian Carlo Menotti, Julia Migenes Johnson, Sherrill Milnes, Leona Mitchell, Richard Mohr, Vicente Molina-Foix, John Mordler, Paul Myers, Milton and Rosemary Okun, Isabelle Partiot, Maurice and Hilde (Beal) Pearton, David Rendall, David Reuben, Adelita Rocha, Vicki Romaine, José Luis Rubio, Julius Rudel, Emilio Sagi, Robin Scott, Margaret Shackleton, Thomas Z. Shepard, Alan Sievewright, Catherine Siné, Margherita Stafford, Vivienne Taylor, John Treays, Dame Eva Turner, John Vernon, Lillian Watson, Katharine Wilkinson, Marilyn Zschau.

Brief passages from the text were first published in the *Sunday Times* magazine of 8 November 1981.

Finally, my thanks to Janet and to Ben and Anna who saw to it that such non-operatic characters as Robin Hood, Darth Vader, Snow White and Superman joined forces in a successful rearguard action against the onrush of Cavaradossi, Otello, Ernani, des Grieux and Don José, thus preventing the latter from taking over and monopolizing the entire imaginative life of the Snowman household!

OVERTURE

The theatre lights dim and the buzz of expectant conversation comes to a halt. A smattering of applause is heard as the conductor appears. In the orchestra pit close to a hundred players in evening dress sit patiently with faces impassive. They know tonight's score well, have been thoroughly rehearsed (they think over-rehearsed), and are in the hands of a conductor none of them particularly likes but most respect.

A few yards away, on the other side of the giant curtain of rich, embossed velvet, are another hundred people, one or two (about to make a speedy exit) wearing sweatshirts and jeans, the rest in period costume, fidgety, shifting from foot to foot, one checking yet again that a wig is securely fastened, another unpinning and re-pinning a cape. In the wings are yet others. Here the jeans and sweatshirts outnumber the period costumes though there are plenty of both. One man, taller and broader-chested than most, handsome head topped with a crown of wavy black hair, himself in jeans a few hours ago, is now sporting the most magnificent of all the period costumes on display this evening. He, too, shifts from foot to foot, clears his throat as quietly as his great reverberative chest cavity will permit, and steals a reassuring wink at his nearby colleagues.

Suddenly—it is always quicker than those behind the curtain expect—the orchestra plunges into the opening bars. The velvet curtain opens to reveal a spectacular set populated by a vigorous and well-drilled chorus. When the time comes for the tall, dark man in the distinguished costume to appear, he does so to the accompani-

6

ment of sizzlingly exciting music from the orchestra. Throughout the performance he sings with a dark, poignant, perfectly controlled flow of sound that projects clearly to the very back of the house. He does not sing especially loud most of the time, which makes one or two of those who had expected him to do so look at each other in the half-light with concern. His acting, too, while appropriate and convincing, is never show-stopping, even a little self-effacing at times. Not the way a 'star' is supposed to behave. But then, the musical and dramatic demands of the work have not so far required great assertiveness from the hero. Later, when the opera approaches its climax and the emotions become correspondingly grander, he opens up his chest and lungs with a display of glorious vocal power that nobody present will ever forget—and from which he withdraws the moment the score requires it.

To those to whom opera is a branch of athletics, it at last becomes obvious why this man is so celebrated. To those with more sensitive aesthetic antennae it has been obvious all evening: his genius consists not of flaunting his outstanding musical, dramatic and vocal gifts but of integrating them with those of his colleagues to try and create a fully-rounded performance. He knows how to let out all the stops and nobody experiencing his performances can doubt the man's exceptional talents. Yet it is never a one-man show. He is, paradoxically, too great a star ever to be merely a star.

A roar of sustained applause greets his curtain appearance at the end of the evening and a smile of pleasure flashes on to his face as he eagerly accepts the delight and gratitude of the wild audience at his feet. For the preceding three hours they have been silent witness to a performance of sustained and surpassing artistry. Many have been deeply moved by the beauty, pathos, nobility and tragedy that here unfolded before them.

Backstage, a final scene is added. It is in a way a surprisingly casual scene, full of the most banal *bonhomie*. 'What are you doing over the weekend?' asks one chorus member, naked to the waist but still wearing period tights, as he swabs off his stage make-up. His colleague, who has popped over to say goodnight, is taking the kids to the zoo on Saturday but has a recording session on Sunday. 'Good luck with both!' The members of the orchestra are already out of the

7

house, most well on their way home even before the applause has finally subsided.

For the soloists, the post-performance rituals last longer. And as for the principal single cause of the tumult after tonight's performance, he is virtually besieged by well-wishers. How does he himself feel and behave in the immediate aftermath of one of those towering performances for which he has become legendary? In what sort of state do his performances leave his own emotions, to say nothing of his voice? Glimpse him in the midst of all those people, every one of whom claims a special right to his attention. The man is wreathed in smiles, his dark eyes flashing with pleasure at a compliment here, an embrace there, the unexpected appearance of an old friend, a request for an autograph. He is obviously tired, yet visibly gains strength from the enthusiasm of those to whom he has been performing. Is he still performing? Not really. He is one of nature's mixers, at his most relaxed when surrounded by people to talk to, chatting warmly about his boys who, alas, were not able to be with him on this particular occasion, telling an impresario from another opera house about his forthcoming schedule, giving a brief extempore interview to a local radio representative who has been pursuing him and who is at last rewarded for his persistence. 'Can we have lunch some time?' asks a record executive, in town specially to try and persuade him to undertake a new project. 'When can we talk about our TV show?' asks another voice in another language. 'Will you have time for the photo session between performances?' asks one more visitor anxious to pin down the elusive star. The questions come thick and fast, and much as he would like to respond properly to each, he is constantly interrupted by new calls upon his attention. Autographs can be signed, hands shaken and beautiful women kissed here and now: future arrangements can be agreed in principle and the details worked out later.

His patience is enormous but he knows there is yet more work to be done tonight. As he eventually works his way out towards the exit he can already see and hear an excited crowd of perhaps a hundred more fans who refuse to leave until he leaves. He signs their programmes and talks to each of them as well. Some seem a little shell-shocked from the performance; as he signs they mutter extravagant metaphysical praise. Others feel their hearts pounding as their moment of personal proximity approaches. He himself remains calm and courteous, as though he had all the time in the world.

In a sense he does. He knows he has no obligations until noon the following day when his agent is coming round to discuss some of those future projects. And then he has nothing much to do until the next performance three days later. Except that he will try and squeeze in a quick flight to see his sons half a continent away, over-dub part of his role in a recent opera recording which he had to miss because of a conflicting engagement, sign records at a local store and give a television interview. And at some point he will also need to go through on the piano a role he has to perform in two months' time . . .

Tonight a group of close friends is assembled at one of his favourite restaurants with instructions to get on with the preliminaries and not wait for him. Once he arrives, the meal and the talk and the drink and the laughter can go on until all hours. A short, dark lady with rich brown hair and bright darting eyes behind thick spectacles leaves the theatre and goes off to the restaurant to take charge of introductions and seating. Marta Domingo is a skilful and experienced hostess. She ensures that there is a happy and relaxed atmosphere by the time he eventually appears. When he does so his guests turn to greet him with affectionate applause. He grins like an *ingénu* unaccustomed to recognition, goes the rounds shaking every male hand and kissing every female cheek, then takes his place at the centre of the table opposite his proud and smiling wife. Everyone present is made to feel that he is their special friend and they his. But there is something else that nobody around that privileged table will forget for a moment: that Plácido Domingo is one of the world's busiest jet-setters, a one-man multi-national business, an operatic megastar comparable this century only with Maria Callas and Enrico Caruso.

Plácido Domingo was born in Madrid on 21 January 1941, a child of the theatre, for his parents were well-known performers of that quintessentially Spanish form of light romantic musical known as the *zarzuela*. He recalls that he and his younger sister had a happy home and childhood, though their parents' departure from Spain on a

9

protracted Latin American tour in 1946 must have been wrenching. Things went well for the Domingo parents and when the tour was finally over they decided to stay in Mexico, start their own *zarzuela* company there, and send for their children. It was not until January 1949, when Plácido was just days short of his eighth birthday, that he and his sister were at last reunited with their parents.

Accounts of Domingo's adolescence in Mexico suggest that the seeds of his adult personality were sown early. The voracious interest in all kinds of music and the compulsion to perform it, the sunny sociability, the unflagging energy, all this was evident in the boy. His formal education was somewhat restricted; when music was not distracting his attention, football and girlfriends probably were. The principal influence was in any case not school but parents, particularly it appears the powerful personality of his mother, and it was from his parents that Plácido acquired his consuming love of the musical theatre. Sometimes Plácido was asked to sing small parts in performances for his parents' company, and he was also called upon for his growing expertise at the piano—on which he was having private lessons.

It was chiefly as a budding pianist, indeed, that Plácido entered the National Conservatory of Music in his early teens. Few of the instructors had much impact on him, he says now, though the Chilean baritone Carlo Morelli gave voice lessons that Plácido learnt to appreciate, and he also thinks back affectionately to classes in conducting by Igor Markevitch that he attended as an observer.

Plácido's parents were quite often away from home, and it was while they were on a tour of Europe that Plácido, aged sixteen, left home and moved in with a girlfriend he had met in class. They married secretly and in due course had a baby son, José. Plácido's formal education, such as it was, came to an end when it became necessary for him to earn money for his wife and baby. His parents, although not pleased at the turn his life had taken, gave him work in their company, and he also found himself playing the piano in nightclubs and singing baritone parts in Mexican productions of *My Fair Lady* and similar musicals. Before long, the marriage fell apart and ended in divorce.

At eighteen Plácido felt confident enough of his singing to

audition for the Mexican National Opera. They told him he was really a tenor and to his delight offered him a number of small roles. At about this time he began to develop what slowly grew into a serious relationship with a fellow singer, the soprano Marta Ornelas. Marta was a sophisticated girl, more interested in German *lieder* than in musical comedy, and she was at first no more attracted to Plácido than he to her. The relationship crept up on them both, however, with all the impact of the unexpected, and in August 1962 they were married.

By this time both were established young singers on the Mexican operatic circuit. Marta's career was more advanced, though Plácido gained local fame as presenter of a regular music show on television. Each needed experience, however, and opportunities in Mexico were limited. Then Marta and Plácido, with their friend the baritone Franco Iglesias, obtained just what they needed—a six-month contract to perform major roles with the Hebrew National Opera in Tel Aviv.

The Domingos went to Israel for six months and stayed for thirty, during which time Plácido sang some 280 performances of ten operas. If he was ever likely to have sung himself into the ground it would have been in those relentless years in the hot and clammy opera house in Tel Aviv. In fact, Plácido considers he left Israel a far better singer than when he arrived. Not only did he become a seasoned performer—he feels his proper knowledge of breathing and diaphragm support date back to the informal tutelage he received from Marta and Franco during their days in Israel.

When the Domingos left Tel Aviv in the summer of 1965 Marta was pregnant. After an emotional visit to Spain (Plácido's first for over sixteen years) the couple went on to the USA where his engagements soon included performances for the New York City Opera—notably the lead in Ginastera's *Don Rodrigo* on 22 February 1966, the night the NYCO opened its new theatre in Lincoln Center. In 1967 came Domingo's débuts in Hamburg and Vienna and by the end of 1968 he was also starring at New York's Metropolitan Opera. La Scala followed in 1969, Covent Garden in 1971, and as Domingo settled down into his thirties he was already one of the most highly regarded singers in the business in all the major houses of Europe and

America. Marta's singing career effectively came to an end with the birth of her two sons, Plácido (Placi) and Alvaro. A loving and supportive wife and mother, Marta was never content to be merely these things, and she always tried to keep the shrewd eyes and ears of an expert ex-performer on her husband's developing career and to remain his most observant and conscientious critic.

Throughout the 1970s Domingo gave a constant stream of performances in all parts of the musical world, recorded most of the standard repertoire, and appeared increasingly on television. At the age of forty he might have been forgiven for resting on his laurels. 'If my voice had disappeared at that point,' he says realistically, 'I would still have had a career that any singer might be proud of.' Instead, he continued to broaden the scope of his activities and to hasten the transition, documented in the pages that follow, from star of the opera to world celebrity. The shift was gradual and cumulative, but a revealing moment at which to plug into the process is provided by an event that took place in New York a few months after Domingo's fortieth birthday.

The Performer

Tosca in Central Park

'It's as free as the air,' say the hand-outs, sporting a picture of a big leafy tree. It is June 1981 and tonight sees the opening performance of the New York Metropolitan Opera's summer season of free open-air performances. The Met used to take over Lewisohn Stadium for these giant ventures in opera for the people. Then the old stadium building became unsound and 'Opera in the Park' was born—not just Central Park, where tonight's performance is to take place, but several of the other large parks around the boroughs of New York as well. For these annual events, the New York parks—so long synonymous, at least at night, with murder, mugging and mayhem—are transformed into a massive party in celebration of opera. Courting couples lie on the grass under the stars and let the strains of *Faust* or *Rigoletto* waft over them. People bring picnics, parents come accompanied by their children. If you want to make the parks of New York safe at night, bring in the opera.

This year, Plácido Domingo has been invited to star on the opening night. He has a series of performances of Donizetti's *Lucia di Lammermoor* in Madrid ending four days before the Central Park date, and *Otello* in Buenos Aires beginning five days after. Could he fit in a visit to New York? No trouble. He would even find time to squeeze in some recordings.

While the Madrid newspapers are trumpeting the heroic feats of their favourite son and those of Buenos Aires building up the pre-publicity for Domingo's first *Otello* in the city, the New York press whips up excitement for the Central Park *Tosca*. When the day dawns the radio weathermen all predict a real scorcher, but this does not stop an intrepid few turning up around eight o'clock in the morning —twelve and a half hours before kick-off—to stake out their territory and stay firmly put.

By 11 a.m. the thermometer has already crept up to the mid-eighties and on Central Park's Great Lawn the squatters now number several hundred. Elsewhere in Central Park there are the usual array of cyclists, joggers, softball players, dog-owners and, doubtless, muggers and rapists. Here on the Great Lawn, in addition to the settler population, workmen are putting the finishing touches to a huge temporary dais and erecting massive loudspeakers on either side of it. Behind the dais a number of musicians seek shelter from the sun and gulp down gallons of iced orange juice. One of them is a chubby young man with a round Jewish face, a bushy Afro hairstyle and a casual blue shirt. This is James Levine (rhymes with fine), Music Director of the Metropolitan Opera since 1976 and Principal Conductor for the past ten years—which must mean since he was about twelve by the looks of him. The maestro climbs up onto the dais and his orchestra settles for what will surely be one of the more desultory rehearsals in the history of opera. Everybody knows *Tosca* inside out, the day is already ferociously hot and sticky, and the job of the men and women on this dais tonight will be to give not the most subtle but the most projected performance of their lives. Those two giant speakers will carry the sound a mile or more across the park. But unless Levine's troops point everything they play or sing with the utmost clarity, the result will be merely a vast undifferentiated Puccinian mush.

The orchestra strikes up the opening notes of *Tosca*, the big, ominous chords associated with the evil police chief Scarpia, a role performed tonight by Sherrill Milnes. Milnes is not there yet, nor Domingo, who is to sing the hero, the painter Cavaradossi. The title-role is to be sung by Renata Scotto, with whom Domingo has recently recorded the opera. She turns up wearing a blue denim suit, and joins the people playing the smaller parts who are all at their places. Levine takes everyone through the first act, quite happy, it seems, to sing the parts of his absentee stars himself, though this is not much help to the sound engineers, who want to tune their loudspeakers correctly for the volume they will have to carry.

14

The squatter camp has grown quite large by now. A rustle of excitement whistles through it as a vast black limousine draws up behind the dais and Sherrill Milnes emerges. As tall and ruggedly good-looking as Domingo, he wears a pale blue shirt stretched tight across his broad chest, and delicate finger and wrist jewellery to match. Milnes is a product of the American Mid-West and every inch looks super-nourished since babyhood. He is probably the finest Scarpia since Tito Gobbi and really plays the part like a man accustomed to having his every demand satisfied. 'I so *hated* you tonight,' giggles a girl admirer after the show to Milnes as he signs his autograph. 'Great!' answers the genial villain. 'The more you hate me the better I feel!'

Eventually, one final 'limo' turns up with its silent motor, smoked windows, air-conditioning, and three rows of seats. Out of this compilation of modern American technology comes Domingo sporting a long-sleeved, light blue, striped shirt and a pair of sparkling white trousers. He looks like an off-duty admiral come to survey his fleet at anchor. Domingo is in his element in this heat and his eyes immediately adjust to the midday glare. After chatting briefly to a few people at the back of the dais, he climbs its steps and walks slowly round to his place beside Scotto, Milnes and Levine. As he appears, there is a smattering of applause from the squatters out in front, happy that, for their pains and at the risk of a severe bout of sunstroke, they will have a good one and a half performances of *Tosca* before the day is done. Domingo smiles back at them. He and the other principals sing along as the rehearsal progresses, every now and then singing out just to test the equipment—their own and that alongside the platform. None of the three has a score. Domingo has performed the work some 150 times, most recently in Naples a few months back. He will be doing it again in London in November.

Domingo wanders off the dais as casually as he had wandered on and is immediately waylaid by friends, admirers, well-wishers and hordes of press and television people who attach themselves to him like leeches. Tonight's performance will get a lot of coverage and all the newshounds, including many from foreign radio and television organizations, want to send back their 'exclusive' interview. Domingo seems unperturbed and gives extempore interviews in

15

English, Spanish, German, French or Italian. No question, it seems, of 'saving his voice' for tonight's performance. He seeks out his 'cover', the Italian Carlo Bini who is to sing the tenor lead in later Met performances of the opera in the various parks of New York, and the two men have some pictures taken together.

Not everyone is in quite such high and relaxed spirits. Sherrill Milnes's 'cover', the British baritone Peter Glossop, walks around in the shadows clearly wishing that he and not Milnes were singing in this opening performance. Not that he wishes Milnes any harm . . . Glossop will doubtless make a convincing villain when his turn comes to sing Scarpia in Marine Park, Brooklyn, three days later.

By the time the performance is due to begin at 8.30 p.m., the first few hundred squatters have been joined by something like another quarter of a million—some in sweatshirts and torn-off jeans, with beads and with beards, some with tents, most with blankets and many with great hampers of food and drink. It is a sort of vast, democratic Glyndebourne-gardens-for-the-masses, spread out over a dozen acres of park.

The stage lights come on as the sun conveniently—and after a day of relentless heat, mercifully—begins its descent. Some had predicted a post-heatwave storm but the night proves blessedly cloudless and, wonder of wonders, a superb full moon appears. Anthony Bliss, the Met's Executive Director, comes on to the podium and makes a brief speech of welcome. He thanks Chemical Bank and the other contributing organizations for their sponsorship. Also New York's own vigilante group the Guardian Angels, a sort of scout troop in red berets that compensates for New York's short-staffed police force and patrols the city's subway system. Tonight they are all over the Park to keep the customary malefactors at bay. The applause that greets the conclusion of Bliss's speech is not because he was good but because he was brief. Chemical Bank and Guardian Angels are instantly forgotten as Levine, still wearing a casual open-neck shirt, strikes up the big Scarpia chords and *Tosca* begins.

On cue, each of the principals appears on the dais, Scotto in a fetching long dress, Domingo and Milnes each in a smart, loose evening waistcoat—Domingo's specially designed for him by Oscar de la Renta. Tonight's is not an acted performance; scenery and costumes would make no sense for an audience much of which is sitting nearly a mile away. But each of the principals projects as much drama and personality as the circumstances permit. All three sing with immense *brio*, as though trying to reach their colossal audience directly and by-passing the loudspeaker system.

The occasion is a great success. The big moments, such as Domingo's long, high, sustained 'Vittoria! Vittoria!' or his aria 'The Stars Were Brightly Shining', sung with melting lyricism under authentic stars and authentic helicopters, are greeted by a vast roar of approval like that of a World Cup football crowd. During the intermissions the singers retire to the temporary trailers erected for them at the back of the dais, but Domingo is not good at sitting around in intervals. Tonight he breaks all the rules and emerges from his trailer to chat to friends, sign autographs, give more interviews, embrace the bevy of beautiful women who seem to materialize wherever he appears and generally to do all the things you would least expect a singer to do in mid-performance. None of this seems in the least to affect the stunning beauty of his singing and at the end the whole of Central Park, as far as the eye can see and beyond into the darkness, goes wild.

It takes a long time before the massive crowd seems ready to disperse—half of it to the space behind the dais where the performers chat and unwind. Domingo's compulsive socializing now takes on a new intensity and he works the crowd like an American politician running for office. A man of enormous energy, he is still chatting and kissing and signing and handshaking long after most people have left the Park and it is well into the early hours before he finally gets back to his apartment in mid-town Manhattan for a few hours' sleep. He has to get up early in the morning, for a five-hour recording session awaits him and in the evening he has to fly off to Buenos Aires.

Otello in Bregenz

A month after the New York *Tosca* Domingo is due to arrive in Bregenz, a small lakeside town in the far western corner of Austria nestling between the borders of Switzerland, Germany and Liechtenstein. In the past four weeks he has been in Buenos Aires, Los Angeles, Mexico, New York again, and Spain. The opening of this year's Bregenz Festival is to be marked by a new production of Verdi's *Otello* and, on the floating stage on the edge of the lake outside the Festival Theatre, a German-language version of *West Side Story* by a composer billed locally as 'Leonhard' Bernstein.

Bregenz has been on the European summer festival circuit for many years, not in the class of Salzburg, Aix or Edinburgh but a popular and enjoyable festival none the less. Its most famous feature is the stage on which its principal productions have usually been performed, floating on the edges of the Bodensee (or Lake Constance as it is known to non-Teutons). On the safety of dry land are tiers of seats—there is room for almost 5,000 spectators—and many excellent productions of opera and musical comedy have been enjoyed there. Every now and then rain drives in from the surrounding mountains and players and spectators alike have to scatter for cover as though for lifeboats. This year, too, as the festival looms, the Bodensee weather is wet, and in truth a burst of squally weather might be rather appropriate for at least the first tempestuous minutes of *Otello*. But *Otello* is to be performed indoors in the new, luxurious theatre inside the Festspielhaus underneath the tiers of outdoor seats, a theatre opened only a year before, and as the rehearsing Jets and Sharks battle with each other and the elements on the floating stage, the *Otello* cast gets down to work in the theatre beneath.

Domingo is due to spend something like a full week in Bregenz as the rehearsal period builds up towards opening night. Most of the *Otello* cast, which includes Bulgarian soprano Anna Tomowa-Sintow and Italian baritone Silvano Carroli, have already been there for a fortnight when word comes that Domingo will be delayed. His wife Marta has been suffering from stomach pains for some time and is to have a gallstone operation in Barcelona. Domingo is determined to remain with her for as long as he can. He will definitely arrive in

Bregenz the day before the dress rehearsal. But not until late afternoon.

Everybody's nerves are a little on edge. This is a complex production, complete with revolving scenery that is forever revolving at the wrong speed. Rehearsals are at that tense and tetchy stage when nobody quite knows whether or how things can jell in time for the first night. On the afternoon Domingo is due to arrive, producer and designer Piero Faggioni holds a stage rehearsal with piano and shouts incessant instructions to his German-speaking chorus and off-stage crew in a colourful and often unprintable stream of English and Italian. The opening five minutes of *Otello*, full of storm, fear, fury, prayer and salvation, culminating in Otello's trumpet-like entry on the word 'Esultate!', are among the most riveting ever written, and Faggioni is anxious to sharpen and polish the movements of the chorus (not to mention those of the revolving set) until they completely match the demands of Verdi's music. Again and again he rehearses those opening minutes. Conductor Nello Santi, unruffled by the histrionics before and behind him, patiently conducts his pianist and his chorus from the beginning each time Faggioni asks him to. They reach Otello's entrance but everything that can go wrong does so and they never seem able to get beyond it. 'Thank God Domingo isn't arriving until later,' an exasperated Faggioni is heard to mutter. One or two disgruntled chorus members think Faggioni is over-rehearsing them.

Outside the Festspielhaus on the vast floating stage, aesthetic young men and women put the finishing touches to the stylized re-creation of Manhattan that is to serve as the background for *West Side Story*. As the band strikes up 'I Like to Be in Amer-i-ca!' a girl with an aerosol can carefully sprays authentic-looking graffiti on to the set.

Domingo arrives on time at Zürich airport from Barcelona and is immediately whisked across eastern Switzerland towards the Austrian border and Bregenz. In an uncanny way the *Otello* scene being acted out again and again on stage in the Festival Theatre, the tense but excited anticipation of Otello's first appearance, mirrors closely the real-life tensions as everybody awaits the appearance of Domingo. Finally, around 4.45 p.m., he reaches the theatre. He has not unpacked his bags or even seen the house he has rented and which is to be his home for the next two weeks. He is taken straight to his dressing-room and knows he must now plunge into five or six hours of rehearsal. He puts on his Otello cloak and Faggioni takes him over the set, giving him in Italian a detailed run-down of his moves. By about 6.30 Act I begins yet again. This time, however, things progress with no serious hitch. The first three acts are rehearsed that evening and they leave Act IV for the next day.

That night Domingo sleeps badly. He is pushing himself, is concerned about Marta, and knows that, along with the sympathy, there is some resentment at his late arrival among the *Otello* groundlings. He is woken at 5 a.m. by the relentless pounding of rain on the roof and windows of his unfamiliar temporary home. He dozes off again and does not rise until mid-morning. It is still pouring with rain and it is noon before he gets to the theatre.

The floating stage alongside the Festspielhaus is almost a drowning stage and *West Side Story* rehearsals have had to be brought indoors. In the corridors of the theatre Jets and Sharks mingle amiably with Cypriot warriors and Venetian diplomats. After rehearsal of the last act of *Otello* there is a two-hour break—and then the full dress rehearsal is due to begin. Domingo is chased by the usual well-wishers, autograph-hunters and the rest and he tries to be as accommodating as he can. He gives an interview in German to a local radio station, then, dressed in jeans and a casual shirt, saunters into the staff canteen, buys himself a couple of ham rolls and a black coffee, and chats up some of the *West Side Story* cast at the next table. How have their rehearsals been going? Too bad about all that rain. They should rename the show *Wet Side Story*! One of the Americans in the cast playing a Puerto Rican gang leader wonders if he should try to pronounce his German lines with a Spanish accent. 'Oh, you should listen to me,' jokes Domingo, 'I'm a real expert!' A very pretty girl has a copy of the *International Herald Tribune*. Can Domingo have a look? He'd like to check the sports results . . .

Even slouching over a canteen table munching a ham sandwich Domingo looks impressive. But when he assumes a role like Verdi's Otello, a real transformation is effected. He stands erect, carries his flowing robes with immense dignity, and with his olive skin darkened and his wavy black hair now flecked with grey and gently crinkled, he becomes an imposing figure of unassailable authority. In Bregenz, the noble Moorish general who emerges from Domingo's dressing-room at the start of the *Otello* dress rehearsal is scarcely recognizable as the easygoing, talkative Spaniard who entered it ninety minutes earlier. From his first entry, when he sings the 'Esultate!' in full voice, Domingo shows complete mastery not only of the music but also of the complex details of Faggioni's staging. He has absorbed in twenty-four hectic hours what the company have been working towards for weeks.

Domingo has two free days between the dress rehearsal and the opening night, two days in which to look out at the almost ceaseless rain that sweeps across the region. In parts of adjacent Switzerland this week they are having severe and unprecedented summer snow storms. Domingo would much prefer to be in Barcelona with Marta but has long since adjusted to a life of alternating hyper-activity and enforced immobility.

As it happens, Lord Snowdon is to visit Domingo during his off-days. I should explain that my own presence at Bregenz arises out of a feature on Domingo I was writing for the British *Sunday Times* magazine and Snowdon was to do some special photography to accompany my article. Snowdon is a thoughtful, serious, somewhat shy person, fastidious in his tastes, aesthetic to his fingertips, anxious when on a professional assignment to avoid as far as possible the glamour that has sometimes been heaped too excessively upon him. Small in stature, unassuming in manner, but accustomed to having his way, Snowdon arrived in Bregenz with his assistant, Richard Dudley-Smith, the evening before he was due to photograph Domingo.

'You realize,' Snowdon tells me drily as we sit down to dinner, 'that you are talking to a man who knows nothing whatever about opera.' 'That's all right,' I reciprocate, and assure him I know even less about photography. He knows about Domingo, though, has been listening to his records and studying photos and press cuttings about him. 'What makes Domingo tick?' he asks me. 'What sort of friends does he have? What does he eat? What does he do in his spare time? Is he a happy person? What drives him? Tell me about his family.' I answer as best I can—and then Snowdon fixes his penetrating blue eyes on me and asks me equally direct questions about myself, my interests, my BBC work, my home life. This may be a shy man deflecting conversation away from himself, the celebrity *malgré lui*. But it is also the supremely professional artist immersing himself in his current assignment.

Snowdon's professionalism gets Richard and me up at an unearthly hour the next morning to go exploring. The clouds still lower but the rain temporarily keeps off and we must find suitable locations to photograph Domingo. Since Bregenz is on the edges of spectacular alpine scenery, we drive up and over the hills surrounding the town, clamber over damp, mossy rocks towards hillside churches or cafés, all still shut at this early hour, break all the rules and wander over the deserted *West Side Story* set on the floating stage, and eventually return tired and clammy to our hotel for some welcome mid-morning coffee.

Word of Tony Snowdon's presence in town has begun to spread and on our return various smooth Austrians press their attentions on him. And sometimes, mistakenly, on me. One or two get not just our persons but also our names confused and I revel in the unaccustomed experience of being addressed as 'Lord Snowman'. I think Mr Snowdon is amused too.

Snowdon may be an early riser but Domingo is not, and it is noon before he calls us over to his house. We drive up again into the mountain foothills and, in ten minutes, approach a great chalet with a sweeping A-frame roof. The tall, gregarious Spaniard steps out and greets the fair, dapper British earl and the two immediately click. And get down to business. They find an austere, unused, unfurnished upstairs kitchen and Tony and Richard set to work to turn it into a temporary studio. Snowdon brings in a chair and table, Domingo opens a skylight window, Richard sets up a tripod and prepares rolls of film—and, hey presto, the studio is ready.

Domingo has always had a keen appreciation of the value of publicity and is well aware that a memorable study by Lord Snowdon will do him no harm. He changes into a clean shirt—indeed, produces a number and asks Snowdon which colours he would like him to wear. He worries that his deep, dark eyes may look tired and applies a little light-coloured make-up. Then for an hour or more

Domingo sits at the kitchen table, looking at a music score (the only one in the house is *Norma* which he has to polish for performances at the Met a few weeks later), staring straight at Snowdon or his camera, glancing thoughtfully up at the skylight. He smiles very little and Snowdon feels (but does not say) that Domingo's 'Great Artist' look does not adequately capture the man's natural exuberance and energy.

There is not a lot more Snowdon can get out of this 'studio' session and when Domingo cheerily suggests that we all go into town for some lunch Snowdon is happy to comply. Work is not over for the day, however. In the restaurant my job is to talk to Domingo, Snowdon's to snap him chatting to me. The weather outside is as dull as ever but the gossip inside the restaurant sparkles. Snowdon tells some very funny self-abnegatory stories about his supposedly dissolute youth, while Domingo chats away about his career and childhood, his family and his friends, and at one point is provoked into a full-voiced rendition of 'Happy Birthday', much to the delight of everyone else in the restaurant.

It is now four o'clock and Domingo is supposed to be resting himself and his voice in preparation for tomorrow's opening night. But a little fresh air would do no harm, rain or no rain, and we head out for a stroll around the floating stage. Something in Snowdon's bones tells him that the mock-up of New York City in this bizarre location might make a suitable background for a series of pictures. Domingo, still visibly enjoying himself and apparently as unconcerned as ever with conserving his energies, dons his raincoat and clowns in front of the drab Manhattan skyline. A handful of spectators accumulates in the soggy aisles and Domingo plays up to them with glee and they clap back to him. 'I've never had so much applause without actually singing anything!' he jokes, while all the time the earnest-faced Lord Snowdon continues to snap away.

Eventually it really is time to split up. Domingo has been talking and exposing himself to the inclement elements for more time than can possibly be good for him. He goes off to his house in the hills while Snowdon and Richard and I return to our hotel. There is a birthday celebration going on there, complete with tables groaning under piles of stupendous Austrian gourmandise. Won't Lord Snowdon come and photograph the happy birthday party? 'Ve vould be so honoured if you vould schnap us all!' says their overdressed olea-ginous spokeslady, and I watch with awe as Snowdon edges his way out of that one with the deftest courtesies.

The next day dawns cold and cloudy and when I get up Snowdon and Richard are already on their way back to London. It rains all day and as performance time approaches I am undecided whether to wear suit and tie or sou'wester and gum boots, but finally opt for the former. Inside the Festspielhaus everybody is, in fact, dressed imma-culately and very expensively. As the orchestra under Maestro Santi strikes up the various anthems, national and regional, that have to be played, an air of excited expectation descends. There is still one anthem to go when suddenly the computerized *Otello* lighting plan commences, bathing the fashionable audience in embarrassing and premature darkness. Never mind. A certain amount of tension never did a performance of *Otello* any harm.

As the curtain goes up on Act I a huge, curved, grey battlement turns slowly and reveals—more or less on their appropriate cues —great phalanxes of soldiers and sailors, individual characters like Roderigo and Iago, and crowds of praying women. The Festspielhaus stage revolves the full 360 degrees so that, in that opening act, a great variety of stony crenellations, stairways and platforms appears before the massive structure returns to its original position. Tonight, miraculously, the set and the music turn in harmony and at times Faggioni's conception looks quite brilliant. In Act III, for example, Iago appears to lead Cassio literally all over Otello's castle, while Otello constantly has to creep along from one pillar to the next if he is to keep up with the conversation he is trying to overhear. Occasion-ally, Faggioni does not know when to let go of a good thing; although the stage is quite often at rest it is distracting to have Iago begin his *Credo* while heading slowly for the wings and even more so for Otello's great outburst 'Ora e per sempre addio' to be sung on the move.

In the first interval Domingo says that he is a little uncomfortable perched on top of some of Faggioni's high moving sets; it feels vertiginous up there and he is worried his voice is getting lost up in the stage curtains. But his performance throughout is a powerful, commanding one. His colleagues are in good voice too—Carroli having the presence of mind to carry on singing his first aria (the *Credo*) even though, in the midst of it, the out-of-sync lighting plan suddenly plunges the stage into another pall of irrelevant if temporary darkness.

At each interval Faggioni looks more relaxed. There is, it is true, some muttering over the unnecessarily audible fountain in Act II, and Desdemona's bed in the final scene puts one in mind of the vast Vittorio Emanuele monument in Rome. Some in the audience feel that more light would have been a blessing, even in those scenes in which the lighting plan worked successfully, and someone is heard to remark that if you didn't know the principal character was supposed to be darker-skinned than everyone else you would not have been able to tell most of the time. But as the evening progresses it becomes increasingly clear that the production is going to go down as a memorable feat of imaginative staging. When the great tragedy reaches its conclusion the audience goes wild. Everybody is cheered to the rafters and Domingo smiles broadly in the knowledge that he has added one more city to the list of his triumphs.

Backstage, Domingo receives the usual handshakes and embraces, and jokes that any girl getting too close will get tell-tale black make-up on her cheeks. He has two more performances of *Otello* here—between them he will snatch a couple of days back in Barcelona with Marta—then on to Salzburg and *The Tales of Hoffmann*. His next *Otello* performances are with La Scala of Milan when they visit Japan in September. While in Tokyo he is told that, next to Argentina, Japan is expected to prove the biggest market for his forthcoming record of Spanish tangos . . .

Later that autumn my article about Domingo appears in the *Sunday Times* magazine. It is timed for the tenth anniversary of his Covent Garden début as Cavaradossi in *Tosca*, a role he is repeating to mark the occasion. Plácido and I had both hoped the article would be the cover story, and it is. What we had not bargained for was the picture they would use on the cover. After all the time and expense of getting one of the world's most famous photographers to and from Bregenz, and the fact that a superb Snowdon photo of Domingo in front of the *West Side Story* set is featured inside the magazine, the cover photo is not by Snowdon at all. Instead, the editor chooses a grotesque close-up picture of the back of Domingo's wide open throat. The story has been entitled 'The Man with the Golden Larynx'.

ENTR'ACTE
Having to Perform

We all need to communicate with others and crave and seek love and admiration in return. Performing artists have this need, or at least work at its fulfilment, more than most. 'After all,' said one American former prima donna to me realistically, 'we don't perform for ourselves, you know!' There is indeed something of a recognizable 'showbiz' personality: extrovert, super-sociable, larger than life, in which everything—personal appearance, language, clothes, voice —is designed to advertise one's 'presence', to demand attention and recognition. Recognition is commonly thought to be a form of approval. We consider ourselves complimented when recognized by acquaintances, insulted when not. This may be irrational. People are as often recognized, after all, because acquaintances recall *un*attractive traits. But in general, none the less, we all like to give and receive recognition, attention, and thereby approval and admiration.

Social gifts are not distributed evenly and shy people can find these fulfilments hard to attain. Odd though it may seem at first, many performing artists are fundamentally shy people whose needs for social fulfilment are to some extent achieved through the roles they are professionally required to play. The tragic clown is the classic example of a man acting out a public part at variance with his private feelings. But chat to any group of actors or opera singers and you will soon detect among some of them a less extreme version of the same pattern: the person whose inner uncertainties can be disguised or, indeed, quite productively sublimated through the assumption, on or off the stage, of a very different public role.

Plácido Domingo is not this kind of person. He cannot by any stretch of the imagination be said to be shy, nor is he a Pierrot or Pagliaccio disguising inner sadness by means of public bombast. But he is a showman, a person whose life is devoted to communication with others and the quest for recognition and approval from them. In this, the private individual and the public artist converge, and an examination of the first throws interesting light on the second.

In a sense, Domingo can only really be understood inasmuch as he relates to other people. This is obviously true of Domingo the artist; but it is largely true of the man as well, for he is an intensely sociable person, a man who spends relatively little time alone. We have already likened him to an American politician in the way he will have a brief chat with every acquaintance he sees in a crowd that has come to see him. He remembers who everybody is (or pretends convincingly to do so), is good at names, and does not let any friend go untouched and unaddressed. We have seen him in the staff canteen at the Bregenz Festspielhaus chatting to the *West Side Story* cast about the weather and the football results, and will later observe him moving about in the darkened auditoria of the world's opera houses during rehearsals, seeking out friends and acquaintances whenever he himself is not required on stage. Consider, too, his reluctance to give concerts in which he has to appear alone before an audience; there are good artistic reasons for this, but there is undoubtedly something in Domingo's character that is more comfortable if he can attune his individuality to the ensemble of which he is part. If there is no crowd, Domingo will seek and make one; if there is he will assuredly be in the middle of it.

This almost compulsive gregariousness is carried out with unfailing good humour and is never imposed upon an unwilling recipient. In the right company he enjoys the cut and thrust of verbal wit. 'For a tenor you're quite a big fellow,' said one female colleague provocatively during a break in rehearsals. Immediately Domingo replied with a grin: 'You mean, for a big fellow I'm quite a tenor!' Domingo's conversation is rather like the game of a good tennis partner: he will adjust his game to yours so that the rallies are as fulfilling or as demanding as you wish them to be. I have seen him chatting with complete ease to the King and Queen of Spain and to the cleaning ladies at Covent Garden, in the first case with respect but no artificial reverence, in the second with simplicity but not a whiff of condescension.

This graceful sociability seems to constitute a central feature of Domingo's make-up. It appears important to him that he should chat pleasantly to everybody he knows, however briefly, whenever he sees them, that he should always have someone to talk to, something or someone to engage in. He is very bad at sitting around with nothing to do and it is impossible to imagine Domingo remaining alone at the edge of a crowd absorbed in a book. If ever there was a man of action, this is it, a man whose jaw or fingers or leg will begin to twitch if he has to suffer enforced immobility even for a matter of minutes.

The easy explanations will not do. It is simply not enough to say that Domingo's restless sociability compensates for deep inner uncertainties or that he has a stronger need to be loved than the rest of us. The socializing has no sense of frenetic insecurity about it; on the contrary, Domingo comes across as a man of inner strength and certainty whose gregariousness arises out of love of his fellow beings rather than any sense of inner self-doubt. He palpably enjoys the pleasure he gives and receives from his exchanges with friends and acquaintances, and if his instincts prove so fruitful, why not follow them?

A link between the style of the man and the career of the artist is provided if we consider all this alongside other patterns in Domingo's life. For if every friend's hand is regularly shaken or cheek kissed, so Domingo also makes a point of visiting most of the world's major opera houses and several of the minor ones each season, while new Domingo recordings continue to appear regularly from several different record companies. Consider the charm with which he loves to entertain, at least in principle, the many attractive propositions that are constantly heaped upon him by ambitious entrepreneurs —and the positively Byzantine diplomacy with which the hopelessly interwoven threads then have to be unravelled. 'He has a deep inner need to get everybody's vote,' says one who has known him well for many years, 'and to leave no friend or opera house or impresario or colleague or record company too long without a new gesture of trust and friendship.' All of which is fine in itself, adds the friend, 'but wanting to say yes to everybody, he often lands up having to make most of them wait as a result'.

Everyone who has had dealings with Domingo has a story to illustrate the point: how it took him years to fulfil a promise to make this recording, give that interview, perform in such-and-such a city. I recall with wry amusement the problems Domingo had even finding time to work on his own autobiography, *My First Forty Years*, with his patient 'ghost', Harvey Sachs. 'If I don't get on with it soon,' Domingo would quip guiltily, 'it will have to be retitled *My First Fifty Years!*' One day in Domingo's dressing-room at La Scala, Harvey tactfully pressed Plácido on when they could get together to tape the final sections of the book. It could all be wrapped up over a period of three days. By now Plácido was feeling really bad at the way he had been keeping Harvey waiting for so long. 'OK,' he said eventually, glancing at Marta for approval, 'why don't you come to Barcelona over Christmas, Harvey? We can surely have our three years then!' Everyone guffawed at the Freudian slip. Domingo may have meant three days, but he often keeps people waiting for years.

People are forever accusing Domingo of making too many commitments, of jetting around too much, of taking on too much work. The contention is doubtless exaggerated but not without foundation. By the time Domingo was forty he had clocked up 1,500 operatic performances and nearly fifty complete operatic recordings. But does he really do 'too much'? And if so, what would constitute 'enough'?

First, a comparison. Domingo certainly travels incessantly and rarely stops for long in one place. Even when he is appearing in a run of performances in, say, Milan or Vienna, he is likely to be flying off between times to London, Paris or Madrid. Caruso was not able to do this kind of thing, of course, and would spend months at a time based in New York. He may have made the occasional trip up or down the north-east coast of the USA to do a performance in Philadelphia, say, or a recording in nearby Camden, NJ, but his expressive eyes would have popped out of his head at the thought of spending thirty-six hours in Mexico City or Puerto Rico between performances at the Met. To Domingo, this sort of excursion is nothing out of the ordinary.

But look at the performance schedule Caruso set himself. In his first London season, in the spring of 1902, for example, Caruso sang twenty-four performances of eight different operas in two and a half months. Giulio Gatti-Casazza records that in his first week as director of the New York Metropolitan Opera in 1908, his star tenor sang in *Faust* (at the newly opened Brooklyn Academy of Music), *Aida* at the Met, *Bohème* in Philadelphia, then *Butterfly*, *Traviata* and *Tosca* at the Met—six performances of six different roles in three theatres in eight days. Nor was Caruso a reluctant traveller. In an era in which travel took time, he appeared in Italy, Russia, Germany, France, Belgium, Portugal, Spain, Monaco, Austria, Hungary, Czechoslovakia, England, Ireland, Scotland, Argentina, Brazil, Uruguay, Mexico, Cuba, Canada and, of course, the United States. At the Met alone in eighteen years he sang over 600 performances.

Let us try and put this into a further perspective. However hard a Domingo or a Caruso might work, there can be no comparison with the performance schedule undertaken by the busy instrumentalist. A singer uses up his instrument as he talks. If he is physically below par, so is his instrument. If he uses it one day it will inevitably be more tired the next than if he did not. A pianist, however, can perform every day with no physical wear and tear. There may be mental strain, of course, and a tired pianist or violinist will not play as well as a relaxed, fresh one. But a Paderewski or Pachman, a Rubinstein or Heifetz, Stern or Brendel, can notch up a string of performances —twenty or more during a one-month tour of the United States or Europe—that not even the most tireless singer could match. Domingo, unlike some other leading opera singers, rarely performs other than in opera, and has certainly not gone in for regular or frequent public concerts. By the standards of the busy opera singer who also has a thriving concert career, indeed, Domingo might almost be considered as working at a fairly modest rate!

The only realistic criterion by which an artist's schedule can be appraised is whether he delivers what he promises. Some take on what, for others, would be a reasonably light load of responsibilities yet fail to deliver the goods. Others take on a load that would overwhelm the rest of us yet appear to relish it. Domingo seems to be in the latter category. He does take on a great amount of work and intersperses his public commitments with many other demands on his time, energies and talents, yet he seems to thrive on such a life. He works hard, in other words, not because he is (as one concerned friend put it) riding a tiger and is scared to get off, but because he knows life suits him best this way. He is like a rechargeable battery, said another experienced Domingo-watcher: all the activity he demands of himself does not wear him out so much as give him renewed energy. He takes on as much as he does not primarily because he is a tense workaholic, uneasy unless he is 'achieving', but because he seems to be a robust and talented man who thrives on healthy activity.

Colleagues make fun of Domingo's non-stop round of engagements. The great Swedish soprano Birgit Nilsson once said affectionately that among all Plácido's talents he is also a brilliant linguist —'but, alas, he has not yet learnt to say "no" in any language!' Domingo adores Nilsson but gets irritated at the frequency with which this quotation is disinterred. 'Look,' he says emphatically, 'it is not that I *cannot* say no. It's that I feel no need to. I know people say this about me out of affection and concern, but they need not worry. If anybody knows and cares about my career and my voice, it is me!' What upsets him is that although everybody complains about how hard he pushes himself, they really want it that way. 'Nobody ever says to me, "OK, Plácido, don't come to us, you'll tire yourself and hurt the voice."' On the one hand, everybody wants Domingo to come and sing for *them*, and the demands on his time and on his voice are relentless. On the other hand, he complains that the people who accuse him of taking on too much work are often the very ones who are, collectively, responsible. He sometimes feels inclined to retaliate. 'One day I will say to them all "Sorry, but I have changed my plans. I'm cancelling all my engagements for a year, spending more time with my family, and simply taking on engagements where and when I feel like it!"' An appealing fantasy for someone whose diary regularly contains fixed points four years ahead, but one that nobody seriously expects Domingo to act upon. 'The more I sing the better I sing,' he once said, without conceit, and this still seems by and large to be true.

From the earliest days of his career Domingo would take on a vast amount of work; there are still people in the musical world in Tel Aviv who talk with awe of Domingo singing one night in three for two and a half years during his stint there in the early 1960s. From Israel he systematically undertook a series of auditions in the major houses of Europe, and by the time he was giving his débuts in them a few years later he was already retaining in several locations the services of a publicity agent. Domingo is a naturally expansive and generous man, fond of throwing a backstage party to mark his birthday or each time his number of performances reaches a new, significant statistic, or of taking the cast out for dinner. Like a good politician, he has carefully kept in touch with friends and colleagues by means of carefully placed phone calls, flowers, telegrams, gifts of various kinds. In much the same way, he is careful to schedule at least a few performances for each season in some half a dozen countries. Amidst all this there will be television and radio shows plus occasional concert appearances, record-signing sessions and the like. All this suggests something akin to the chairman of a big multi-national corporation, or a general anxious to keep all the far-flung troops in line. Since the Domingo schedule is certainly not the result of an artist forced to accept whatever engagements he can get, if he regularly keeps the entire circuit assiduously watered, so to speak, it can only be because he has chosen to.

On the face of it, Domingo must by any standards be a man driven by an abnormally powerful and restless ambition to be the Number One in his field. More—the fact that he is also making a bid to become widely known as a popular entertainer and taking on conducting engagements suggests that his ambitions may be even broader than some Domingo-watchers had suspected.

The ambition, the competitiveness have clearly been present since childhood. Yet Domingo also has a high reputation in a notoriously backbiting profession for being courteous and helpful towards colleagues. Several well-known singers talk movingly about ways he has helped nurse them through vocal problems. One soprano recalls a performance that was to be televised and the gentle way Domingo helped show her how to play more effectively to the cameras. Another remembers how he helped direct her towards a repertoire more appropriate for her voice. A third singer who was having agent trouble took up a Domingo recommendation and has been grateful ever since. American soprano Leona Mitchell told me of the gratitude she felt when Plácido, already one of the great stars of opera, made her feel one of the team when she made her début at the New York Metropolitan as Micaela in *Carmen* in 1976 at the age of twenty-four. Film director John Schlesinger, a giant in his own accustomed field, but a novice to operatic production when he directed Domingo in *Hoffmann* at Covent Garden in late 1980, told me he found Plácido a tower of strength. 'He virtually held my hand in early rehearsals,' yet was quite prepared to take direction from Schlesinger as though he had never sung the role before. Even fellow tenors (most of them, anyway!) speak warmly of Domingo's kindnesses. David Rendall, who took over a run of *Traviatas* from Domingo at the Met in 1981, tells of the practical help Domingo gave him when they discussed details of the role of Alfredo. 'Whenever I am working on a part that is in Plácido's repertoire,' Rendall says now, 'I go over it with him and he is the most marvellous friend, helping me to pace myself through the role as a whole and giving me practical tips about some of the awkward details.'

Domingo seems to be a man of genuine inner serenity, secure in his knowledge of his own capacities and able, therefore, to regard others pursuing the same ends as colleagues and not rivals. 'Competitive? Yes, he is,' a fellow singer agreed, 'but only with himself. It's his own artistic achievement, not anyone else's, that he always wants to improve upon.' Domingo is frank and open with strangers. When I first got to know him I was astonished at the candid way he would talk about various possible projects, some of which were still at a delicate stage of negotiation. When I asked him about details of past performances he lent me his private diaries. Most people in his exposed position would be more reserved in what they revealed to someone they scarcely knew. How, I wondered then and have often wondered since, can so obviously ambitious and work-driven a man remain at the same time so relaxed, helpful, generous and trusting? Was he as open with others who came to interview him as he was with me and, if so, had not some of them abused his trust? The answer to both questions, as I later came to know, was 'yes'. Some very inaccurate or indiscreet things have been written about him from time to time, partly because any rich, handsome and talented international celebrity is bound to get misrepresented in the press, but partly, too, because Domingo, being so open, has sometimes told journalists more than he probably should.

Competitive yet trusting, ambitious yet a generous team-player, a brilliant performer yet revealingly frank in conversation: the successful integration of both sets of characteristics in a single well-adjusted temperament is not common, certainly in the world of grand opera, and can scarcely arise at all except on the basis of a pattern already established in childhood. An important clue as to what makes Domingo tick may indeed lie in the extent to which his adult personality has managed to incorporate qualities that were of particular value to him as a child.

All adults retain qualities more obviously conspicuous among children. Among them is the desire to 'perform'. We are all to some extent performers, and psychologists suggest that the desire to perform, to display our talents in public, may be a primitive instinct, a residue of childhood, possibly even a sublimated form of infantile sexual self-revelation. Certainly, many performing artists seem to be people who have conspicuously managed to maintain into adulthood something of the innocent, open-minded responsiveness of childhood, to combine youthful freshness of perception with the disciplined talent acquired with maturity.

A child's responses to people and things are not dulled by familiarity, and he or she creates new words, new worlds, new categories in describing them. But a child does not have the discipline or the organizing skill to create a satisfying whole out of these new perceptions. What a child can do is to perform, to show off skills, dress up, put on funny hats and voices, climb up a tree, stick his tongue out, giggle and cry and, in general, to 'dramatize'—and always, in effect, to shout out 'Look at me!'

What a child does, adults describe as 'playing'. We tend to look patronizingly on 'play' and 'games' as something children do because they cannot take on anything more serious, something we adults only do in our leisure time, an activity to be contrasted with 'work'. But playing games is a deep and essential element in human activity, a voluntary activity (like art) that can help us impose some order upon a

35

disordered world. We learn about military strategy by playing 'war games', learn about relationships with fellow beings by 'role play' or by studying 'games people play', seek or confirm our national stereotypes from the way this or that country plays football, appreciate Brendel or Perlman playing Mozart or Beethoven. It may sound like coincidence that all these apparently unrelated activities are referred to as 'play' and be stretching a point to suggest they all have something in common with the activities of the child in the nursery. But they have this in common: they all represent attempts to work one's way through a problem, by means of a series of more or less flexible rules, towards a greater mastery of experiences presented by the outside world. We all 'play' with new experiences, knead them, mould them, bring earlier solutions temporarily to bear upon them, and by a dialectical process come to impose order upon what was formless before. This is, in essence, what a child does while 'playing', what we all do when faced with a new situation at work or at home, and pre-eminently what the creative or interpretative artist does as he struggles to breathe new life into, and mould new meaning out of, his fragmented material.

Finally, the child typically has a richer fantasy life than the adult. Indeed, children sometimes cannot or will not differentiate fully between fantasy and reality. Here, too, the artist retains something of the child's fantastical imagination and weds it to the skills of discipline acquired with adulthood to create a new, imaginative synthesis of the two.

Thus, the artist is likely to have maintained into adulthood something valuable from childhood that many people lose as they acquire 'maturity', something of the freshness of response of the child, the inclination to use 'play' as a means of trying to impose order upon a stubbornly inchoate world, and the capacity to create imaginative fantasy out of reality. The performing artist will, in addition, probably have in his make-up a vestige of the child's natural desire to call attention to himself, to show off, to appeal for adult approval by displaying his skills before others whose role is to assess and where appropriate to allot praise but not to participate.

These characteristics are not, of course, exclusive to 'artists' nor are they abnormal. We all share them to some extent and live richer lives as a result. Childhood and adulthood, the worlds of fantasy and reality, of play and work are interrelated, and the fulfilled and adjusted person will keep in touch with aspects of both throughout life. But whereas if you were to repress the vestiges of childhood you might still become a successful banker or oil executive, you would be unlikely to permit your aesthetic instincts full scope for expression, and would certainly never become a good performing artist. I am not, of course, saying that the performing artist is a childish or immature adult, although this is doubtless true of some. What I *am* saying is that the performing artist is more likely to have retained some of the characteristics of childhood which many lose or undervalue.

Here perhaps lies an important key to the achievement, personal as well as aesthetic, of an interpretative artist like Plácido Domingo: that he can reconcile to an unusual degree the contradictory thrusts that 'children' are hopelessly buffeted by and that 'adults' are all too often taught to repress. Domingo has the courage to let go of physical and emotional restraints and to liberate enormous reserves of energy while at the same time having the resources to control and direct these energies and never be at their mercy. This double talent helps explain Domingo's magnitude as an artist, but it also lies at the root of his social personality for in the last analysis the two are one. The capacity to give full weight to all aspects of his art while yet managing to integrate them on to a single continuum, is merely the public expression of an inner balance. Ultimately, it is this temperamental equilibrium, not 'merely' the voice or the musicianship, that seems to lie at the foundation of Domingo's achievement.

ACT II
Keeping a Record

Recording Opera

Until the twentieth century the only people who could experience a performance of opera were those in the audience on the night. For all the descriptions of how a singer sounded or acted, nobody who was not there could actually *know*. In the present century a virtual revolution has been wrought by the development of techniques of broadcasting, recording and reproducing both sound and vision. We can have no real idea what Grisi or Mario sounded like. But the voices of Melba and Caruso are captured, if inadequately, for all to hear, while the leading operatic performers of today are not only to be heard but also, increasingly, seen by worldwide audiences numbered in the millions. This revolution continues to have a profound impact upon both performers and audiences, upon the way each perceives the other, perhaps upon the very nature of performance.

As recordings have become better in quality and more available to more people, we have become less bewitched or awestruck by them than our ancestors were. We smile when told that people listening to Fred Gaisberg's early recordings of Caruso's voice found them indistinguishable from the real thing. Nowadays, most people have heard their own voice recorded, seen photos and possibly moving film of themselves, and know that the stars of the electronic entertainment media are creatures of flesh and blood. But if we are more blasé and less star-struck than our predecessors, we also tend to be more demanding. We want to have not just an occasional miraculous recording of Caruso singing a couple of arias, but entire operas recorded by the most outstanding casts. We have learnt to expect

38

excellence from the electronic media almost as a right and are far more critical than earlier generations if what we are offered falls short of expectation.

What does all this mean for an artist like Plácido Domingo? For a start he knows that at every live performance there will be many familiar with his voice from recordings. And since recordings are normally made up by editing together the best of a number of 'takes', he is constantly in competition with some of his own finest achievements. In a sense, this is inevitably a losing battle for him and for his audiences. Suppose you have been listening to one of his operatic recordings on excellent equipment with two well-separated speakers pouring out a massive decibelage of glorious sound. Or, maybe, to spare the neighbours the pain of half-heard music, you prefer the rich spaciousness provided by headphones. You can adjust not only the volume but also the degree of 'treble' or 'bass'. Nobody around you coughs or shuffles or wears a digital alarm watch. And the passages that particularly appeal can be played and replayed at will. If you then go to a live performance of the same opera, even with some of the same artists, you may be disappointed. The singers cannot possibly come across quite as loud and spacious or the orchestral detail be as clear and differentiated as on your sophisticated electronic equipment.

Every live performance is, in any case, likely to contain small errors of intonation, balance or ensemble, for no artist, however distinguished, can get everything right every night. Moreover, the very nature of a public performance necessitates for the listener, sitting in the darkened auditorium, a degree of physical distance and acoustical distortion that are absent in a recording.

Live performance by its very nature offers a different type of experience from that of a recording, less 'perfect' perhaps, more gritty, but often more exciting. Part of the thrill of live opera, like that of the circus (an analogy to which we will have occasion to return) is the possibility that the people before you may fail to pull off what they are attempting. The stakes are high, the effort needed to get things right so great, and the ways of getting them wrong legion and often very funny. But when everything really goes right the impact can be all the more overwhelming. There is an excitement in watching

39

opera live—when you do not know for certain how things will go—
that can never be recaptured if you are watching or listening to a
recording.

For all this, the fact remains that far more people have access to
opera via the electronic media than through live performance.
Broadcasts and recordings are comparatively cheap and have become
less expensive in real terms in the past few years; this is not true of live
performances of opera. Broadcasts have a 'democratic' appeal and
can be enjoyed by virtually anyone regardless of social or economic
status; this too is not always true of live performances. It is often said
that opera has broadened its appeal in recent years, that houses are
fuller, standards higher, companies more numerous and repertoires
wider than a generation ago, and much of this is surely in part a
response to the efforts of the radio and recording (and, in more recent
times, television) companies.

Ask Domingo about all this and his eyes flash with the conviction
of a missionary. He thinks of himself almost as an ambassador who
has to use his gifts to help bring his art to an ever wider public, and to
do this he is convinced that the modern electronic media are the
primary means. He knows that opera on record lacks the impact of
the real thing for all the technical perfection it can achieve and that
opera on the television screen can diminish to absurdity the larger-
than-life passions being acted out. But if he appears almost promis-
cuous in his readiness to record everything he can sing and to appear
at or on any media occasion that comes within his radar range, he
says this is because, ultimately, he wants his name and therefore his
art to become the possession of every household. 'Domingo?
Domingo? Let me see now . . . I know the name . . . isn't he the
one who sang with John Denver?' One may smile indulgently at the
commissionaire guarding the studio entrance on being told the name
of tonight's star—but Domingo himself is delighted. Maybe next
time the commissionaire sees the name it will be in connection with
an opera telecast, and maybe he will then watch opera, albeit on the
TV screen, and perhaps buy a recording of opera for the first time in
his life. And if that happens, nobody would be happier than Plácido
Domingo.

It is for his recordings of opera that Domingo is best known, of course, though, as the following story suggests, recording companies and their artists often have to surmount awkward hurdles before the results of their labours become available to the public.

All is set for a new recording of Puccini's *Madama Butterfly* and the sessions with tenor are to begin in London in two days. Suddenly another record company insists that the leading tenor is contracted to *them* for this role and they threaten to slap an injunction on the rival firm to prevent the recording going ahead. What is to be done? The resourceful administrative manager in London sits on the phone, calls every hotel in Las Palmas until she tracks down Plácido Domingo whom she knows is singing there, and explains her company's plight. Yes, he would love to help them out but he has a performance of *Tosca* tomorrow night and the next day there are no flights to London. Never mind, she says, greatly relieved at his helpful attitude, we'll think of something. She does. On the morning after his performance in Las Palmas Domingo flies to Madrid where he links up with a connecting flight to London. He arrives at Heathrow around 7 p.m. A car takes him straight to All Saints' Church in Tooting in south London where the *Butterfly* sessions are just about to begin. When he arrives, the conductor, Lorin Maazel, is already rehearsing the orchestra. Domingo steps straight in and by the time the session ends late that evening a healthy chunk of Act I is 'in the can'.

The company was the American-based CBS, the year 1978. The classical division of CBS is merely a small part of CBS Records, itself a subdivision of the giant Columbia Broadcasting System built up by William Paley, a conglomerate that owns one of America's principal television networks, several publishing companies, the piano company Steinway & Son, a host of finance and development enterprises, with subsidiaries in some forty different countries dotted around the world.

CBS Records, not unnaturally, has always been anxious to make a profit and to be seen to do so by the parent company, and by their principal American rival RCA Records, part of another giant conglomerate, the Radio Corporation of America. RCA was set up long before CBS and had its own father-figure in the doughty shape of radio and recording pioneer General David Sarnoff. For years RCA had a virtual monopoly of the record industry in the USA and its roster of performers reads like a Who's Who of twentieth-century music-making. One of the first and perhaps the greatest of all recording tenors, Enrico Caruso, was on contract to RCA and it is a moot point whether they did more for his career or he for theirs. But RCA artists have also included Toscanini, Rubinstein, Heifetz, Horowitz and, more recently, opera singers of the calibre of Leontyne Price and Sherrill Milnes.

CBS Records really came into its own with the dawning of the era of the LP (which RCA first tried to resist and then, with the marketing of 45s, to side-step) and in the 1950s and 1960s CBS produced a stream of magnificent classical recordings. They were the home company of Bruno Walter and some of the finest early recordings of Mahler's music were on the CBS label. CBS were also at this time making definitive versions of modern classics: Stravinsky conducting his own works and Boulez conducting the entire opus of Webern, for example. Opera, however, they tended to leave to the British and European companies and to their American rival RCA. The president of CBS Classical Division during these years, Goddard Lieberson, himself no opera fan, did not think most opera was really good music, felt its public to be philistine and fickle, and was not in any case convinced that opera recordings on the CBS label would sell. At RCA, on the other hand, the roster of singers on contract was spectacular and the house had an impressive string of opera recordings in its catalogue. So when a bright new tenor appeared on the American horizon in the late 1960s it was natural, to both him and them, that he should sign an exclusive contract to RCA.

Domingo was already being spasmodically courted by other companies. The British company Decca, for example, gave him a solo recital disc conducted by Nello Santi, first issued in 1970, and you might even catch the voice of the nineteen-year-old Plácido on a recording of *Mi Bella Dama*, the Mexican version of *My Fair Lady*, recorded in Mexico City in 1960. But right from the outset of his recording career Domingo gravitated towards RCA. A month before his début at the Metropolitan Opera in September 1968, he recorded a solo album for RCA and its producer Richard Mohr. The disc was issued in 1969 and the cover shows a rather earnest, round-faced, Mediterranean-looking young man in a dark jacket glaring uncompromisingly at Fred Schnell's camera.

Before long Domingo was recording up to four or five complete operas a year. Recordings for RCA in the late 1960s and early and mid-1970s include his first complete *Aida* (to date he has recorded this opera three times), *La Bohème, Andrea Chénier, Norma, Simon Boccanegra, Tosca, Il Trovatore, I Vespri Siciliani, La Forza del Destino* and many others. In those days Domingo's appetite for work was almost insatiable and even so opera-oriented a company as RCA could not accommodate all the recordings he wanted to make. So when an outside opportunity presented itself to which RCA had no objection, or regarding which it was prepared to have its arm twisted (*Don Carlos* for EMI under Giulini, an EMI *Aida* partnering Caballé, *Carmen* for Decca under Solti), Domingo eagerly snapped it up.

But what if an irresistible outside opportunity should present itself and RCA refuse to grant release? This was bound to happen sooner or later as the various companies came trooping to Domingo's door with increasingly enticing offers. Deutsche Grammophon were particularly anxious to have him on their books and in due course he was signed up to record several attractive projects. Meanwhile, RCA's great rival CBS had been quietly reconsidering its opera policy. Goddard Lieberson had retired and new people were coming to the fore in the company. In particular, Paul Myers, an Englishman who had worked in radio and in CBS Records in New York for many years, returned to London to take charge of the European offices of CBS Classical Division.

London was the right place to be in the mid-1970s. In many ways it was the musical capital of the world. Where New York could boast one symphony orchestra of international standard, London had five. Like New York, London had benefited enormously from the outpouring of mid-European talent occasioned by the Hitlerian holocaust. It was physically at the centre of the music world so that, in the era of the jet plane, people whose careers had them commuting back and forth around Europe and between Europe and the USA would find London a convenient stopping-off place. London was certainly the ideal place to make records. The plethora of orchestral talent and the legendary sight-reading ability of British players meant that it was always possible for a producer to book a first-class orchestra that could go straight into recording sessions able to play what was required. In addition, the Musicians' Union, while solicitous for the welfare of its members, had not pushed the pay of orchestral players to the prohibitive heights achieved in the USA, so that the overall cost of recording in London was lower than anywhere else where comparable artistic and technical quality might have been available.

Once Paul Myers was back in London, he and his enthusiastic assistant Vivienne Taylor set to work to unfold the new CBS policy. CBS would do opera, but would not—not at first, anyway—compete with the existing giants, Decca and EMI in Britain, Philips and Deutsche Grammophon on the Continent, and, above all, RCA back in the States. Thus, instead of going straight for their own *Tosca*, *Bohème*, *Rigoletto*, *Traviata* or *Carmen*, Myers and CBS went instead for a less well known repertoire. In 1975 CBS recorded Massenet's one-act opera *La Navarraise*—and to their unfeigned delight discovered that RCA was itself setting up a recording of this very work with Domingo, but that CBS had beaten them to it. A year later they decided to record Charpentier's *Louise*, a charming opera straight out of a Renoir painting (which CBS shrewdly displayed on the box cover). For *Louise* they engaged that most *simpatica* of sopranos, Ileana Cotrubas, for the title part and for her lover Julien (Charpentier's own *alter ego*) Plácido Domingo. Domingo had already worked for CBS. Back in 1970 he had come as a last-minute replacement into Bernstein's recording of the Verdi Requiem and had recorded the small but very exposed part of the 'Italian tenor' in that same conductor's *Rosenkavalier* a year later, one of the few opera recordings to get through the Lieberson net. For these recordings, RCA had been prepared to release Domingo as, indeed, they were for *Louise*.

As Paul Myers and his colleagues at CBS gained confidence in opera, they edged closer and closer towards the centre of the standard repertoire. When Covent Garden mounted a delicious production of

Donizetti's *L'Elisir d'Amore*, all pinks and yellows and mauves with scenery on pulleys operated by the 'country bumpkins' of the chorus, Myers felt that the time was ripe for a new recording of the opera. CBS offered Domingo a contract and, again, RCA released him.

By this stage in Domingo's career he was finding the exclusive RCA contract distinctly limiting. He was asking for release so often, indeed, that his RCA exclusivity was almost more honoured in the breach than in the observance. For several years he tried to wriggle free from the shackles of exclusivity. By the time CBS were considering recording *Butterfly* Domingo's contract with RCA stated merely that they had first refusal on a handful of stated operas; otherwise he was free to sell his services to whomever he wished. The trouble was that one of the core operas on which RCA had a hold was *Madama Butterfly*—something of which Paul Myers was unaware when he set up his CBS recording. Domingo had agreed enthusiastically to Myers's proposal—but then Domingo has a disarming habit of agreeing verbally to all sorts of attractive projects and then having trouble finding the time to deliver. In this instance, he *had* found the time: two full days in a crowded schedule would be put aside in which he would record for CBS all the sections of *Butterfly* which included Pinkerton, the tenor role. These would be the opening two days of the recording schedule—the only dates on which Domingo could possibly be free. He would fly in from the States for the sessions—and back again immediately after.

Paul Myers recalls that he was in his New York office preparing to go off to Cleveland for a couple of days to record the Beethoven *Eroica* symphony with Lorin Maazel. After the Cleveland sessions the two men would come to London for *Butterfly* . . .

A message is hand-delivered to Myers's office. It is from his RCA counterpart, Thomas Shepard, who declares that Domingo is under contract to RCA for a number of core repertoire operas, of which *Butterfly* is one, and that RCA cannot possibly release him. Myers's face goes ashen. He has known Tom Shepard many years. They are rivals but friends and both care about good music and good recordings. Myers remembers giving Shepard a call. 'Plácido is dying to do our *Butterfly*,' he pleads. 'He and I were talking about it just the other day and he's so looking forward to it.' 'I'm sure,' replies Tom, 'but as a matter of fact I must tell you we have our own plans to do a *Butterfly* with Plácido so I really can't release him on this.' Sigh of bitter resignation from Paul . . .

Madama Butterfly is one of the first CBS forays into the core operatic repertoire, their first major bid to compete with their old US rival RCA on ground so far largely dominated by the latter. There is no time for head-holding. The only question Myers and Maazel consider as they fly to Cleveland is not whether the *Butterfly* will go ahead but how and with whom . . . In Cleveland, Maazel works the orchestra hard. They are used to it. This, after all, was for years the orchestra of that martinet among modern maestros, the late George Szell. Between *Eroica* sessions Myers and Maazel hurriedly confer about *Butterfly*. There is no question of cancelling the London sessions. That is, they could be cancelled but the cast and orchestra and studio fees would all have to be paid. The non-tenor sections of the opera could perhaps be recorded and the rest deferred until a tenor is found. But that would still leave two days of unused studio time to be paid for. Maazel generously offers to save CBS a packet and use the sessions to record an album of Wagner overtures.

The part of Butterfly is to be sung by Renata Scotto, who was due to do the role under Maazel at La Scala, Milan. Scotto and Maazel had withdrawn from this production, but the obvious solution to the CBS dilemma would be to engage the Scala tenor, Giacomo Aragall, for the recording. Aragall has one of the most ingratiating voices in the business and if he is not an artist of the stature or box-office appeal of Domingo, his voice is scarcely less beautiful. In any case, Myers rationalizes, Pinkerton is a small part as leading tenor roles go. He is on for a lot of Act I but only appears again briefly towards the end of the opera. Aragall is invited and is delighted to accept—though, inevitably, the recording sessions for the sections with tenor have to be rescheduled.

Three months later all the non-tenor sections of *Butterfly* are substantially edited. Everybody looks forward to recording the rest of the opera with Aragall. But when the dates for the Aragall sessions finally approach, Myers is assaulted by a second bombshell. Aragall is apparently committed, not by contract but by a comprehensive letter which he has signed, to record *Butterfly* for a Canadian company.

Will the Canadian company please release him? Will they, hell! They threaten to slap an injunction on CBS forbidding *Butterfly* to go ahead with Aragall in the cast.

This time Myers is desperate. In a fit of bravado he calls up Tom Shepard in New York once more and explains his acute dilemma. Is there no way CBS could call upon Domingo to help them out? Just this once? Shepard is genuinely sympathetic but still cannot see his way to releasing Domingo. RCA, he repeats, have their own plans to do *Butterfly* with Domingo. Myers, trying to keep his mounting fears from surfacing, keeps the chat going. 'Oh, yes, I remember you mentioned that,' he says weakly. 'By the way, who's going to sing the title-role?' 'Kiri Te Kanawa,' Tom Shepard replies. Myers has to think fast. He knows and likes Te Kanawa. But he also knows that *Butterfly* is not one of her roles and that it would take her a long time to get the part up to the standard required for a recording. She is not one of those artists like Domingo who can sit at the piano and learn a new role almost at sight. In the nicest possible way Paul points this out to Tom who has to acknowledge that, realistically, no Domingo-Te Kanawa *Butterfly* could be set up and recorded for some years. Shepard reconsiders Myers's problem—all those tenor-less scenes of *Butterfly* already in the can—and knows that if he were in a similar fix Myers would do all he could to help him. 'OK, Paul,' he says at last with a smile audible along the transatlantic line, 'you're on!' Verbal hugs and handshakes—and Myers is off and running. There are now just three days to go before the postponed tenor sessions are to commence. Domingo must be found. And fast. Vivienne Taylor has already ascertained that he is in Las Palmas and the frantic telephoning back and forth begins. The rest is gramophone history, as anyone who has enjoyed the splendid 1978 CBS *Butterfly* can testify.

It may just be worth adding that there was a two-day break between the first and second recording sessions and Domingo spent it quietly with his family. In Barcelona.

From Op to Pop

Domingo's recordings have not all been of opera. Indeed, to many people he is familiar primarily as a singer of middle-of-the-road popular songs. His record with John Denver, 'Perhaps Love', sold over one and a half million copies in its first two years while subsequent 'crossover' albums are also cruising comfortably through the international charts.

Domingo's career as a singer of pop songs has landed him, as he knew it would, in controversy, particularly from those who say that 'serious' and 'popular' music cannot mix. 'Why does he waste his talent doing that stuff?' one famous colleague asked me, hands thrown up in exasperation. 'Can he still want to be rich and famous?' 'All this pop business,' sniffed another, 'why, he doesn't even do it well. Plácido's a great opera singer but a lousy crooner.' 'Plácido is one of the great artists of the century,' yet another regaled me. 'Why should such a man crave the adulation of the pop star? It's so demeaning.' Some Domingo-watchers put the 'crossover' career and the attendant publicity down to jealousy of the popular hysteria, not to mention the income, that for years accompanied Pavarotti. 'Plácido is by far the greater artist but he resents the way the public, particularly in the United States, has been gulled into thinking that Luciano is *numero uno*,' one soprano colleague of both men put it to me. 'He's trying to get his own back.'

Domingo is naturally hurt by the sniping but tries to brush it off philosophically. 'I just love to sing anything that is good music,' he says. 'The best *zarzuela* songs or those of Lennon and McCartney or Sammy Cahn or John Denver are the *lieder* of today and I want to sing these just as much as the greatest operas.' In addition, he never fails to remind questioners that he is not exactly the first classical singer to perform the popular repertoire of his day. Patti and Melba, Caruso and Gigli, Tauber and Schipa and Pinza—all had a substantial repertoire of popular songs. As for the Pavarotti jibe, Domingo easily points out that his crossover career (and his classical career for that matter) has covered territory far further afield than anything attempted by his Italian rival; Domingo is quite prepared to concede his annoyance at all the newspaper talk about which of them is the greatest, but not at all prepared to concede that the much-bruited rivalry has made the slightest difference to the nature of the work he has chosen to undertake.

What about the question of commercialism? There is no denying that Domingo makes a great deal of money from his crossover albums. 'When I record an opera,' he points out, 'the effort is enormous but the sales low. *Oberon* or even *Aida* won't provide much of an income for my children or grandchildren, but they may stand to benefit from an album like "Perhaps Love".' They may indeed. Classical records account for a paltry four or five per cent of overall sales; once you become a household name and record genuinely popular albums, however, your records can sell not in the thousands but in the hundreds of thousands and even the millions. But money does not seem to be the principal motive. If it were, Domingo could greatly increase his annual income simply by taking on more popular solo engagements and recordings than he does and less opera.

Far more important to Domingo is his belief that, by making his art and his name more widely known through his pop recordings, he may perhaps help win a new audience for his first love, opera. 'You should see the letters I get,' he offers enthusiastically, 'from people saying they're coming to the opera because they heard me sing "Perhaps Love" or saw me launch one of my pop albums on TV.' Also, Domingo feels that if he is to keep up with the musical developments of his own time, middle-of-the-road pop is one of the few roads not barred to him and his talents. The dissonant frontiers of 'serious' music he finds unsingable, likewise the latest trends in rock music. The one form of singable contemporary music that genuinely attracts him is the work of composers like Andrew Lloyd Webber and Lee Holdridge, men who know a good tune when they hear or invent one and know, too, how to arrange it in an appealing and (to singer and audience alike) accessible manner.

There is a further factor, more deeply embedded in Domingo's personality, that leads him to want to master both 'classical' and 'popular' music, to appeal to two kinds of audience, to make social and cultural bridges. He himself, when asked why he sings popular music, often retorts that he is returning to the idiom of his youth. As a boy he hung around the performers in his parents' company, helped rehearse them at the piano, knew everybody's lines and lyrics, and was occasionally on the boards himself. To those among his critics who say he cheapens himself by performing middle-of-the-road pop, he can legitimately answer that this is close to his authentic musical roots.

How close is it? Does the idiom of John Denver and Henry Mancini come naturally to a man brought up on *zarzuela*? The recordings offer a clue. Listen to Domingo singing *zarzuelas* or Spanish tangos, and then turn to 'Perhaps Love' or 'My Life for a Song'. The voice is stronger, more passionate in the Spanish music, a little breathy at times in the others. The popular songs that classical singers turn to most successfully tend to be those in an idiom closest to them: John McCormack's Irish ballads and Stuart Burrows's Welsh songs, Richard Tauber in Viennese operetta or Richard Tucker in Jewish *chazzanot*, Caruso or Gigli (or Pavarotti) in Leoncavallo's 'Mattinata' or the songs of Tosti. Some argue that Domingo should stick to *zarzuelas* and 'Granada'.

This is too purist. Italian or French opera, after all, is a long way from the native idiom of a Spaniard raised in Mexico, yet Domingo's achievements in these have the stamp of total authority. But when Domingo sings American or American-style popular music, some critics detect a sense of toning down, of switching off several cylinders, of changing gear to accommodate something unfamiliar and lightweight. As Domingo approaches one of those soft, sweet phrases a smile creeps into the edge of his voice rather like that of an adult trying to win over a small child—none the less appealing for that but perhaps a trifle forced. One can almost hear the chin and eyebrows raised to caress the microphone, the lower lip protruding, the hands spread out towards the listeners.

What this suggests is not any serious artistic shortcoming so much as an insight into personality—and ultimately, perhaps, motivation. For Domingo appears driven not only to become an artist of the most rarefied achievement but at the same time to succeed as a casual, friendly approachable entertainer, the greatest master of the esoteric world of grand opera and also the guy next door.

There is no reason on the face of it why one should not aspire to

being both Great Artist and Nice Guy and Domingo's career to date
suggests that he has the capacity to ride both horses better than most
could ride either. He does not pretend he is not endowed with
exceptional talent. He knows his artistic worth and realistically rates it
highly. But he is also by nature a genuinely friendly person with a
desire to perform popular music and be seen as 'just folks'. He has,
one might almost say, a populist, sentimental streak that can lead
him at the drop of a hat to the piano to sing Rodgers and Hammerstein or Irving Berlin or to gossip with anyone within range about the
latest football results. Thus his operatic and crossover careers are both
authentic reflections of his talents, tastes and personality. But the
dual path Domingo has chosen to walk involves a careful balancing
of personal and professional considerations and he knows that his
undertakings must continue to reflect authentic inner urges if the
tightrope act is to continue to succeed. All high-wire artists face the
possibility of falling off; the higher they walk the further the possible
fall. As Domingo marches resolutely across, aware of the sharks that
will eat him alive if his pop career causes him to trip up as an opera
singer and of the derision that would await an unsuccessful pop
record, he remains confident, cool, apparently in careful balance.
Certainly, this is how he appears when making the pop records
themselves . . .

The studio is in a grubby corner of New York's entertainment district,
on top of Manhattan Community College. To get up there you go
through an unmarked side entrance, through a rusty door and into a
service elevator that looks as though it has not been used for thirty
years. Upstairs, along a coffee-stained corridor or two and through an
unpainted door marked 'Studio' is, almost surprisingly, a studio. It is
in here that Plácido Domingo will be singing for the next five hours.

The title song, 'Perhaps Love', is a duet between Plácido and John
Denver and written by John. It was initially committed to tape back in
March but now, in June 1981, Domingo is to re-record his own
contribution to give the engineers more leeway when they come to
edit the tapes. In the earlier sessions, Domingo sang some of his
songs, including the duet with Denver, to the accompaniment of a
rhythm section. In the weeks since, while Domingo has been in

Europe, an orchestral 'sweetening' by Lee Holdridge has been recorded in Los Angeles and grafted onto the sound-track and now Domingo has this full orchestration fed to him through earphones as he sings through 'Perhaps Love' and the remaining numbers. He is sight-reading some of the songs as he goes, but with each run-through there is added strength and line and poignancy and musical meaning. In the Tony Renis song 'He Couldn't Love You More' he develops a sense of jealousy and desperation worthy of the world's greatest exponent of Verdi's Otello.

Much of the initiative not just for this album but for Domingo's crossover career as a whole came from producer Milton Okun. Classically trained, Okun started professionally as a music teacher in New York and then branched out as an arranger, particularly of folk music. For several years he worked with Harry Belafonte. Then came the folk boom of the 1960s which did Okun's career a power of good and throughout that period he worked as arranger and/or record producer for many of the top folk performers including the Chad Mitchell Trio and Peter, Paul and Mary. Through his work with the Mitchell Trio he came to know John Denver and in due course, when Denver branched out on his own, Okun was his regular record producer. By the time of 'Perhaps Love' Okun was long since established as one of the most successful producers of popular music records in the industry.

Throughout all this success in the highly exposed world of popular music Okun retained a deep and special affection for his first love, classical music, particularly opera. Most of the leading opera singers of the 1960s disappointed him, but he found himself intrigued by the emergence of Domingo. Here was a new artist who, at least according to his records, was an almost unbelievable paragon of every virtue one could dream of in a singer: not only a voice in a million but also an outstanding musician and vocal actor into the bargain. Okun was a record producer and maintained a healthy scepticism about recordings. Perhaps these early Domingo discs were flukes, or greatly edited. But as one complete opera after another appeared and Domingo maintained the same uncanny standard of vocal artistry, Okun found himself forced to believe the evidence of his own ears. He developed a fantasy: one day he would get to know Domingo, maybe even work with him.

In the mid-70s the two men chanced to meet. They were both up for a Grammy Award, the Oscar of the record industry, and at the ceremony were placed at the same table. Okun won an award and Domingo did not, and Milt went home that night bathed in genuine incredulity and despair, doubtless the only award winner that night to do so. He could not believe the insensitivity and wrongheadedness of the people who allotted the prizes. When he got home he burst out to his wife Rosemary that he had met Plácido Domingo (and presumably also remembered to tell her that in the course of the evening he had won a Grammy Award!)—and for the next five years he tried every trick he knew to persuade RCA (still Domingo's principal company) or any other record company that would listen to let him produce a recording with Plácido Domingo. He came up with several ideas—Domingo singing Spanish art songs or folk songs, for example, perhaps to guitar accompaniment by Segovia. None of this got anywhere with the company executives and Domingo does not remember being told about any of Okun's brainwaves. Meanwhile, Okun took in every Domingo performance he could catch and sometimes went round after the show. Once he was introduced to Domingo by the president of RCA Records who said, 'Milt is the man who produces the records of John Denver'—to which Domingo was only able to reply, 'You must excuse me but I don't know the name.'

Things seemed at a stalemate. Then one night the Okuns saw Domingo on television on the Johnny Carson show. Chatting about his background in popular musicals in Mexico he sang an excerpt or two from *My Fair Lady*. As he launched into a few bars of 'On the Street Where You Live' Rosemary turned to her husband, riveted, and said, 'Milt! *That's* the sort of record you should make with him. Get him to sing some popular music!'

More time elapsed. By now it was 1980. Finally, Rosemary insisted that if Milt really had the courage of his convictions he should write Domingo a letter setting out clearly what he wanted to propose: an album of popular music that would lie well within Domingo's voice and would enable him to reach a wider audience. Her instincts proved right. The letter was dispatched, and eventually, after several follow-up calls and many weeks of further waiting, the Okuns' phone rang. A gentle voice said, 'Meelton? This is Plácido . . .'

Okun is not a demonstrative man, but he still describes that phone call as just possibly the happiest moment of his professional life. The two men agreed to meet in Los Angeles in November when Domingo was to give a concert at the Dorothy Chandler Pavilion and record an album of arias at the Shrine Auditorium, both with the Los Angeles Philharmonic and Giulini. Milt was making a record with John Denver in Los Angeles at the time and took John as his guest to the concert. They sat in the fourth row and John could not believe that stupendous voice when he first heard it up close. Milt recalls that Denver kept peering round the auditorium, and later discovered that he was looking for the loudspeakers!

By now Domingo knew who John Denver was and had asked Okun to bring him round after the concert. It meant waiting in line with everybody else for over an hour as Domingo and Giulini were being photographed for the album cover, but Denver had no complaints. When the two men finally met, Domingo complimented Denver on 'Annie's Song'. 'I had dinner with Jimmy Galway in New York the other day and he was going into raptures about your beautiful song.' Denver, still a little awestruck at the voice belonging to the gentleman before him, was naturally delighted—and Okun immediately asked Domingo, not entirely casually, whether he might not consider emulating Galway and record 'Annie's Song' himself. Everybody smiled politely, then Domingo added that 'The song sounds as though it belongs in my throat.'

From this conversation, Okun conceived the extravagant idea of recording 'Annie's Song' with Domingo singing, Galway on flute, and Denver on guitar. This ambitious project ('overkill' one friend called it) never reached fruition—but from it arose the idea of Domingo and Denver working together.

In December 1980 Domingo flew to London for Covent Garden's spectacular new *Tales of Hoffmann* produced by John Schlesinger. Okun, who had finished his recording with Denver, flew over too. So, as it happened, did Joe Dash of CBS who had come to London with the express intention of encouraging Domingo to consider expanding his market by making a crossover record. Funny you should mention that, says Plácido, because there's a popular music producer from America who's been pursuing me for quite a while with the same idea. 'What's his name?' asks Dash. 'Milton Okun.' 'Okun?' says Dash. 'Why, he's one of the tops!' From then on it was only a matter of time before Domingo would make his first crossover record, with Milton Okun, for CBS.

And not, in the event, very much time. Okun left London for the States after the first night of *Hoffmann*. Six weeks later he came by appointment to Domingo's New York apartment (he was then living in the Hampshire House on Central Park South) to go through an initial selection of possible songs. Domingo said he would put aside a couple of dates in March for the recording and Okun agreed that new arrangements of all the songs finally selected would be ready by then. The two men decided to have a quick bite of lunch before getting down to work. As they sat down to eat Domingo said, 'We're recording in March, yes?'

'Right.'

'Well, let's see; I'm doing a new production of *Andrea Chénier* in Vienna at the end of April and I'll have a little time to spare . . . I'd like to record a Christmas album—would you like to produce that too?'

'Yes!' says Okun, without pausing for breath—and reflects silently that it took him five years to get his first Domingo record and five minutes to get his second.

After lunch they go through the songs Okun has brought, Domingo playing them through on the piano, vocalizing them, transposing them into various alternative keys, boiling the selection down to a short list for the March recording.

If Domingo's career at this point was at some sort of crossroads, so was John Denver's. Domingo was about to let himself in for a departure he knew would be controversial but which he was prepared to try. Denver, on the other hand, once America's number one popular singer, had not had a hit in several years. The greatest blow to his spirits—and to Okun's—was when they submitted the songs Denver had recorded in Los Angeles at the time of the Domingo concert, and RCA had refused to issue the disc. It might not have proved Denver's greatest selling record but it did contain a new song called 'Perhaps Love' that Denver and Okun both felt could be a hit.

Today John tells audiences that 'Perhaps Love' is one of his personal favourites, possibly the best song he's ever written. 'I was driving down the California coast one day,' he says, 'feeling real sorry for myself' (this was a time when his marriage was breaking up), 'and then I began to think of you wonderful people and that cheered me up a real lot. And just then'—he gives his quizzical boyish grin—'just then, this song jes' comes a-floating by my mind. So I grabbed it quick before it could escape'—another grin—'and here it is, specially for you!' And of course his audiences sing along with him and go wild at the end. But back in 1980, prospects for 'Perhaps Love' were not bright. Indeed, RCA not only refused to issue the disc but took Denver away from Okun and assigned him to a different producer.

By now Okun was immersed in his new assignment to find suitable songs for Plácido Domingo. One day he had a call from John Denver saying he was not comfortable with his new RCA producer and, in particular, Denver wanted to share with Okun the melancholy news that the new producer did not even want to record 'Perhaps Love'. This flowed through the filter of Okun's new obsession and he came up with an idea.

'John, you want that song on record, right?'

'Right.'

'And RCA won't let you sing it?'

'No.'

'Do you mind if I give it to Plácido to sing for CBS—with you playing guitar?'

'Great!' John exclaims with delight.

Okun goes one further. 'Maybe you and Plácido could do it as a vocal duet?'

Denver does not think RCA will give him permission to sing on another label.

'Let's record it anyway,' says Milt. 'If it doesn't work, we can forget it. But if it sounds good, RCA can't say they haven't had first refusal on the song, and a Denver hit from another company can only help sales of RCA Denver discs.'

John is absolutely ecstatic. But he is also apprehensive. He remembers that giant, unamplified voice.

A month later, in March 1981, Denver and Domingo meet again, this time in the CBS studio on 52nd Street in New York. The chemistry works from the start and the recording goes well. The two singers, so different in training, background, talents and tastes, enjoy working together. Once Denver has left, Domingo records a few more tracks. One of them is 'On the Street Where You Live' from *My Fair Lady*. It was his rendition of a few bars of this song on the Johnny Carson show that unwittingly provided the genesis of his new crossover career. In the event this particular track is not included in the album as issued, for Plácido in his enthusiasm has insisted on recording twelve songs for a disc that cannot hold more than ten.

That night Plácido goes to the opening of the new Broadway show *Woman of the Year* starring Lauren Bacall. He loves the show, gives Bacall a congratulatory hug afterwards—and next day reports to Okun that the show contains a song that he would like to try called 'Sometimes a Day Goes By'. They chase up the music, clear the copyright—and a day later Plácido records it. By now his relentless schedule catches up with him and he is due in Europe so the sessions have to be suspended until he is back in New York again three months later. When Plácido has gone, Okun plays over the 'Perhaps Love' duet and is convinced he has a major hit on his hands. But he still cannot be quite sure that RCA will permit Denver's voice to appear on the CBS label. Thus, the first order of business when the sessions resume in June will be to re-record the whole song in Domingo's own voice so that there are enough versions with and without Denver to satisfy any contingency. When the time comes, Domingo does not object. He loves singing the song.

In the studio in June—the shabby studio above Manhattan Community College—everyone is relaxed. Never mind that Domingo was singing *Tosca* to a crowd of 250,000 in New York's Central Park the night before and has only had a few hours' sleep since. Today he is in good form, happy to spend as much time on each song as is required to get it absolutely right. There is no hurry. The studio has been booked for six hours and Domingo has nothing else to do for the rest of the day—except fly that night across a continent and a half to Buenos Aires.

The opening phrase of 'Perhaps Love' gives trouble today just as it did in March. It starts low and has to be sung very softly. At times the voice loses its customary focus and sounds breathy. In the control room the problem is not too worrying as Domingo's voice is mixed with the reverberant orchestral sweetening by Lee Holdridge. But inside the studio itself, Domingo's voice does undeniably sound drier than it should and he is a little phlegmy this morning. He works at the phrase repeatedly until not only Okun and the engineers but he himself feels he has got it right.

Back in the control room he listens to the latest take. The sound is wonderful and flowing. Domingo in his enthusiasm compliments Okun; he feels Milt records his voice better than has been done in any of his other recordings. Okun is seized by the further fantasy that maybe one day he could produce a classical album with Domingo too . . .

Domingo is a fluent and witty talker in English (though he has a chronic habit of saying 'than' when he means 'that')—but recording songs in English is something else again. In opera, the words are often well known, easy to project (particularly in Italian), or, in certain passages, so subordinate to the music that their detailed meaning is unimportant. But in new, solo songs, unplaced in any dramatic context and unfamiliar to listeners, the lyrics can be all-important and Domingo's warm, Mediterranean pronunciation can occasionally make the words hard to understand. In the Renis song 'He Couldn't Love You More', Domingo's pronunciation is below par in a couple of places. Plácido himself is worried about the phrase 'the stranger at the party': should it be par*ty* or, in the American idiom, par*dy*? Jokes circulate about whether the record is primarily aimed at a British or American market and the eventual pronunciation is mid-Atlantic. Earlier it was the phrase 'Love is like a resting place' from 'Perhaps Love' that bothered him. 'Doesn't it sound too much like "Love is like a *wrestling* place?"' he had asked, frowning. And someone suggested with a wink that, well, yes, it sometimes is . . .

There is no time for lunch. Domingo drinks black coffee from a machine and munches from a plate of sandwiches someone has thoughtfully provided—then back to work. There is a Spanish television team present; they are preparing a documentary about him for the programme 300,000,000—a feature that gets shown throughout the Spanish-speaking world to an audience of potentially 300,000,000 people. Domingo gives them an *ad hoc* explanation of what is going on and why, even lets them into the studio as he records yet another take of 'Perhaps Love'. Present at the session, too, is a journalist from *People* magazine preparing a feature article on him. The phone goes; *Newsweek* want to know when and where they can interview him. He'll call them back later when the session is over—before going off to the airport.

One final take of the final song—and then Plácido agrees to record it yet again, this time at the request of the Spanish television team. He still seems to have the stamina to carry on. 'Where do you get all that energy from?' someone asks. 'Perhaps love!' Domingo quips.

He makes his Buenos Aires flight that evening and goes on to give a series of sensational performances of Verdi's *Otello* in the Argentinian capital. Everywhere he goes in Buenos Aires he is fêted like a conquering hero. He is offered what he himself calls a stratospheric fee to add a concert appearance to an already crowded schedule, and he refuses. He is in Argentina to perform *Otello*. But one night, after all the post-*Otello* kisses and interviews and autographs and handshakes are over and everyone else from the theatre has gone home to bed, Domingo slips into a studio and spends the rest of the night pouring out his heart into what will become his best-selling album of tangos.

Milton Okun, to his immense relief, eventually got RCA to agree that Denver's voice could appear in the duet with Domingo, even though it was a CBS record. But Okun wanted more than that. He wanted RCA to give permission for the duet to go out as a CBS single. It could sell millions. Also, Domingo is an ex-RCA exclusive artist and it would not exactly harm sales of RCA's back catalogue of classical recordings to have Domingo's name on a million lips. Okun was so convinced of the rightness of his case that he went straight to the top and called the president of RCA Records, Bob Summers. '"Perhaps Love" has *got* to be a single. It's a great record,' he said. And got the firm answer 'No'.

The LP was issued in October 1981. The title song was played on radio station WFIL in Philadelphia who immediately received calls requesting details of the record. Several other big pop music stations had the same experience within days—stations that in some cases had not played a new Denver record for years. Okun remembers going back to Summers and pleading yet again for RCA permission for CBS to release the song as a single. Or couldn't RCA themselves issue it as a single? He was sure CBS could be persuaded to agree to that. Anything to make it available in the shops. Fast. Again, the answer was 'No'. Okun's spleen was really flowing. As he recalls it, he told the president of RCA, 'It's rarely given to an executive of a major record company to kill a hit twice but that's what you've just done!'

The LP was a runaway success far beyond anybody's imaginings. Okun expected sales of perhaps 200,000; within a year of its release it topped a million. For months the title song 'Perhaps Love' cropped up constantly on radio stations all over America, Britain and beyond. For weeks the record was number two in Spain. In Austria its sales were such that if the same pattern were repeated in the other countries where the record was available it would have sold ten million in its first year.

One result was that countless people came to hear and love Domingo's voice for the first time, if only as 'the man who sings with John Denver'. At the Met and Covent Garden, in Vienna and Milan, Domingo noticed with pleasure that stage hands who used to be distant and deferential began to call him Plácido and tell him that they had heard one of his songs on a local pop radio station.

Okun had initially underwritten the costs of this record himself and his faith in what he was doing was amply rewarded. The people in CBS Masterworks duly took note and approached Domingo about a long-term contract—a six-year agreement, say, during which Domingo would do one CBS crossover album a year. Plácido was tempted. He knew that, for all the advantages of recording for several different labels, he was possibly reducing the publicity effort any one company would be prepared to make for him. If he were to sign an exclusive contract with CBS, at least for his crossover albums, they would be more likely to push him as a hot marketable product than if he did an occasional one-off for them and other discs for rival companies. Also, it would be good to have several years and several albums guaranteed. This would mean Domingo could plan strategically, build up a reasonably rounded corpus of popular recordings and thereby a definable popular profile, which he could not do if each album were a purely discrete affair. If the scenario worked well, he might be able to continue making popular albums after his operatic career had begun to wind down. The CBS offer gave him the opportunity of some welcome long-term thinking. On the other hand, he was by any criterion primarily a 'classical' artist, to opera lovers one of the greatest of them all, but to the people at CBS, who had to balance their books each year, a far less saleable product than, say, a Neil Diamond or a Kenny Rogers and worth therefore a considerably less generous contract.

Domingo, so sensitive to personality and politics in the world of opera, was still something of an innocent when it came to that of mass entertainment. He knew CBS were offering him a low advance (the equivalent for each record of roughly what he was paid for a single operatic performance) and a poor royalty agreement, but had no way of being sure he could command more. Something in his bones told him not to sign the proffered contract and for once his instinct not to foreclose options held him in good stead. Milt Okun advised him not to sign too. Meanwhile, 'Perhaps Love' was continuing to climb the charts, notching up 50,000 sales in one country, 25,000 in another, a further 50,000 in a third—and the logic was not lost at CBS. By the time Domingo eventually signed for them they had multiplied their original offer by a factor of twenty. This colossal increase still left Domingo well behind the real pop giants, some of whom are offered guarantees of thirty or forty million dollars for their exclusive services, but at least he now felt he was being offered a more realistic approximation to his genuine market—not to say artistic—value.

One outcome of the astonishing success of 'Perhaps Love' was that Milton Okun was flooded with hundreds of new songs that composers of popular music wanted Domingo to perform on his next crossover record. The crossover career had clearly 'taken' and the only question, by now obvious to everyone, was not *whether* there would be another disc like 'Perhaps Love' but when, and precisely what.

Over the next few months these matters got sorted out. Okun followed Domingo around Europe and America throughout the rest of 1981, snatching a telephone conversation with him in one place, going round after a performance in another. They considered a range of songs and eventually decided on a short list of perhaps twenty possibles, almost all new, but with one or two old favourites.

Okun used to do all his own arranging but nowadays often employs the services of Lee Holdridge, one of the masters of the medium. Holdridge is an American born in Costa Rica, a sturdy young man with a dark moustache and Plácido Domingo hairstyle. Classically trained by a teacher broadminded enough to demonstrate sonata form from the example of 'Smoke Gets in Your Eyes', Holdridge has a number of serious orchestral works to his credit but makes most of his money writing music for films and television. He lives in Los Angeles and is one of those fortunate people whose talents wedge nicely into the opportunities available to him. He was not only the arranger of Domingo's Denver and Christmas albums but the composer of a few of the items—notably the 'American Hymn' (theme of the television series *East of Eden*). During the first half of 1982 Holdridge's facility as an arranger was again put to the test as he battled with the scores for Domingo's next pop album and tried to write an appropriate backing for each song while giving the record as a whole a consistent texture.

Lee gets the work done in record time and also writes an original song which will be the title number of the new album. In late August, he flies across to London for the recording sessions. Milton Okun and his family have been holidaying in France while Domingo has been performing *Hoffmann* in Salzburg, filming *Traviata* for Zeffirelli in Paris and Rome, and snatching some rest in his home in Monte Carlo. All now converge on a rainy London and the CBS studios just off Goodge Street. Awaiting them is a five-man backing team, British session musicians assembled for the occasion—piano, guitars and drums—who will play Holdridge's music under his direction. A full orchestra will be assembled later in the week.

Domingo's summer plans have gone awry. The *Traviata* filming over-ran and ate into time that he had at first put by for other things. As the shooting schedule became more and more protracted,

62

Domingo found himself spending much of the summer commuting between half a dozen cities in Europe, often giving a performance on one night in one country and filming *Traviata* the very next day in another.

He has other problems too. The gossip columns of the popular newspapers have been trumpeting a supposed liaison between Plácido and Gina Lollobrigida with reports full of snide and unsubstantiated innuendo. La Lollo had been watching and photographing some of the shooting of the Zeffirelli *Traviata* and had taken a number of pictures of Domingo. They had talked about films and filming and had been photographed together, and he had made a few suggestions about ways in which she might consider getting her once legendary film career moving again. This casual acquaintanceship is pounced upon and represented as a passionate illicit romance by the American scandal-sheet the *National Enquirer* and Domingo is incensed. He knows what groundless pain all this will cause Marta when the story reaches her. When you are a rich, famous, attractive man you are inevitably likely to call upon yourself a certain amount of publicity of this sort and your domestic existence will naturally become the object of public curiosity and tittle-tattle. But Domingo's professional life is already so ferociously programmed that it seems a little harsh that he has to deal with adverse publicity about his private life as well. Little of this shows when he turns up at the CBS studios in London, however. He radiates his usual relaxed good humour, looks tanned and healthy in jeans and casual shirt, and has already put back some of the stomach he lost for the Zeffirelli movie. When he sees me he grins and puts on his best *Sunday Times* magazine cover face—huge mouth as wide open as it will go—and asks from a distance of six inches, 'Recognize me, Daniel?'

His appetite for work is prodigious and seems unjaded by the pace of the past fifteen years. His enthusiasm for the current job in hand is always a little like that of a child for a new toy and on this occasion it infects everyone in the studio. With his hands in his pockets, huge head hunched forwards, eyes wide open and alert, his left leg twitching with impatience, he is all electricity. 'Nye-e-e-e-eh,' he begins to vocalize in a low arpeggio. 'Nye-e-e-e-eh' a semitone up, and so on until he is hitting Es and Fs. He goes into his sound-proof cubicle where he can vocalize all he wants without disturbing anyone, while the engineers, eavesdropping on the orchestra tuning up in the studio and Plácido vocalizing in his cubicle, gradually get everything in balance.

One day a television crew is allowed in the studio and asks if it may film Domingo recording one of the songs. Can they shoot him singing 'My Life for a Song'? This is the new piece by Lee Holdridge which is to be the lead song of the album.

Domingo sings it through once unfilmed, just to get the feel of the thing, and then he and Holdridge come into the control room for a playback. Playbacks are at a monstrously high volume but nobody seems to object, least of all the principals. Sound engineers in the pop world tend to play their machines at a higher level than those recording classical music. George Martin has recalled how, during all-night recording sessions with the Beatles, playbacks got louder and louder, perhaps to counter growing torpor, so that anybody who chanced into one of those sessions at five in the morning would have been in danger of having an ear-drum burst.

Domingo listens to his own work with the cool detachment of an outsider. Yes, he acknowledges, it was pretty good. 'But I feel I am pushing you,' he says to Lee and points to a few places in the score which he thinks drag. It is Lee's music, of course, and he argues that it needs to be a little stately to get the right effect. Maybe, Plácido muses, but he recalls another of Lee's pieces, the 'American Hymn' which brought to a conclusion the 'Perhaps Love' album. 'I've seen *East of Eden* on television several times,' Plácido says, 'and the song works marvellously there as a signature tune.' Holdridge is flattered. 'But'—there was bound to be a but—'but the TV version is quicker than the way we did it and I feel that in this piece, too, "My Life for a Song", we will do more justice to the music if we do it a fraction faster. Or perhaps not faster but more urgently. What do you think?'

'Let's leave it until the orchestra's here,' Okun decides. Plácido will be at one of the orchestral sessions later in the week and this particular song seems to need a proper co-ordination of all the forces. The TV team will have to film something else. Other songs on the list present fewer problems and can be recorded with the five-man backing and mixed later with the orchestral sound.

'Blue Moon' is one such. Actually it is a mix of 'Blue Moon' and 'Moon River', a touch of the first, the soaring tune of the second, then back to the first again by way of conclusion. A quick-slow-quick moon sandwich. They run through the piece and come in for a playback. The piece is sweet. And very short. Blessedly so for everybody's assaulted eardrums. But isn't it *too* short, Plácido asks? What was it—about two minutes? Two minutes and four seconds, he is told. It begins with a very simple, almost childlike series of honky-tonk chords, the archetypal vamping accompaniment, and Plácido feels the song at present comes and goes too casually. Some of Domingo's low notes get lost under the orchestra, and his pronunciation still needs work. His eldest son Joe, who has turned up in his motorcycling gear, kids Plácido about the way he sang 'Moon Reever' on a television show some months back, and Plácido takes the point by jokingly singing whole phrases with an exaggeratedly Spanish accent. The piece is not quite right yet and various suggestions surface from around the control room about how to improve it. 'No good,' says Holdridge to one which would mean re-writing the whole orchestral score. Someone else's bright idea would mean making the piece too long by half. Eventually it is, as so often, Domingo himself who gradually works his way towards the solution that seems most manageable. He lengthens and adapts the first third of the sandwich, including the interpolation of a quick high note on the third appearance of the word 'blue' so as to relieve any suggestion of repetitiveness—and the new version has a far more comfortable feel about it.

The backing musicians take a break, their place in the studio immediately taken by the patient television crew still anxious to film Domingo singing. Quickly they set up their lights, Plácido obligingly gets back into his little cubicle, dons earphones, and then mouths his way through one of the songs recorded at the previous day's session, a powerful tearjerker called 'I Couldn't Live Without You'. Okun's engineers play the tape through to the studio and Plácido does, as they say in the trade, a 'lip-sync'. He does more than that. He not only mouths the words with tremendous passion and energy, he also moves his hands and his body with the music to suggest, with absolute conviction, not just the emotion of the music but the physical effort involved in singing. Watching from the control cubicle it is impossible to tell that he is miming. And when the song is over he offers to do it again just in case his mouth wasn't in sync throughout.

It is getting late. The day's work began at 2 p.m. It is now 9.15 p.m. and the session has to end at ten. Yesterday was the same story. Two double sessions in two days and there seems little point in trying to get anything else 'in the can' today. 'But shouldn't we try the next song, "Remembering"?' Plácido asks. His speaking voice is getting a little frayed and Milton thinks it probably wiser to leave this piece for the next session. 'Let's just give it one run-through,' Plácido suggests, seemingly the least worried of all present about the strain to The Voice.

It is a difficult piece. The *tessitura* is high and there are a lot of fast words for Plácido to get his tongue round, though he negotiates most of the verbal hoops successfully. More than that, he takes the run-through in full throttle with some of the most thrilling high notes he has sung all day. He comes bounding in for a playback. He is not quite satisfied with his pronunciation. What is the exact difference between the vowel sounds in 'warmth' and 'worth' he asks—and never does get the distinction quite right. And how much 'r' should he pronounce? There are musical problems as well. 'Those high A flats, do I give them too much voice?' he asks. 'I sing them as though this were an operatic aria,' he says, genuinely uncertain whether he has got the musical idiom quite right or whether it is appropriate in this kind of music for him to open up his voice with quite so much power and intensity. People start mumbling about his resilience; won't he get tired, shouldn't he rest his voice for tomorrow? He lets his jaw sag and pretends to croak. 'Tomorrow, tomorrow, and tomorrow,' he intones in a cracked voice, simultaneously quoting *Annie* and *Macbeth*.

He puts the croak away and goes back yet again into his recording cubicle. It is 9.45 p.m. He performs 'Remembering' again. Holdridge is not satisfied. One of his musicians came in late a few bars from the end. 'We can probably get it right by editing,' Lee says, but does not sound totally convinced. 'Come on, Lee,' says Domingo, 'let's get it right.' And in they go, one more time, into the studio.

They record the last half of the song again, the bit with all the high notes. And do it yet once more for luck. The high notes are all big and round and powerful and dark and vibrant. Domingo *does* sing them as though the piece were an operatic aria. But he was clearly right to do so.

It is ten o'clock and people begin to disperse. The musicians leave, except for one guitarist who has a small passage to re-record. Holdridge asks Okun if they can do a couple of little edits just to make sure that the ending of 'Remembering' really can be made to work properly. Little edits have a habit of becoming big edits and it is well after 10.30 before everyone finally packs it in for the day. Domingo bows out of an invitation to supper on the ground that he'd be tempted to talk too much. The Golden Voice that seems so tireless does, apparently, sometimes need rest.

As a matter of fact it gets a whole day of rest as the next day is a British bank holiday and the session musicians cannot be inveigled into a recording studio except for an exorbitant fee. When the sessions resume, Domingo is fighting fit, looking dashing in a thick colourful woollen cardigan he bought when he was last in Italy, and in which he will be photographed later for the album cover. It is true he has not shaved on this particular day and is lacking the characteristic aura of after-shave that usually accompanies him everywhere he goes. But the thick shadow around his jaw gives him an even more rugged appearance than usual and certainly none of the women who appear in the studio during the next few hours seem to object to his typically demonstrative affability.

Today a full orchestra assembles—forty-five players as opposed to the five for the earlier sessions. And it is for today's double session that Domingo, Okun and Holdridge have reserved those items that require the greatest co-ordination and concentration. Tomorrow Domingo flies off to Vienna and the orchestra can record the backing for the tracks already committed to tape. Today, and only today, all the elements will work together.

Plácido is deeply immersed in the Italian football reports in yesterday's *Corriere dello Sport*. He is in good spirits, though wounded at the baseless Lollobrigida story that has now made the rounds in the press of several countries. He is thinking of taking some sort of legal action. Should he call Lollobrigida and find out from her how the story originated? No, because that might simply lead to further headlines about 'Spanish tenor on hot line to La Lollo'. Better do nothing and let the whole thing simply die. He goes back to the sports reports.

The orchestra assemble and Holdridge is in place on the podium. It is time to think of music, and the mental shadows, if not the stubbly ones, lift off Domingo's face as he goes into his soundproof recording booth and dons his earphones. The session begins with the title piece, 'My Life for a Song'. This is Lee Holdridge's own composition, a powerful, surging melody to a lyric by Carol Connors.

> My life for a song
>> More than anything I just knew I had to sing.
> Was it wrong to give the best of me
>> When my destiny was in my song? . . .
> My life for a song I would gladly give
>> If I knew my song would live for all time.
> There'll be a part of me
>> That will always be in my song.

Banal on paper perhaps and no doubt so if you or I sang it. But with the irresistible appropriateness of this man singing these words, the whole composition takes on a stature that surprises even its delighted composer. Holdridge is thrilled at the transformation his creation is undergoing and jokes that he almost forgets he is supposed to be conducting. He and Plácido come into the control room for the first playback, Lee standing between the two giant loudspeakers, Plácido seated next to Milton at the control desk. Plácido is wearing his 'Lee' jeans; there cannot be too many singers who wear their composers' names on their hips . . .

The music pours out of the two speakers with great washes of sound that make one expect a cinemascope presentation. Much of Holdridge's work is for movies and he certainly has the knack of building up great waves of luscious sound. The first take is good. But it is not quite right. Plácido, as usual, wants to put more expression, more contrast, more intensity, into his interpretation. For example, that slightly introspective question, 'Was it wrong to give the best of me . . . ?' Shouldn't he sing that a little more quietly? In which case Lee would have to bring the orchestra down, no? Lee is happy to try anything and the men go back to their allotted places to do a retake. This time Plácido sings with his whole body, fists clenched, arms outstretched, brow set, jaw firm and low. The take sounds almost flawless but before Milton can call everyone in for a playback Plácido asks if they can do it once more, this time singing the reprise with a softer head tone than before. By the break he has recorded no less than six complete takes of 'My Life for a Song' and a further seven takes of separate sections of the piece. Thirteen full-voiced takes in all.

Everybody reassembles and gets to work on the Tim Rice/ Andrew Lloyd Webber song, 'I Don't Talk to Strangers', written specially for Plácido. Domingo tried it out on a television show some months earlier but was not happy with it. 'For TV appearances they usually fix a single mike on you,' he explains, 'and you can't play it, approaching it for the more intimate bits, moving away when the music requires more voice, the way I can here.' He then treats everyone to an object lesson in 'playing the mike' as he records several versions of this song. In the pre-electric days Caruso and Melba used to have to dodge around their primitive microphone in order not to over-record or under-record or obliterate the orchestra. Recording techniques have come a long way since then, but even so Plácido moves about in his cubicle and alternately caresses his mike with his lips or scolds it from a distance with all his power according to the musical requirements. He makes great play with the word 'madly', starting the long 'm' earlier and earlier take by take. He makes it sound as passionate as can be, then sneaks a grin at his little audience through the glass. The passionate pronunciation is almost too over-emphatic, though there is something alluring about his Spanish delivery: 'm-m-*mud*dly!'

He is comfortable in his cubicle. He hears the orchestra and his own voice through earphones and can thus instinctively adjust his own contribution to the overall balance. 'In opera recordings you usually have to sing over the orchestra and cannot judge your own contribution or deficiencies. Here I find I can. I'd love to do opera this way one day.'

'But you'd have to re-record the entire operatic repertoire once you started doing that,' someone says. Plácido puts on his mock impish look and actually seems to relish the prospect.

'Let's do Placi's song.' Placi is Plácido Domingo III, a bright and talented seventeen-year-old of whom his father is immensely proud. Last month in Salzburg young Placi was extemporizing on the piano and came up with an attractive melody which he recorded on cassette. Since then Milton Okun has written out the tune properly, given it to Holdridge for orchestral arrangement, had a lyric written for the piece—and, lo and behold, a new song called 'There Will Be Love' is about to be born. One tiny clue to what lies behind the obvious pleasure Domingo obtains from his crossover recordings may lie in his closeness to his sons. There is something boyish about him and he is clearly anxious to remain as far as he can on the same wavelength as his children. Perhaps singing music that is popular among a younger age group is one way of doing that. Certainly singing a song actually written by one of his boys is a pretty good method.

He goes off into his cubicle and does a run-through. Young Placi has laid some traps for his father. The song, set in the key of G flat, has almost a two-octave range, from low B flat to top A flat, and Domingo is worried that the *tessitura* of the earlier part of the song lies too low for his voice. As the first couple of takes are played back it seems he is right. 'Should we try it up a semitone,' he wonders, 'in G rather than G flat?' Holdridge asks the orchestra if they can manage the transposition, reports back favourably, and Domingo goes once more into his glass cage. Lee starts the orchestra in its new key of G and Plácido begins to sing. Consternation. He is not hearing his own voice in his earphones properly and so cannot judge his own volume. He waves for everyone to stop and calls out in his own idiosyncratic brand of English, 'I need more my own voice, please.' To which Milt retorts: 'The whole world does!' Everything is put in order and Placi's song takes on a brilliance it did not quite have before. His father's voice soars up to the high As (he is now into his fifth hour of singing today) and at playback all agree that he was right to suggest pushing the piece up. 'There is only one problem,' he says gravely. 'We'll have to check the change is acceptable to the composer!' He then reveals amid laughter that Placi does not even know they are recording his song.

Holdridge brings word that the musicians have a complaint. 'This guy's supposed to have the greatest voice in the world and we haven't had a chance to hear it. Couldn't he come and rehearse something in front of us instead of in his cubicle? And couldn't a playback be relayed into the studio for us to hear?' Okun is flabbergasted. No session players in his long experience have ever made that kind of request and for the next song, the final item, he is only too happy to oblige.

This last song is to be the Jacques Prévert lyric *'Feuilles Mortes'* or 'Autumn Leaves', made famous twenty years ago by Yves Montand, a gentle, wistful song. Domingo had some reservations about doing it. Was it right for his voice? Wasn't Montand making a come-back? Montand's imminent American tour was to include a concert inside the hallowed walls of the Metropolitan Opera, no less; mightn't it look as though Domingo were trying to ride on somebody else's success? On the other hand, it was a song he loved and he felt he could do it his own kind of justice. Earlier this very day he has been chatting away on the phone in French to a friend in Paris checking details of pronunciation—when should the 's' at the end of *'tous'* be pronounced, should there be a liaison in the middle of *'deux ensemble'*? And now, while everybody else takes a break, he listens to a Montand recording to make sure of every one of those troubling words.

The clock shows nearly nine o'clock and it is time for everybody to get into position for the last time. 'Autumn Leaves' Take One. It starts in English and then goes into French. There is nothing wrong with the first take but it lacks fire. The big sweeping tune should be faster—almost a predictable Domingo suggestion by now. Also, that semi-*parlando* verse in French—does it work? Well, no, it doesn't. In any case, says Lee, everyone knows the big tune but nobody even knows there's that bit of verse in the middle. It can't really be cut but maybe it could be shortened. Or delivered with more urgency. Domingo considers the structure of the piece, its duration, its key changes, the transition passages that would be necessary if this or that section were cut. And he also keeps firmly in mind the audience at whom the album is targeted. The mind is alert though by now a roughness is beginning to enter his speaking voice. There are further takes of further versions. Domingo is tired. His head is sagging and with his dark unshaven shadow he is beginning to resemble his own representation of Hoffmann in the tavern scenes of the opera.

He makes a big final effort, lifts his head, grips the music and goes back once again into his cubicle. The take is superb and he comes out beaming, patently ready to do another version if anyone wants him to. But everybody is punch-drunk. For many it is evidently even more exhausting watching Plácido Domingo at work than *being* Plácido Domingo at work.

In any case, Plácido Domingo still has more work to do. For, sitting patiently throughout the latter part of the session, is a representative of another of his recording companies, Deutsche Grammophon. Plácido has promised to give her a promotional interview for two of his forthcoming DG recordings for distribution to local radio stations around Britain. As everyone else packs up and says a weary goodbye to Plácido, he clears his throat and his mind and prepares to talk with enthusiasm for his radio audience about *Turandot* and *Aida*.

Fanciulla on Television

If many people get more of their opera from recordings than from live performances, for millions virtually the only exposure to opera is via television. Domingo has always been prepared to go to great lengths and make considerable sacrifices in order to appear on TV, not just in opera but in chat shows, interviews, variety shows—anything that might enable him to reach the widest possible audience. He first became a household name among the general, non-opera-going public, indeed, when he began to appear as a frequent guest on television chat shows. When Rosemary Okun saw him singing snatches of *My Fair Lady* on the Johnny Carson Show in the USA, a major new career as a singer of middle-of-the-road popular songs was first conceived, while in Britain Domingo shot to popular celebrity-hood the night he starred, with Sammy Cahn and Cliff Richard, on the BBC's Michael Parkinson Show. On TV Domingo will talk eagerly about his art, illustrate it with an excerpt from his repertoire—and then change gear smoothly back into standard chat-show routine with no sense of condescension or loss of dignity. The grandeur of his singing is often something of a shock to television viewers unfamiliar with it and is perhaps of too great an intensity to be easily enjoyed on a small screen with poor sound quality. Yet the obvious intelligence of the man (not to mention his macho Latin good looks) invariably wins over viewers who might at first acquaint-ance find the voice alone too awe-inspiring for comfort.

Domingo is a great believer in the value of television if well used, and considers it the most potent single method of bridging the notorious gap between the few who go to opera and the millions who feel that it is not for the likes of them. But if he is keen that his television appearances should help encourage people to want to listen to opera, he is also anxious that his opera appearances should, as far as possible, be made available on television and/or video. To date he has made some fifty opera telecasts, surely a virtually unsurpassable record. He is the ideal performer in the new medium. Very few singers have the voice, the looks *and* the acting ability.

It is 2 November 1982, 4.45 p.m. Television history is being made, for at this very moment Britain's fourth TV channel is inaugurated. Few countries have four nationwide TV networks, and if Channel Four fulfils even a fraction of its many promises, British viewers will be blessed with genuine options in the years to come and not, as in many other countries, merely a choice of pap.

At this historic moment Plácido Domingo is in London in a television scanner van watching a TV screen, but he is not watching Channel Four. The van is one of several parked outside the Dominion Theatre in Tottenham Court Road and Domingo is watching Kiri Te Kanawa—Dame Kiri as she has recently become—inside the theatre rehearsing a show. The BBC's Humphrey Burton is making a Christmas Special, 'Call Me Kiri', and Plácido is to be one of her star guests. Others include soprano Norma Burrowes, dancer Doreen Wells, and that unique Welsh concoction of comedian and tenor, Sir Harry Secombe. A couple of years ago the BBC mounted a special Plácido Domingo Christmas Show with Kiri as his star guest; today Kiri is reciprocating.

The chief reason Domingo is in London is to add Puccini's *La Fanciulla del West* (The Girl of the Golden West) to his list of video recordings. *Fanciulla*, like the same composer's *Madama Butterfly*, is based on a play by the American dramatist David Belasco and is really the first of the Spaghetti Westerns, a story of good and evil and lust and blood in the days when the West was really Wild—more specifically Gold Rush California. The girl of the title, Minnie, is a gun-toting, Bible-swinging All-American blonde who civilizes the miners and loves, protects and eventually rescues from execution the reformed bandit Ramirez, alias Dick Johnson. It is a silent movie plot, complete with evil, dark-coated, lustful Sheriff Jack Rance. Like many silent movies but few other operas, it has a melodramatically happy ending as last-minute rescuer and rescuee walk away hand in hand and bid farewell forever to their beloved California. Domingo/Ramirez/Johnson has spent four hours this morning rehearsing *Fanciulla* at Covent Garden. He starred when this production opened in 1977, but it needs re-working and the original director, Piero Faggioni, is in town to whip everybody back into shape. The dress rehearsal is tomorrow morning and the opening performance a couple of days later. The third performance is the one to be filmed.

There is television and television. Chat-show appearances do not take up a great deal of time or effort; Domingo has been known to step into one or two of these straight off a transatlantic flight. Telecasts of operas are more complicated, especially if, as at Covent Garden, the film people cannot bring cameras in for earlier performances so that the telecast requires special rehearsals. But the sort of operation that requires most work is probably the TV special such as the one in which Domingo is guesting for Kiri Te Kanawa. A one-hour television show can require of its stars a total of fifteen or twenty hours of rehearsal and recording time.

Domingo looks up at the TV monitor in the scanner and sees Dame

Kiri reading and re-reading her cue card. Her frequent stumbles take time to rectify but undoubtedly add to her charm, especially when she introduces the Maori rugby team, a formidable squad of sportsmen whom, she says, 'I am glad to have on *my* side!' She and they sing a Maori song. Portly Harry Secombe appears among them in football togs, causes uncontrollable giggles all round and is then carried off bodily by the Maori team as though he were the ball.

Kiri goes off to change from a long dress into a fetching golden pantsuit, while Burton's stage hands set up a pastoral scene: a swan here, a few rushes there, and rocks on which sit a group of children dressed to represent the ethnic variety of the world. Kiri appears and sits on a rock among this motley crew of little Africans, Indians (of both kinds), and the rest, and sings to them 'The Ugly Duckling', the song based on the Hans Andersen story and made famous by Danny Kaye. The TV lights are hot and a little boy in a thick Eskimo coat begins to reel and needs a cold drink, while a stage hand comes over to fan him. The spotlight is casting a mike shadow on Kiri but the spot operator does not seem to be reachable through the talk-back.

'All quiet now, please,' calls the stage director as he and conductor Robin Stapleton hear their instructions over earphones and Kiri prepares to sing her song once more to the patient children. 'Ten, nine, eight, seven . . . ' One little boy leans over and whispers to Dame Kiri that he needs to go to the bathroom, so there is a further delay.

As he watches the monitoring screen, Domingo is uncharacteristically out of sorts. He has banged his leg hard against the door of the scanner van and for a while thinks he may have injured himself. He is in any case tired. He has just come from four hours of *Fanciulla* rehearsal at Covent Garden, only to discover that instead of being able to rehearse his TV contribution on schedule he will probably have to stay on here all evening. Tomorrow he has to appear in a public dress rehearsal of *Fanciulla* during the day and appear again in the evening at the Dominion Theatre in front of an audience for the final shooting of the Kiri show.

A busy timetable even by Domingo standards. In the past three weeks he has been singing in New York (where he had to pull out of *La Gioconda* at the Met in mid-performance because of a heavy

75

cold), Chicago and Mexico, has come to London to start *Fanciulla* rehearsals, has flown off to Rome for three days to sing for, and be decorated by, the Pope, and has now plunged back into Covent Garden rehearsals with the BBC show somehow meshed in between. Yet Domingo's physical fatigue is only part of the story. 'It's my head,' he says, 'that's really tired.' He needs a month with no obligations to have to think about, no demands to be slotted into a busy schedule, no operatic roles to think himself into, no planes to catch, costumes to be fitted, phone calls to make or await, contracts to discuss. It's not just the singing, it is the relentless and complex *thinking* that Domingo's schedule imposes that contributes most to the strain he is feeling now. He dare not let his mind relax.

'The Ugly Duckling' is eventually in the can to everybody's satisfaction, the tea interval comes and goes, and Domingo appears on stage at last, wearing dinner jacket and black tie. His big, round shoulders give him a tendency to stoop but today the tendency is more pronounced than usual. He will sing one short aria—'Ch'ella mi creda libero e lontano' from *Fanciulla*. It is an aria sung by a character who wishes he were free, and a long way away. Plácido will sing it just once. He does. Harry Secombe cannot believe his ears and the orchestra tap their music stands in appreciation. Robin Stapleton is delighted and says so. Domingo gives a wan smile and walks his small-stepped stooping walk off the stage again. He goes back into the TV van where Burton is sitting. 'That was terrific, Plácido!' Domingo is not convinced. He wants to hear a playback. It is, by Domingo standards, a little throaty, slightly lacking in the ultimate golden ring of confidence, but it is pretty good none the less. Anticipating problems, Burton had taken the precaution of recording it with several different microphone balances—floor mikes, a stand mike and a boom were all available. One way and another, Domingo is more pleased than he expected to be and says he will agree to stay on and do his remaining items. Burton, who had no idea Domingo was even considering pulling out, feels a heavy shadow touch him and pass by. Domingo does not often walk out of shows he is committed to, but on this occasion he nearly did. He steps slowly out of the TV van and shuffles back into the theatre. 'I can sing that aria so much better,' he murmurs in self-disgust as he climbs wearily up the three

flights of dingy steps past all the ethnic children to his dressing-room.
There is an hour's break and then he and Kiri have to start work on
several numbers from *West Side Story*.

In his dressing-room, sprawled over a *chaise-longue*, Domingo
tries to unwind. He would not have done this show were it not for his
friendship with Humphrey Burton and Kiri. 'I thought the *Fanciulla*
dress rehearsal was today so that I could have done that, come and
done Humphrey's show, and then had two free days before the
opening night at Covent Garden.' He makes a decision. He will sing
the *West Side Story* pieces as well as he can and Humphrey must film
them tonight; Plácido really cannot come again tomorrow night,
after the *Fanciulla* dress rehearsal, and sing again. 'I sometimes wish
I were a pianist,' he muses. 'A person like Maurizio Pollini can play
all morning and then, if necessary, play something else for some
other occasion later in the day. But nobody seems to understand that
the voice is not like other instruments. It is part of you. If you use it,
you are using yourself. Everywhere I go I am expected to have the
voice there with me.' During this stay in London he is to be made an
honorary Fellow of the Royal College of Music. A great honour
rarely accorded a non-Briton—but they want him to sing for them
too . . .

A young man brings the refreshment Plácido has requested: a take-
away cup of black coffee and a warm apple pie from McDonald's over
the road. In the background, Plácido's lean and conscientious dresser
carefully hangs up his dinner jacket and prepares a pink shirt for *West
Side Story*. 'God, I wish I were a pianist or a violinist,' Domingo
mutters again as he nibbles half-heartedly at his apple pie.

Record producer Milton Okun has brought a couple of new lyrics
which Domingo reads avidly. Plácido tells Milt enthusiastically
about the *Traviata* film which he has now seen in its edited form. He
thinks Zeffirelli has done a superb job and is extravagant in his praise
of Teresa Stratas. He also tells Milt of the latest romances he is said to
be having by the gutter press. One paper suggests a liaison with
Raquel Welch, and another links his name with a woman he has
never even met, but would certainly like to, Claudia Cardinale. It is
all rather funny in a way. But if he ever meets the people who invent
all these absurd stories he will personally smash their heads in.

Domingo pulls himself up on his *chaise-longue* and looks in the glass. His eyes look tired. For a split second, reflected in the pair of facing mirrors, are a thousand identical, receding images of an exhausted Plácido Domingo, all gazing sadly at each other.

He turns again to Okun. Milt has played him the edited versions of some recently recorded popular songs. There are passages Plácido wants to re-record. Milt is happy to oblige. But when? That is always the big question with Plácido. 'Milt, you know when we could do them? One night after a performance of *Fanciulla*,' Plácido suggests. 'After all, I will be well sung in by then, and *Fanciulla* doesn't leave you drained the way, say—*Pagliacci* does.' *Pagliacci* is a slightly surprising way for that particular thought to have ended. But then, Domingo is feeling right now rather like Canio in the opera who has to perform even when he least wants to.

'At night after *Fanciulla*? Yes, Plácido, of course,' says Okun, scarcely able to believe that this weary hulk sprawled before him is seriously proposing such a procedure.

'Anyway,' Plácido adds pensively, but does not sound convinced by his own words, 'that might help give me a free day.'

He drags his tired frame up from the *chaise-longue* and begins to think of the *West Side Story* pieces. Tonight, tonight. Maria, Maria, Maria, Maria, Maria, Maria, Maria—Maria! So many Marias, how will he ever remember the right number? He'll need a rosary to count them all. 'With your recent Papal connections you'll have no trouble!' Humphrey Burton assures him.

Domingo lopes onto the Dominion stage in his pink shirt and a pair of black trousers and black waistcoat. Dame Kiri is in a long, elegant dress, too elegant for Maria but it will look good on television. Plácido and Kiri stand together before a representation of Manhattan's West Side. Not an elaborate, colourful one like the outdoor set at Bregenz but a sort of grey Mondrian structure with a staircase and doorway as realistic props. The spotlight needs adjustment. Plácido has a mike shadow on his face; would different lighting obliterate this, or should the mike, or Plácido, be moved? The 'laundry' in the Mondrian structure has to be shifted slightly to get the set balanced correctly; this means finding a ladder. The minutes tick away and Plácido and Kiri are still standing, standing, standing—and still nothing has been rehearsed, much less recorded. Tonight, tonight. It's got to be tonight. Plácido won't be here tomorrow night . . .

Kiri Te Kanawa is, after a full day's rehearsing, still her delightful bubbly self and Domingo wants to please her. They work well together and by 9.15 p.m. their two duets ('Tonight' and 'There's a Place for Us') are finally in the can. Humphrey Burton allows the many press photographers in the house to come on stage for a quick photo call. Harry Secombe has also been waiting patiently in the darkened theatre all these hours as he is due to sing, of all things, 'On With the Motley' from *Pagliacci*. He does not sing his aria today, but is the life and soul of the photo call, telling Kiri rude Antipodean limericks (which she is quite prepared to cap), joking about how they are both knights of the realm, blowing raspberries that have Plácido laughing as he has not laughed all day, and generally gooning around to the delight of all. Doreen Wells, too, has been in the theatre much of the day as she was scheduled to rehearse the Dying Swan. But her hair is in curlers and while she will join in the frivolities she does not want to be photographed. So naturally someone snaps her.

All the stars except Domingo finally leave. He still has to record 'Maria' and, of course, sings the song (and counts the Marias) perfectly. Then he asks if he can re-do the final section, the bit with the difficult soft high notes. He had brought himself off one bar before the orchestra and would prefer to end with them. By now it is well after official closing time and the television crew are dismantling their equipment and mumbling about overtime. They have to be here tomorrow morning and need some rest. Domingo, mindful of Burton's problems as well as his own, suggests they re-record the sound only. 'You will see that I kept my mouth open during that final bar so the dubbing will be no problem!' Burton is sceptical but does not say so. He and his sound men agree that Domingo can do the ending once more. Silence, please. Final take. And Plácido just stands there, the mikes recording but with no lighting on him, and sings once more the final high cadence from his final song. Mar-i-aah. Everyone applauds. He comes off the stage looking yellow and drawn. Tomorrow, while Kiri is rehearsing Rossini's Cat Duet with Norma Burrowes and 'We're a Couple of Swells' with Harry Secombe, and while Doreen Wells will eventually do her dance routines, Domingo will be at Covent Garden for the dress rehearsal of *La Fanciulla del West*. Someone wishes him luck. He pretends to slit his throat and mutters that he won't sing tomorrow. 'I'll just mime,' he says gloomily. And goes home to bed.

Later, when Humphrey Burton comes to edit 'Maria', he finds that Domingo did indeed keep his mouth open during the final bar of the video version and this, plus a little judicious use of slow-motion for a second or two, enables Burton, just as Domingo had anticipated, to graft the final soundtrack of the ending onto the film.

The day after his marathon session at the Dominion Theatre, after a good night's sleep, Domingo duly appears at the *Fanciulla* dress rehearsal as the good-guy-cum-bandit Ramirez, alias Dick Johnson, complete with the cowboy hat in which he features on posters all over London's tube stations but minus the moustache he happened to be sporting at the time the photo was taken. He swaggers, he plays with his gun and his saddle, dances with the heroine Minnie, and sings with a subdued but deliciously golden tone. The audience, made up of Friends of Covent Garden, are obviously enthusiastic and Domingo responds. When Johnson is shot in Act II and has to drag himself up a ladder to hide, his acting is genuinely pained. And when he reaches his last-act aria, the one he felt so bad about the evening before at the Dominion Theatre, he comes to the footlights and gives a ravishing performance with all the power and pathos at his command. By the end he is standing better, his head is more erect, his walking steps more measured. He is all smiles at the final curtain. And over a late lunch at a nearby restaurant with his family and fellow *Fanciulla* principals, he is full of his accustomed energy and good humour.

For the next week or so he has to live, eat, sleep and dream *La Fanciulla del West*. The first night is a great success, the packed audience clapping and shouting the usual 'bravos' and in some sections screaming as well. The press hail Domingo's 'triumphant' return to this production—he 'soars away at his burnished best', lyricizes one reviewer, while another compliments him on looking the part as well as he sings it.

Next morning, a Saturday, while his colleagues and many in the first night audience are doubtless resting after the excitements of the previous evening, Domingo goes to the Roundhouse in London's Camden Town to over-dub some sections from Puccini's little-known *La Rondine*, helping Kiri Te Kanawa get through some awkward passages that did not quite work when they recorded the opera earlier in the year.

Will Plácido Domingo at least have a peaceful Sunday? On the contrary—the entire *Fanciulla* cast is required back at the Royal Opera House for a 10 a.m. call and they can expect to remain here for a solid twelve hours. The next performance but one is to be filmed and every shot and frame and bar has to be laboriously rehearsed and co-ordinated. There are more television rehearsals lined up for the Wednesday and Thursday—as well as three performances to give within the week. With this sort of pressure, you can go off even the best operas.

La Fanciulla del West does not come quite under this category, though it carries the indelible stamp of its composer, Giacomo Puccini, the creator of *Bohème*, *Tosca*, *Butterfly* and *Turandot*, which are among the most successful and beloved of all musical works for the stage. *Fanciulla* was written at a troubled time for Puccini. His wife Elvira had publicly accused him of having an affair with their young servant girl Doria and while Puccini's affections undoubtedly wandered every now and then from his difficult and headstrong wife, this accusation caused him terrible anguish. The girl suffered even more deeply, however, committed suicide, and an ugly domestic scandal took on the proportions of genuine tragedy—a tragedy, moreover, not a million miles removed from the sub-conscious obsessions of a man whose creative opus regularly featured the sufferings and death of innocent young women. Puccini was devastated by the horrific turn of events and, if his personal honour was vindicated by the inquest which found Doria to have died a virgin, his domestic peace of mind was scarcely restored.

Some of this may help explain the opera's anomalies. Puccini spends too much time in Act I setting the scene and establishing the many miners who figure peripherally in the plot. The orchestration throughout is rich and varied but disjointed as though several styles and functions are jostling for dominance. The melodramatic and sugary ending is not in the same class as those spine-chilling *coups de théâtre* with which Puccini's masterpieces conclude. But for all this, his Californian opera is packed with nuggets of gold for those prepared to dig. Its big moments—the Minnie–Johnson duet at the end of Act I, the Scarpia-like figure of Sheriff Rance playing cards with Minnie for Johnson's life, Johnson's pre-scaffold aria—etch themselves on the memory along with the best of Puccini's work, while its subtle thematic details become clearer with every hearing. *Fanciulla* is a work that grows on you.

The Sunday session is obviously going to be a marathon, and everybody on stage tries to conserve his energies. The singers merely mouth—and in some cases deliberately overact—their parts with no more than piano accompaniment, the imperturbable Nello Santi conducting. At times it all resembles Charlie Chaplin's *Gold Rush*—particularly on one of the various black-and-white monitor screens. At one point in Act II, hero and heroine embrace passionately in Minnie's log cabin as a fierce snowstorm outside causes the door to blow violently and repeatedly open and shut. Valentino movies were not more melodramatically romantic than that, and movie analogies step still closer when at one point the BBC producer John Vernon asks everyone to perform (and the piano to play) a complicated scene at half the normal speed so that he can get all his camera angles properly rehearsed.

Vernon and the original stage director Piero Faggioni decide to work their way backwards, as it were, starting with Act III. Like the first act this contains various initial pieces of more or less fragmented ensemble, notably a manhunt through the hills, and eventually the bandit Johnson/Ramirez is dragged on, hands bound together. So if Domingo himself comes a little late to the house this particular morning, it will not matter, and when at last his entry arrives, various substitutes act his part as the prisoner is brought on by his captors. Maestro Santi sings, if that is the word, Johnson's lines. It is all a little tame, though from Vernon's point of view, since it is the positioning of people that counts, one body is pretty much the same as another for present purposes. Not so to Faggioni, however. He constantly leaps over the rickety bridge erected over the orchestra pit on to the stage, pushing one group of chorus members hither, another thither, repositioning soloists. Time and again the action has to stop as Faggioni and Vernon go into a huddle behind the production desk to discuss details, Faggioni rattling out his thoughts in quick-fire fractured English, Vernon responding in his controlled fashion and communicating the latest decisions along the wires to his relevant cameraman. 'Can we go from *"andiamo"*, please, everyone,' Vernon calls out with his clipped British pronunciation. And everybody trots back to the *andiamo* position and the silent movie cranks over once more.

This is a big, spectacular production, and if there is to be a permanent visual record it is worth getting things right. Each act contains great wooden structures—beams, bridges, balustrades, boardwalks—that give an authentic sense of period and place among the hills and forests of nineteenth-century northern California, and this final act, set in a mountain gorge, even contains a wooden water wheel that begins to turn as the final curtain falls. The designer was Ken Adam, veteran of *Dr Strangelove, Chitty, Chitty, Bang, Bang, Barry Lyndon* and most of the James Bond and Len Deighton movies. He, too, wants the video recording to go well and with his Italian wife hovers near Faggioni and Vernon as the TV rehearsal wends its weary way.

The video version is being made by an all-BBC team and will be broadcast by BBC television in early 1983. After that one transmission the rights revert to a recently formed company called Covent Garden Video Productions Ltd (CGVP), a subsidiary of the even more recently formed National Video Corporation. NVC arose at the confluence of various converging currents. As the Royal Opera House felt the increasingly drastic effects of inflation and recession, General Director Sir John Tooley and his colleagues had to ask themselves whether there were new ways in which Covent Garden could augment its funding. Naturally, the house and its artists obtained fees from television relays just as they had always done for live or delayed radio broadcasts, and BBC TV seemed to be taking a growing number of Covent Garden productions. But television gives essentially transient pleasure. Might not the television relays be developed into some sort of permanently available resource, perhaps marketed by the BBC in conjunction with Covent Garden, to the growing army of people who possessed, or would soon possess, their own domestic video machines? Indeed, since there was every likelihood that those home video-owners would soon be illegally recording material off the air just as many already pirated sound tracks of radio programmes, there seemed to be some urgency in getting a proper filming, marketing and distributing mechanism organized as soon as possible. If it could be done, everybody—Covent Garden, the BBC, the viewing public—stood to benefit.

At the time that Tooley and his colleagues began to have thoughts along these lines, the Controller of BBC-2, the British television network most concerned with relays of ballet, opera, and the like, was Robin Scott. In 1977 Scott was promoted to become Deputy Managing Director of BBC Television and one of his specific briefs was to investigate ways in which the rapidly developing new technologies of satellite, cable and video might usefully be exploited by the BBC. The BBC was faced with a number of exciting new opportunities but also possible threats. In particular, it had built up over the years an enthusiastic, if minority, audience for relays of opera and ballet. How could it maintain that audience if a major bid for its attention was made by the commercial purveyors of the new technology? The BBC could not itself make commercial use of video—it was a broadcasting organization not a publisher, a public corporation not a private business. But suppose the BBC could have transmission rights to programmes which the video business might legitimately market thereafter . . .

A passionate believer in the video revolution and its capacity to bring 'élite' arts to a wide audience, Scott, a former television director and producer, had also shown himself at the BBC an outstanding arts administrator. Although he was due to leave the BBC in 1980, he knew he could not simply leave behind him all the interests that had absorbed his mind and energies over recent years. Perhaps in retirement from the BBC he could do work that might also be of benefit to his former colleagues. As it happened, a City financier named Julian Wills was at that very time exploring ways of combining investment in Covent Garden productions of opera and ballet with television and video expertise and distribution skill, and it was Wills, with his fortuitous mix of money and enthusiasm, who was

84

able to give Scott the fillip he was looking for. Before long, the two, in conjunction with their friends at the BBC and the Royal Opera House, had drawn up a tripartite agreement which issued in the formation of a company to be called Covent Garden Video Productions Limited. The agreement anticipated a minimum of fifteen Covent Garden television recordings over the next five years. The BBC would provide its production expertise and equipment. Artists' fees and all above-the-line costs would be paid by CGVP. The BBC would receive rights to one broadcast of each production while CGVP would market the programmes commercially to worldwide television and video outlets, the artists being paid a royalty in accordance with the number of foreign television transmissions or video-cassette or disc sales CGVP could negotiate. If the BBC ever wished to re-transmit one of the programmes it would have to pay repeat fees in the normal way.

The first fruit of the new agreement, tied up with the various unions just in the nick of time, was the Royal Opera House's spectacular *Tales of Hoffmann*, produced by John Schlesinger and with Domingo as the star. Wills and Scott did not expect quick profits. In the event, that opening *Hoffmann*, for which CGVP put down something in the region of £200,000, paid for itself in television and video sales within two years.

Wills, Scott and their colleagues felt they were on to a winning formula and it was not long before they extended their activities. Wills created a holding company for CGVP to be called the National Video Corporation and NVC began to negotiate similar agreements with other bodies in addition to Covent Garden. Soon NVC was recording and marketing a London Festival Ballet double bill and the English National Opera's production of Donizetti's *Mary Stuart* with Janet Baker. NVC also cast its ambitious eye abroad, to Germany and Italy. By November 1982, even as John Vernon got down to the job of rehearsing the Covent Garden *Fanciulla* for the BBC and CGVP, Julian Wills and his associates were negotiating the small print in what would shortly issue as major contracts between NVC and La Scala, Milan, the American Ballet Theater, and also the Kirov and Bolshoi theatres in the USSR. The Covent Garden *Fanciulla* was as handsome as anything the Royal Opera House had mounted in years, and hopes were high that the videotape of this production would sell briskly.

Stage director Piero Faggioni is impatient. Domingo has still not arrived and as the various Johnson substitutes are not acting the part correctly, Faggioni, himself a former actor, runs up on stage to take over. He struggles with his captors, glares at Sheriff Rance, electrifies everyone on stage. Better still, a tenor member of the chorus, John Kerr, goes down into the orchestra pit, stands by the piano facing Santi, and sings Johnson's vocal line. Kerr gets to the big tenor aria 'Ch'ella mi creda' while Faggioni mimes above. Kerr does not often get this sort of opportunity and he launches in for all he is worth. What he does not know but everybody else can see is that at this very moment Domingo himself saunters onto the stage ready to take over. Nobody, least of all Domingo himself, has the heart to interrupt Kerr in mid-flight. But the smiles on stage and in the auditorium gradually break through into Kerr's concentration. 'The other tenor has arrived,' Faggioni tells him gently. Kerr gets a round of applause and slips back into his persona as a choral goldminer.

For much of the next hour, Domingo stands atop the rickety wooden steps under the makeshift gallows alongside the water wheel with a noose around his neck. In the opera, Johnson is prepared for hanging, then Minnie arrives, orders the execution stopped, persuades the goldmining roughnecks to unstring him as he is really a Good Guy, and walks off with him into the proverbial sunset. How should Johnson react when Minnie arrives? On which of them should the camera focus at the pivotal moment? From which position up *her* rickety staircase should Minnie stop and gaze at Johnson?

Today's Minnie is an authentic strapping Californian blonde, Carol Neblett, with Domingo and Silvano Carroli one of the original 1977 team that opened this production. She has just had a baby and the Minnie in the opening performances of this run has been another American singer, Marilyn Zschau, whom we will have occasion to meet again later. But Carol will appear in the performance to be filmed and today she bounces in, full of vigour. 'Stop, stop, stop, stop, stop, stop, stop, stop!' It is Faggioni. Carol has come too far down her staircase and has to go off and enter again. But not before Faggioni has called out to everyone that he proposes 'a little applause for our little Neblett who is back'. He has a habit of calling people by their surnames; it is a sign of affection. There is nothing diminutive about tall, handsome Carol. Perhaps he is thinking of her seven-week-old baby.

Domingo stands patiently at his gibbet, the noose still around his neck, the other end of the rope in the hands of a bunch of desperadoes below, pretending they are about to string him up. It is a faintly comic scene though not without its dangers. 'One false move from someone and you'd have had it!' says a friend to Plácido later. 'I know it,' he rejoins with mock alarm, 'and to think that half of them were tenors!'

The scene is re-rehearsed. Someone on stage goes down on all fours and chats to the man in the prompter's box. Silvano Carroli, the evil sheriff, talks amiably with big blonde Carol/Minnie. The pianist in the pit complains that there is a draught behind him which keeps turning his pages prematurely.

Eventually it gets to what is laughingly referred to as 'lunchtime', which means that everybody is dismissed for an hour. There is nowhere much to go at two o'clock on a November Sunday in London—nowhere, certainly, if you are dressed and made up as a nineteenth-century sheriff or desperado and are expected back within sixty minutes. Some of the cast have brought sandwiches and coffee flasks. Domingo joins the Carrolis and the Adams for a take-away Chinese meal that someone goes off to collect from Soho. They set themselves up around a table in a corner of the costume room on the ground floor of the new Covent Garden extension and await the food. By the time it eventually arrives, Domingo's call for the next act is already booming through the intercom. Never mind. He is a light eater. He puts through a quick telephone call to Marta and goes off towards the stage.

They rehearse Act II. There is not enough snow when the door of Minnie's cabin is open. But if the snow machine pumps too much polystyrene snow on to Domingo's jacket—enough, that is, to be visible to the television audience—won't it be strange that it doesn't melt? Domingo and Neblett embrace again and again before the opening-and-shutting cabin door as the piano beneath thunders out its silent movie accompaniment. Domingo gets shot and hidden, and Carroli comes and performs his card game with Neblett for Domingo's life, and acts more melodramatically each time they go over the scene. Another break while Minnie's hut is demolished and the Polka Saloon erected in its place. Act I is the longest and dramatically the most complex. Every one of those little character-establishing scenes has to be just right—right for Faggioni, that is, *and* right for Vernon and his cameramen. The act is rehearsed, frame by meticulous frame, and by the time the cast have worked through to the end of the act they are aching with exhaustion. It is well into the evening before, at last, everybody is dismissed.

Monday is a rest day. It has to be. They all have a performance on Tuesday. By Tuesday evening everyone is refreshed and the perfor-mance—Neblett's first in this present run—is a great success. The inevitable embracings and handshakings and autographings go on until the early hours—but next morning the entire cast have a ten o'clock call, this time a more or less non-stop run-through of the entire opera for John Vernon's cameras. 'Dunno why I bother to go home at nights or change out of my costume,' says one of the goldminers with resignation. The run-through is likely to be time-consuming but relatively painless. The cast know they can just mouth the words and go through the motions. After a couple of successful performances and all the hard work for Vernon on Sunday they are all in a fairly relaxed mood. Neblett makes her entrance in Minnie's dress but with her hair in curlers.

Trouble is brewing elsewhere, however. Tension builds up at the production desk between Faggioni and Vernon. It has been simmer-ing for several days. Vernon is accused of not capturing on his cameras the pictures Faggioni's production has been designed to create. Faggioni, mercurial, brilliant and impulsive, boils over. He attacks Vernon for undoing all the good work (Faggioni's language is actually far stronger) that everyone has put into this production over the years since its inception in 1977. There is probably an inevitable conflict of interest between the man responsible for the staging and the TV director—though Vernon, one of the most experienced of the BBC's Outside Broadcast producers, has never met this sort of opposition before. He feels that Faggioni is wasting rehearsal time by changing too many details of the production, and confusing everybody, not least Vernon's cameramen, as a result. What happens when unstoppable Italian temperament meets immutable British phlegm? John Vernon, portly, gentlemanly, peering over his half-frame spectacles, tries against the odds to consider, one by one, the details of Faggioni's complaints, and suggests in his quiet but authoritative way that he quite appreciates Piero's point of view, of course, but he should realize that . . . Faggioni will not let him finish and it takes all the diplomacy of General Director Sir John Tooley and his deputy Paul Findlay to iron out the difficulties.

As the cast sit around waiting to be told what to do next, someone asks Domingo how the experience of filming a complex stage production compares with making a movie of an opera. His mind at present is still fresh with the recent memory of filming *La Traviata* with Zeffirelli. 'With a movie the big problem is TIME. Everything always overruns like crazy.' When Domingo was filming *Tosca* for Unitel on location in Rome some years before, the final session had to be scheduled overnight as Domingo had a plane to catch the next morning. 'But at least with a film all the moves and frames and camera angles are worked out meticulously in advance by the director. By the time you come on to the set there is nothing left to do except spend time acting what you are told to act.' 'And here?' 'Here it's the other way round. Here *we* know all the moves, and the film director is having to learn what *he* wants to do from what we are already doing. These rehearsals are really for him rather than for us. But at least here,' Domingo adds gratefully, 'there is a strict deadline. There is no running over schedule. The piece *has* to be in the can on Friday night!'

The Wednesday run-through comes to an end and while Vernon and Faggioni, in a state of uneasy truce, go off to consider the lessons revealed and still to be learnt, the cast disperse.

Domingo has further business to attend to. Deutsche Grammophon have arranged through Covent Garden that Domingo will sign copies of his records at 5.30 this afternoon. Already, shortly after 2 p.m. a queue begins to form and by the time 5.30 approaches hundreds of people line the streets outside and around the house. One performer in tonight's ballet is briefly buoyed up as she arrives early at the stage door thinking the long line must be for her show. Her heart sinks back into her pumps when she is told what has really drawn the crowds.

Inside, Domingo combs his hair, straightens his tie, and sprays liberal dollops of after-shave over his face and head. He looks relaxed and at ease as the Deutsche Grammophon people place him behind a little table ready to receive. He is in one of the principal artists' dressing-rooms in the new backstage extension of the Royal Opera House, opened only a few months before by Prince Charles. Domingo has slight misgivings—it was good, after all, to know in the past that one was changing in the very room occupied by the great tenors of the past stretching back through Gigli, Martinelli and Caruso to the legendary Mario. But what Domingo's new dressing-room lacks in 'ghosts' it more than makes up for by containing such luxuries as its own shower, toilet and piano.

Domingo sits himself down at the little table and tries out his signature on one or two of the records offered by members of the 'family' who are milling around before the crowd is let in. 'To Wally,' Plácido tries to write with a felt-tip pen on one shiny surface, but the ink does not show up legibly. *Che penna infame!* (this pen is awful!) cries Rodolfo in the last act of *Bohème*, and Domingo puts on his Rodolfo face. A ball-point pen is provided which performs little better. Half a dozen pens are offered from all around and Plácido jokes about his 'choice of weapons'.

In the corridor the first dozen people are let in. Prominently on display are Domingo's latest complete recordings, *Turandot* and *Aida*, his most recent Deutsche Grammophon anthology albums, 'Viva Domingo' and 'The Best of Domingo', his tango album, 'Be My Love', *Fanciulla*, of course, and any number of others. For this company alone Domingo has also recorded *Carmen*, *Werther*, *Samson et Dalila*, *Traviata*, *Rigoletto*, *Ballo*, *Luisa Miller*, *Macbeth*, the Requiems of Verdi and Berlioz, Berlioz' *Damnation de Faust* and *Béatrice et Bénédict*, German operas including *Meistersinger* and *Oberon*, and Beethoven's Choral Symphony. The people let into the corridor at any given time have plenty to think about as they await their turn and decide what discs to ask the Mastersinger to sign.

Which is just as well as they also have plenty of time in which to do their thinking and their buying. Domingo is like a good doctor —generosity itself to those who are with him, but that inevitably means keeping a lot of other people waiting a very long time for their turn.

His generosity exceeds itself when lame Mrs Shackleton appears with two friends, and, with difficulty but unaided, walks up to him. Margaret Shackleton comes from the Cheshire suburbs of Manchester and might possibly have been dead were it not for the inspiration of Plácido Domingo. A sufferer from bone marrow cancer who lost one of her legs at sixteen, she managed, through grit, determination and an artificial leg, to live a reasonably normal life and even married and had two children. In time, however, her condition deteriorated and walking proved impossible except with crutches. 'You will never walk again,' the doctors told her and she was not given very long to live. Some gain inspiration from those near and dear to them. Margaret Shackleton gained a new lease on life from a man she had never met but whose voice she knew well, Plácido Domingo. Domingo's records were played over and over again in the Shackleton home—and then, a year ago, Margaret went off, with her crutches, to London to meet the man who had been her inspiration. The occasion was a similar signing session to today's. Plácido was full of smiles and affectionate encouragement, and Margaret concluded her brief meeting by vowing that 'Next time I see you I swear I will walk up to you!'

Today she is as good as her word. She has a new artificial leg, something it was beyond her powers to use a year ago. Proudly carrying the royal blue 'Plácido Domingo' volume she has compiled with its Bible-style gold-embossed page-marker, she walks, shakily but unaided, up to her personal saint.

What is a man to do? Plácido glances through the book (he has an 'Aura' around him, he reads, comparable to that of the Pope) and sees pages and pages of cuttings about himself, photos from every imaginable source, and letters to Mrs Shackleton from record companies, Domingo's agents and managers, the editor of *Opera* magazine, the public relations people at Rolex watches, and many others besides. It is embarrassing, possibly, but also deeply moving.

The evening progresses and somehow Plácido manages to work his way through the colossal crowd. 'I have always wanted to thank you for your wonderful performance of *Pagliacci*,' gushes Angela. Beryl wants him to sign an EMI disc she has brought with her and the ecumenical Domingo sees no reason why he shouldn't oblige. 'To Peter', he writes, as his wrist begins to tire, 'To Joy', 'To Lindsay', 'To Eddie'—and by about 8.30 p.m. the very last members of the queue are let into the corridor to receive their thaumaturgic touch from the man recently dubbed by *Newsweek* 'the King of Opera'. The King vouchsafes his signature to them all, and they leave the presence healed of any ailments they may have contracted during the long wait outside—relieved, also, depending on how many records they bought, of anything from five to fifty pounds.

That night, after the four-hour *Fanciulla* run-through and three hours of autograph-signing, Domingo is driven north along the drizzly Midland motorways to visit his eldest son José. Joe, offspring of Plácido's brief first marriage, has been resident in England for some years, has had an up-and-down career, and has carved a special niche in his father's fond and concerned heart. Plácido telephones and visits Joe whenever he can, often snatching the odd half day in England in the midst of a crowded continental schedule. He tries to be as accessible and accommodating as he can and if there were a prize for depth of parental concern, Plácido would doubtless have won it years ago. But he cannot help feeling that some of the difficulties Joe has faced arise from Plácido being a largely absentee father—one, moreover, long since married to a second wife who has provided Plácido with two boys of her own. The Joe–Plácido relationship is encrusted in various layers of potential disfiguration, and Plácido knows that he must constantly strive hard if this father–son bond is to be successfully maintained.

Plácido has many things on his mind at the moment. Even to find time to talk essential business with Milton Okun he has to drive halfway up the motorway with Milt, his own chauffeur following in the rear-view mirror ready to take Plácido on when Milt is ready to turn back. And what do Plácido and Milt decide on that motorway trip together? The exact schedule of their overnight recording session.

The next day after yet one more run-through of *Fanciulla* for Vernon's cameras, there is the filmed performance itself. Maybe '*Fanciulla* doesn't leave you drained the way *Pagliacci* does', but few performances can have contained greater intensity than this. And not just from Domingo. Carol Neblett throws herself into the role of Minnie with enormous gusto and Carroli's Rance is more snarling and sinister than ever. Everybody fulfils the detailed instructions they have been receiving all week from Faggioni and Vernon. Only one brief section from Act I has to be re-taken and that is because a bass clarinet misses its cue. The audience is delighted, though they are denied such special effects as Robert Lloyd's John Wayne-style gun-twirl or the turning of the water wheel—features possibly too scene-stealing on television for an already action-packed production. No more *Fanciulla* for three whole days—during which time Domingo will slip in a quick trip to Rome to correct a detail or two in the *Traviata* film, to Milan to discuss the forthcoming La Scala production of *Ernani*, and on to Geneva for a hurried visit to Placi and Alvaro at school in Switzerland. And then, back in London a day before yet another *Fanciulla* performance, he has a singularly British ceremony to fit in.

For thirty of its hundred years London's Royal College of Music has had as its President the person who regularly tops the polls as Most Popular Woman in the Country—Queen Elizabeth the Queen Mother, universally and affectionately referred to behind her back as the Queen Mum and in front as Ma'am. With her natural grace, flowery or be-feathered hats, spontaneous and winning smile, and a record of public service that includes authentic courage and leadership in Britain's darkest hours of World War II, the Queen Mother is a genuinely much-loved figure, not least in the world of music for which she, like her grandson Prince Charles, has always had a real fondness. Nobody can know for sure, of course, but whereas many of her Royal chores are doubtless a burden to be endured for the good of the realm, she probably regards her annual visit to the Royal College of Music as a special pleasure.

The occasion of 'The President's Visit' involves the conferring of various honours. Not, usually, honorary doctorates; only five have been given in a century (three of them to music-loving Royals) —though a sixth, to Sir Michael Tippett, is to be granted this afternoon. But bestowal of Fellowship of the Royal College of Music is part of the Queen Mother's annual duties and the list of College Fellows reads a little like a Who's Who of British music. Today's new Fellows include several distinguished British musicians and two of the world's musical superstars, Daniel Barenboim and Plácido Domingo.

Domingo and Barenboim are old friends and the bonds run deep. Several of Domingo's recordings of French works—Saint-Saëns' opera *Samson et Dalila*, Berlioz' Requiem, *Damnation de Faust* and *Béatrice et Bénédict*—have been conducted by Barenboim. Domingo was supposed to be in Barenboim's recording of Berlioz' *Roméo et Juliette*, too, but pulled out at an awkwardly late stage, which annoyed Barenboim at the time. Today, they chat together amiably and animatedly in Spanish—part of Barenboim's boyhood was spent in Argentina, part of Domingo's in Mexico. They have Israel in common too, Barenboim spending his adolescence there, Domingo his early twenties. Domingo's Hebrew is nowadays pretty rudimentary, though he likes to tell how he overheard some Israelis in a New York elevator talking about him, let them finish—and then shocked them by thanking them in their own language for all they had said! The two men are of an age, Domingo forty-one, Barenboim forty this very week. Barenboim, short, stocky, wearing a quiet suit, his hair just beginning to fleck with grey and to thin at the crown, hovers solicitously close to his wife Jacqueline Du Pré. Domingo, huge but hunched, flashes her one of his infectious grins. Jackie, once one of the most brilliant of violoncellists, has been confined to a wheelchair for a decade now since the cruel onset of multiple sclerosis.

A student brass ensemble on stage plays Byrd and Bach as the guests begin to settle. Domingo edges back to his place next to Marta who is dressed in black, hair tightly combed back. She looks a little severe today, but then so does the Royal College. A booming voice projects clearly over several rows of seats and many decibels of brass. 'Placido!'—the 'c' pronounced as an English 'ch' as though the name were Italian. 'Placido!' This is the voice of one of the greatest (and possibly loudest) operatic sopranos of the century, Eva Turner. Never mind the fact that Dame Eva is well over ninety, the voice still carries as far as she wishes. A star at La Scala long before any other British singer had made an international operatic reputation, she was the greatest Turandot and Aida of her day. Her career lasted until she was in her late fifties and now, if no longer singing, she is almost as active as ever.

When Eva Turner is not teaching she is probably off on her frequent transatlantic journeys or else sitting on one of the various arts and opera committees on which she serves. And whenever Plácido Domingo is in town she goes to hear him. Ask Dame Eva what she thinks about Domingo and she will go into raptures—this from a lady who has heard (most of them at close quarters) every major tenor of the past sixty years. 'I'm over the moon every time I hear Plácido's performances,' she says. 'I only wish I were singing today so that he could be my Calaf and Radamès and Manrico.' She rolls the 'r's with true Italianate gusto. 'It's not just the voice, the acting, his looks—and he's such a *handsome* man, isn't he?—no, it's also that he's such a wonderful *musician*. Of how many great singers can you say that?'

Dame Eva, with her white hair, dumpy figure and comfortable hat, looks a little like the Queen Mother; certainly, Plácido responds to her call as to a royal summons. She was absolutely *thrilled* by *Fanciulla* the other night, she says. Plácido has a soft spot for Dame Eva but has to creep back to his seat as the brass ensemble reaches the end of the Bach C minor fugue and the assembled crowd wait in silence for the proceedings to begin.

Presently, amid a ripple of applause and a sea of craning necks, the Queen Mother enters at the back of the hall accompanied by the Director of the Royal College of Music, Sir David Willcocks. Willcocks makes a brief introductory speech and then the Queen Mother comes to the fore to make the presentations. Willcocks's citations are mostly soberly appropriate to an august academic occasion but the Director's tongue is seen to slide ever so discreetly into his cheek as he introduces the next Honorary Fellow. Plácido Domingo, he announces, is 'one of the greatest stars in the operatic firmament. His light shines in the major opera houses of the world and on the television sets in millions of homes.' One or two looks are exchanged in the body of the hall, but Plácido is enjoying himself. He is well practised at shaking hands with royalty and as he does so on this occasion and receives his scroll he seems able to look at the same time at both the Queen Mother and the press cameras. He is enjoying himself all the more in the knowledge that, notwithstanding the original request of the College, he does not have to sing today—or, except at tea, even have to do much talking. It is a rare but welcome experience for Domingo to be able to enjoy silent stardom.

After the Fellowships, a long list of Honorary Memberships of the College. As the Queen Mother eventually steps back towards her seat, she makes a brief detour to Jacqueline Du Pré to say how glad she is to see her there. The gesture is spontaneous and the two ladies exchange warm smiles and a hand clasp.

Tea-time beckons. You might think that on a royal visit tea and cucumber sandwiches would be *de rigueur*, and you would be right. But the spread includes a great array of rich cream cakes as well, and once the Queen Mother is observed through two hundred sidelong glances to have raised her cup of tea to the royal lips, everybody else instantly sets to. Or nearly everybody else. Domingo is besieged throughout the tea party by people wanting him to autograph their copies of the programme and to each he writes a personal message. Within twenty-five minutes the swarm of musical locusts has done its work and there is not a sandwich—much less a cream cake—to be seen. Never mind. Domingo is keen to keep his weight under control. The following evening he has to look like a fugitive Californian bandit. And a week later—such are the exigencies of the operatic profession—another bandit on the run, a Spanish outlaw known as Ernani.

On Tenors and Tenors

Mirror, mirror on the wall, who is the greatest tenor of them all? A silly question to ask and a simple question to answer. Silly, because musical performance is not a branch of athletics to be assessed by universally agreed criteria; simple, because everybody's safe and obvious nomination is Enrico Caruso. But Caruso has been dead for over sixty years, and those who insist on thinking of music as a branch of athletics persist with the questioning: who, then, is the greatest tenor of *our* day? Tenor-watchers can be distressingly like sports fans in the crudity of their judgements of excellence. If Caruso held the title in the first two decades of this century who wears the belt today?

The purely physical aspects of music-making have great appeal and many are fascinated by, for example, how high or low or loud or fast or often someone sings. Nor are these attitudes confined to singing. Many of the most celebrated instrumental performers, too, have been those with (among other more sophisticated skills) the most formidable technical accomplishment, the Paganinis and Liszts and their successors, capable of producing more sounds faster, higher or louder than is given to ordinary mortals. But it is to singers, particularly those at the top end of the voice range, that many direct this somewhat basic approach. The most famous and highly-rewarded singers have often been those capable of pushing their physical resources to perform in a range beyond the point that to most people would be hysteria or strangulation, yet continuing against the odds to produce beautiful, controlled sound. We can all sing a little. Yet, just as we marvel at the athlete who can jump higher or run faster than anyone else (and we can all jump and run a little, too), so there is something particularly exciting in seeing and hearing a human being pushing the voice up and beyond the range available to the rest of us.

Thus, the view of the Singer-as-Athlete is not entirely inapposite inasmuch as a good singer *is* capable of physical feats, necessarily grounded on robust good health, that most could not emulate. And it is particularly applicable to the tenor. Of the other high voices, the castrato is no longer with us, while the counter-tenor and high soprano tend to be lauded more for the controlled accuracy than the muscularity of their top notes. There is something exhilarating, for singer and listener alike, about a powerful, reverberant chest-toned high note from a good tenor, something assertive, too, as though the singer were requiring and displaying confidence and courage similar to those of an athlete approaching and clearing a high bar.

The tenor, capable of singing notes other men cannot reach or at best screech, is also invested with something of the mystique of the circus performer, almost as though he were a sort of Strong Man, Trapeze Artist or Circus Freak. 'Here, ladies and gentlemen, before your eyes and ears, is a man just like the rest of us, yet capable of the most prodigious feats of vocal prowess while managing to retain control throughout.' Control throughout? Normally, yes. But part of the audience thrill is the feeling, the fear (perhaps even the repressed hope) that he may just possibly *lose* control. Nobody consciously wants the high-wire artist to lose his hold, but part of the undoubted fun of the fair is the knowledge that he could. Similarly, part of the thrill of hearing a singer pushing his voice up beyond the normal limits is the repressed anticipation that the voice might break. The most emotionally loaded moments in the opera house can often be when the tenor approaches the big top note of the evening. Will he make it? Will he sustain it? It requires temerity for a man to propel his voice, with full steam, as it were, up and up—in public. As most men try to sing high, the voice tends to become constricted, they close up the back of the throat for fear of what might come out if they continued to apply full power and leave the instrument open. Or they simply opt out and sing falsetto. But the professional tenor has to have, among other ingredients in his make-up, a large pinch of courage, the preparedness to leave everything big and wide and open as he pushes himself up. The orchestra will play a sophisticated equivalent of rolling drums during the big run-up. And, lo: the tenor gets up there, stays there, and, as he comes down again, perhaps even allows a little triumphant flourish and possibly a slight suggestion of strain or even a sob to enter the voice. Everybody breathes with him as he goes up there, releases breath as he comes back safely to earth.

This circus analogy is obviously a crude and inadequate way of regarding operatic singing, but it may offer a clue to a further aspect of what we may call the tenor mystique. He may be an athlete; he may even in the eyes and ears of some be a species of circus freak. But why is it to the tenor voice that most of the great, surging music of love and heroism is regularly given? After all, in 'real life' men with high voices are often weedy little fellows, often with less obvious sex appeal than big, beefy types with lower voices and bigger muscles. Indeed, the high male speaking voice is sometimes associated with effeminacy. Surely it is to the bass, not the tenor, that operatic composers ought to have given all their best romantic music?

The tenor voice is in its highest register only a degree removed from hysteria, from the frantic screams of extreme emotion. We 'raise' our voices, not just in volume but also in pitch, when emotionally aroused; a shout or scream is high not low. Whereas an unusually low timbre or low note as sung by an operatic bass is usually quieter and more resonant than notes in the comfortable middle of the voice (and often associated in opera, therefore, with introspective, magisterial or calming forms of expression), the notes at the top end of the tenor register are usually sung flat out with a fast vibrato. This is the stuff of emotional intensity, of heroic ardour, love, honour, anger, resolution. It is also the stuff of youth—older men tend to have lower voices than young. Thus the ardent young hero, capable of prodigious feats of arms and love—of running and jumping, so to speak, faster and higher than his rivals—has normally been cast as a tenor, the Strong Man of the operatic circus.

Not every tenor looks the part. Just as most men are natural baritones, not capable of singing very high or very low, so most are neither exceptionally tall or short, handsome or ugly. If you *are* unusually tall, you will probably have a long neck and long vocal cords—in which case the odds are that you will have a deep voice. By contrast, the sweet little voice of a Galli-Curci or a Lily Pons, so like that of a child, seems to go naturally with a slight body, while many of the great tenors, too, such as Caruso, Gigli, Bergonzi or Alfredo Kraus, have been fairly short in stature.

By a curious chance, several of the leading tenors of our own times are men of substantial physique. Franco Bonisolli is a towering man from whom you might expect a sonorous bass voice to emanate. Luciano Pavarotti fluctuates between the large and the enormous, but for his size is reasonably lithe and active, as you might expect from a one-time gym teacher. And Domingo? A powerfully built man of six foot two, impressively proportioned with a great barrel of a chest, strong forearms, and a body that leaves the ladies swooning as no major tenor has done since Franco Corelli. He has a tendency to put on weight, his broad shoulders are more rounded than they should be, and his powerful neck can merge too easily with an incipient double chin. But when he is in good physical shape—which is almost always and means when he is within hailing distance of 200 pounds (90 kilos)—Domingo looks most of the parts he has to play.

The art of Domingo represents an uncommon fusion of physique, vocal quality and musical intelligence. Physically, he just happens to be tall, dark, handsome and powerfully built and to have a voice cast in the same mould. Domingo's voice, too, has a strong, heroic quality to it, burnished, covered, almost baritonal in quality,* and is capable on occasion of lifting the roof off the largest auditorium. But like many powerful men Domingo does not flaunt his physical strength, and the moments of great vocal power are carefully rationed and attuned to the demands of the musical and dramatic situation. The real hallmark of Domingo's vocalism at its best lies not in the display of power for its own sake but in the sense of a great instrument being used in the service of music. You rarely feel at a Domingo performance that he is pouring out his final reserves; rather, that his artistry consists of a highly sensitive and intelligent husbanding of

* For a revealing display of how baritonal Domingo's voice can sound, listen to the first half-hour of his *Meistersinger* recording where much of the music goes to the German tenor Horst Laubenthal as David. The occasional Domingo interjections give the music almost the character of a tenor-baritone duet.

unusually well-endowed resources. 'His appeal,' Sir John Tooley once summed it up to me, 'lies not only in his outstanding natural gifts but in his capacity to control and direct them and never to be at their mercy.' A comparison with another great tenor of modern times is instructive. Where Jon Vickers in his prime would almost always give the impression that *this* performance of *Fidelio*, *Otello*, *Pagliacci*, *Peter Grimes* or *Tristan* was *the* one into which he had squeezed his last drop of emotional energy—though, of course, it was not and he would give the same impression again three nights later—Domingo's performances tend to be more measured, the greatest bursts of artistic energy kept in reserve for the appropriate moments. As with Vickers, a Domingo performance is always exciting in a physical way; there is a yearning quality to much of his lyrical singing that tugs at the heart, and the great climaxes of triumph or despair are superbly portrayed by voice, face and body. But the excitement is never gratuitous and is paced by the drama it is helping to unfold.

Domingo's voice has changed very little over the years since he began his international career. Where Caruso's, for instance, became noticeably darker and heavier in his mid-forties, Domingo's is scarcely different from in his late twenties. Listen to recordings of arias committed twice to disc by Domingo over a ten- or twelve-year period and you will be hard pressed to tell simply from the voice which was the earlier and which the later. Domingo himself feels that what has changed is the depth of his interpretations, the emphasis he gives to language, the facility with which he can colour the voice, deal with difficult *tessituras* and alternate between dramatic and lyrical roles. 'People told me after I sang my first *Otello* at thirty-four with all the darkness of tone that opera requires that I would never again be able to sing lyrical works like *Bohème*,' he says. 'But honestly, if you listen to a recording of a performance of *Bohème* I gave ten years ago and one a year ago, the fresher sounding one will be the more recent one, you know.'

The actual quality of Domingo's voice is astonishingly even. If you play a Domingo recording at low speed so that the voice sounds like that of a bass, the natural vibrato remains almost uncannily regular. For all Domingo's power, it is the smooth, dark velvety sound that remains in the aural memory. While his voice has the deeper tones more commonly associated with the *tenore drammàtico*, his sense of lyrical style also puts him in a league with Pavarotti and Bergonzi. Probably no other tenor since Björling, or perhaps even Caruso, has had quite this combination of gifts. The tone is darker, richer, more covered than the honeyed sound of Pavarotti, more nasal perhaps, but less *stretto* or constricted than his famous Italian rival. Where Pavarotti would ride over the assembled forces of a big orchestra with his tight, bright, pin-pointed tone rather as a flute or an oboe can do, Domingo's will blend and balance more like a horn—unless the score requires the independence of a trumpet, in which case Domingo has the resources to oblige. If there is a single musical instrument that Domingo's voice most resembles it is probably the rich, vibrant, generously bowed cello and it is not surprising that his hero among instrumentalists is his late, great compatriot Pablo Casals.

Is there anything specifically 'Spanish' about Domingo's voice? Many have found echoes in Domingo of some of his Spanish predecessors, such as Miguel Fleta, the first Calaf in Puccini's posthumous opera *Turandot*. Spanish voices, Domingo acknowledges, do often have something velvety about them, more velvet than metal, certainly. He thinks that Italian voices on the other hand tend to have a brighter, more 'pinging' resonance that helps them cut through the orchestra. Velvety voices are all very beautiful, but have a tendency to diminish in projection when tired, so Domingo says he has to work hard if he is always to penetrate thicker orchestral sonorities while not losing the essential smoothness of texture.

It is hard to compare one voice with another and records give us only an approximation of the impact singers of the past had in live performance, but the question is often asked: how does Domingo stand alongside the other great tenors? In many ways, his voice quality is reminiscent of the later Caruso, minus the 'protruding jaw' mannerisms and with a cleaner *portamento*. Possibly less heroic than Martinelli or Corelli, without the easy top of a Kraus or Gedda, not always as passionate as Carreras, and for some lacking the silvery seductiveness of a Gigli or quite the supreme aristocratic stylishness of Bergonzi at his best, the greatness of Domingo lies in his capacity to bring together qualities from each of these and other great singers and to combine and synthesize into his own art a dazzling array of qualities rarely if ever found in a single artist.

Vocal artistry consists of a great deal more than merely the sound a singer produces. Domingo's natural vocal centre of gravity is a little lower than that of some leading tenors yet he seems able to cope with the most demanding *tessitura*. *The Tales of Hoffmann*, for example, is usually thought to be an opera for the higher, lighter type of voice of Gedda or Kraus. Hoffmann is on stage almost throughout a long evening and in the final scene has to repeat the high, chromatically ascending *arietta* of the first act, yet I have heard Domingo sing through this scene without a hint of the weariness he must be feeling by this stage. What other basically Italianate tenor—one who, after all, has made a delightfully stylish recording of *L'Elisir d'Amore*—would also be prepared to manoeuvre the pitfalls of *Lohengrin* or (on record) *Die Meistersinger*—in German? One has to go back to the nineteenth century and Jean de Reszke for vocal versatility of that quality.

There is also the question of phrasing, that capacity to sing with the breath, to let the musical and verbal meaning make its own point almost unencumbered by the physical needs of the singer. There are times when Domingo almost seems to refrain from breathing in order to let the music flow uninterrupted. Listen, for instance, to the way he has (twice) recorded the lines sung by Manrico to his ailing mother in the last act of *Il Trovatore* ('Riposa, o madre') in a single breath yet, like Björling, manage to make the herculean phrasing sound the most natural thing in the world. The same is true of the long run in his recording of 'Il mio tesoro' from Mozart's *Don Giovanni* where Domingo on record emerges as a serious competitor to the greatest master of this music, John McCormack.

What of those very high notes that the tenor-as-athlete is supposed to be able to reach? Domingo does not have an easy top C and certainly does not reach that note with the relative facility of lighter tenors such as Kraus or Pavarotti in their prime, though he probably has the richest high Bs and B flats in the business. Like Jussi Björling, one of Domingo's predecessors whom he most admires, Domingo sometimes has a tendency to focus his tone on the sharper end of the highest notes, a quality which, held carefully in control, can add brilliance and excitement to passages of emotional intensity. But what of top C? Baritone Sherrill Milnes recalls Domingo struggling to get the two top Cs at the end of 'Di quella pira' when the two of them were recording Verdi's *Il Trovatore* in 1969. The first was successful; the second proved harder. 'He stood there with a towel round his neck in front of the full male chorus—forty guys, each of them probably thinking they could do better, and Plácido knowing what they're thinking.' Domingo just stood there, sweating under the strain, asking again and again to go back a few bars so that he could have another try. And then, suddenly, he landed on a real beauty. 'Well,' says Milnes now, his face beaming with admiration after all those years, 'you just had to love him for the guts of it, standing full courage in front of the world, so to speak, soaking wet and with that stunning voice cracking until finally he got it right.'

Domingo himself is not shy of talking about his top Cs. A few years ago he said: 'I sing high Cs in the fourth act of *Manon Lescaut* with the soprano, in the duets in *Ballo* and the riddle scene of *Turandot*, plus the single C in *Otello*. I always transpose the arias in *Bohème*, *Trovatore* and *Faust*.' He went on to add that as time passed he was feeling more confident of the note. Top C? Great to have, said the undisputed King of the High Cs in recent years, Luciano Pavarotti in his 1982 *Playboy* interview, but it is like playing soccer. If you score a goal every week, that's fine; but to be rated a really good footballer you must be an all-round team player.

Like all good singers, Domingo integrates the high notes into the texture of the music that surrounds them. He will not hold on to a high note longer than the natural flow of the music permits nor interfere with the musical pulse in order to help his run-up. Indeed, he will often not even pause for breath before a high note but rather take it as part of a single sweep of a phrase. Such feats could only be attempted by a man blessed with large and pliant lungs, tremendous diaphragm support (Domingo's stomach muscles are like those of a weightlifter)—and, above all, great musical sensitivity. Domingo is a showman but not a vulgarian and he knows how to keep the lid on during a performance until there is a good reason in the music and the drama for letting it blow off. Like a good chamber player, indeed,

Domingo knows how not to outsing his colleagues but rather to integrate his own artistry into the work and the current performance as a whole.

All this is not just a matter of singing more *forte* or *piano*, more *legato* or *staccato*, or building up a *crescendo* from an earlier or later starting point, though all this is of course part of it. It is really a question of overall musicianship, of letting the architecture of a work dictate the details rather than considering the details purely in their own terms. It may sound patronizing or platitudinous to commend Domingo's musicality. Is not any successful singer bound, almost by definition, to be musical? Well, yes, of course. But Domingo's scrupulous care for detail, for letting each word and musical phrase make its own point, is always allied to concern for the overall arch of musical meaning—a combination not so common among singers of Grand Opera. Opera lore abounds with jokes about the proverbial stupidity of tenors. Once after a performance of *Tosca* conductor James Levine complimented Domingo on the all-round quality of his singing: 'Plácido,' he said, 'you know you really have the mind of a conductor.' Domingo smiled into the dressing-room mirror and replied, 'It's just as well you don't have the mind of a tenor!'

Domingo's musical intelligence is not in any doubt. Much of it is instinctive. He is a quick and natural learner and tends to refine his performances by doing rather than by analysing. Nor does his schedule allow him a great deal of time to read in detail around a part he is studying. But the intelligence is incisive and penetrating and there is nothing in a Domingo performance left to chance. He talks animatedly about the need to change the colour of the voice when (for example, in the Act III aria from *Trovatore* 'Ah! sì ben mio') the music lifts from minor to major. Or take Alvaro's big aria at the opening of Act II of Verdi's *Forza del Destino*. As Domingo tells it, the tenor has to sing a tricky duet early in the evening, go off for an hour or so—and then come on cold to sing an extraordinarily difficult and varied aria. It starts with a long recitative in which words are all-important, then, with the orchestra just playing simple pizzicato chords, he has to produce a beautiful soaring phrase right up to a *piano* A flat. If he is in good shape it's no great problem, but if he is a little tired or has a frog in his throat he may decide to play safe and attack the note with more volume. The decision may depend upon many factors—even the nature of the audience he is singing to. 'In a place like Hamburg, people expect you to try the *piano* sound even if it does not come out quite right; in Milan, the note has got to come out perfectly, however you attack it, or they'll all be groaning!' Every role creates its own demands and problems. Rodolfo in *Bohème*, for example, requires a more lyrical voice than Otello, for the first is a young poet, the second an experienced general, even though the *Bohème* orchestration in Act III, for example, is much heavier than in the *Otello* love duet.

There are not many opera singers who talk in detail about orchestration. Most are not much more than vaguely aware of what their singing colleagues are doing, let alone of the details of what is going on in the pit. But ever since his early days in his parents' music theatre, Domingo has been interested in all aspects of music-making. Before he began to take his voice seriously he was already an accomplished pianist and is still an excellent player and sight-reader. Thus, he teaches himself his various roles at the piano without having to depend, as most singers do, on the skills and time of a coach or *répétiteur*—and, above all, without having to use his voice. First-class pianism is an extraordinary boon to a singer and one that few possess. Domingo, with some eighty operatic roles under his belt and something like twenty-five of them virtually ready for performance at any one time, can always brush up his lines, without singing, on his own and at his own convenience. Certainly, as he approached the run of performances of Verdi's *Ernani* with which La Scala opened its 1982–3 season, he spent very little time revising a score he had scarcely had occasion to touch for thirteen years. Yet when rehearsals began he was clearly note and word perfect. When did he relearn the opera? He tries to think. In taxis. In London during *Fanciulla* breaks. On the plane to Milan . . .

ACT III

Master of the House

The Opera Business

The great opera houses of the world are in cities like Milan, New York, London, large towns full of busy people not all of whom are opera fans. Indeed, ask the man in the street in these cities what he thinks about opera and he will probably say that he doesn't. Or perhaps he thinks of it as a music-hall joke complete with bosomy fat soprano belting out hideous high notes of tender love to an uncomprehending little Latin lover. He has a point. The Marx Brothers scored a bullseye in A *Night at the Opera* where a crazy plot culminates in the hilariously disrupted performance of an opera, *Il Trovatore*, with a plot almost equally unlikely. *Trovatore* is a notable example of an opera that contains glorious passages of dramatic improbability in which various characters, galvanized into passionate action by some critical news, freeze on stage for minutes on end to tell us how not a moment must be lost. There are good operas and bad operas, opera well done and badly done. At its best it can be a sublime meshing of the three great arts of music, poetry and drama and can convey a depth of feeling perhaps unequalled in any other form. At its worst it can alternate between the embarrassing and the downright ludicrous.

To some extent opera has only itself to blame if it has sometimes received a bad press or no press. Bad opera, or opera badly performed, gives the whole art a bad name. But even good opera well done tends to appeal to the few. To some extent this is a question of idiom; it is not to everybody's taste to hear people singing when you and I would talk, or to sit through the rumbling ruminations of characters whose thoughts—if you or I had them—would be better kept silent. There are other problems: language for example. When opera is performed in its original language before an audience largely unfamiliar with it, much of the detailed meaning is bound to be lost, while the frustration at not catching every word in one's *own* language can be even worse than not understanding someone else's. Some people are simply not responsive to music. There are the deaf, the tone deaf, and the many to whom 'classical' music is of little or no interest.

Possibly a more profound reason why opera does not appeal to everyone is that it is a composite art form which can stir deep and sometimes troubling emotions. Consider the impact a good movie can have, particularly one with a strong musical score. Many of the emotion-packed clichés of film music are more or less direct derivations of standard operatic practice—the harps, flutes and *tremolando* strings associated with moonlit nights of romance, the low brass chords that denote death, the great orchestral climaxes that accompany dramatic release of pent-up feelings. This sort of music can make a powerful impression even when separated from the dramatic situation it was intended to depict, and the film music of Carl Davis or John Williams, for example, or Walton's music for Olivier's Shakespeare films, can be evocative enough even out of context. The same is obviously true of some of the great Wagner or Verdi orchestral set pieces, which always go down well in the concert hall. But the combined assault on the aesthetic senses of powerful music, drama and poetry can be overwhelming. It is not easy or comfortable coming to terms with, say, the infinite sadness of Mozart's Countess or Strauss's Marschallin, Verdi's poignant fathers and daughters, Wagner's woefully misdirected gods and goddesses. These fictional characters can tell us truths about ourselves, the more authentic for the ostensibly fictional and artificial mould in which the message is packaged, that are not always easy to take. Opera notoriously arouses the most passionate and vociferous audience reaction of any of the performing arts and when a great work is superbly performed (or butchered) it is easy to see why. No wonder most people gravitate towards less demanding forms of art, whether for escape, solace or sheer entertainment.

If there are reasons in the realms of aesthetics and psychology why opera does not have mass appeal, the most obvious ones are economic. Opera is expensive entertainment to produce and to attend. A typical Broadway or West End theatre in the 1980s has a payroll of some twenty people and puts on the same play, with maybe five or eight actors, to an audience of under a thousand each night with also a matinée or two. A major modern opera house may pack in two or three times as many people every night, but the management has not twenty but perhaps a thousand salaries to pay, and in a typical week may put on two or three performances each of three or even four different productions.

Opera was always one of the most elaborate arts to promote and costly to attend and no opera house has ever been fully self-supporting. In the seventeenth and eighteenth centuries the costs would generally be underwritten by wealthy aristocratic patrons. In the states of nineteenth-century Italy and Germany, individual patronage by the wealthy political or social leader gradually merged with the idea of local subsidy so that in our own time many Italian and German opera houses are, in effect, still partly subvented by taxes on other local amenities. In addition, the idea of a national subsidy developed so that the Opéra in Paris, for example, like the Comédie Française and other cultural institutions of national importance, receives a sizeable grant direct from the French government. In Britain, the Arts Council pays a substantial proportion of its annual grant (in 1984 £29.6 million out of a total of £100 million) directly to the four 'National Companies' (the National Theatre, Royal Shakespeare Company, English National Opera and Covent Garden), by far the largest single grant (£12.3 million) going to the Royal Opera House. In Eastern Europe, government subsidy takes the form of direct nationalization so that singers and opera house staff are placed on government salaries and blocks of seats are allocated at moderate prices to factory workers who, in any Western system, would never normally be able to afford so expensive an art.

The idea of private patronage has never completely died. Just as early performances of Haydn's new works were paid for by Prince Esterhazy and those of Wagner a century later by the King of Bavaria, so in our own time much of the income of the American opera companies comes from wealthy families and firms. There is, of course, 'private' and 'private'. There is a world of difference between the personal munificence of a Renaissance prince or a wealthy eccentric like John Christie, the founder of Glyndebourne, and a large and efficient American insurance company calculating how best to combine shrewd commercial appeal with a possible tax write-off. Perhaps we do language a disservice to call them both the 'private' sector. But the main point remains: opera has always required external financing.

No major opera house can normally rely on box-office receipts for more than about half its income. * Another way of putting this is to say that if opera houses like the Metropolitan in New York, Covent Garden, Vienna or La Scala had to pay for everything out of box-office receipts alone, then in theory ticket prices would have to be doubled or trebled—in which case, of course, many more would remain unsold so that box-office revenue, instead of rising, would in fact fall.

The cost of tickets and the various methods of raising the necessary additional revenue are integrally related to matters of artistic policy. For example, it would presumably be possible for a house like the Met or Covent Garden to concentrate only on the standard works, such as *Bohème*, *Carmen*, *Tosca* and *Traviata* that more or less guarantee sold-out houses, and to avoid altogether their periodic forays into the modern repertoire. This might save money, but no house pursuing such a policy would be able to defend itself from the accusation, often enough levelled at most of them as it is, of being no more than a museum for an essentially fossilized art. In any case, the amount of revenue lost as a result of empty seats when unfamiliar works are performed is small; works are either performed with relatively inexpensive home-grown casts or, if starily enough cast, the public will tend to come in reasonable numbers anyway.

Then there are the over-lavish new productions that every major house is periodically accused of mounting. This *Aida* or *Ring* or *Turandot*, one is forever hearing in one corner or another of the operatic world, could have paid off the national debt, and it is true

---

* The Met, with nearly 4,000 seats, gets close to two-thirds of its income from ticket sales, many of the European houses more like one-third.

that a new production at a large house can nowadays cost in the region of £250,000 or approaching $½ million. But the main costs of operatic production are not really susceptible to much flexibility. Simple sets and infrequent scene changes can help a little. But new sets and props and costumes have to be designed and made, principals and chorus coached, lighting and staging worked out and practised, new programme notes commissioned, the whole production re-hearsed, re-rehearsed and publicized. If that round figure of £250,000 can be reduced in one way or another, the margin is unlikely to be more than about five per cent or so and is usually more related to the nature of the opera than that of the production.

What about expensive guest stars? Could not the high cost of opera be reduced by paying them less—or employing them less? Perhaps the first thing to say is that no fee paid in modern times to opera singers remotely compares with the sort of sum paid to top popular entertainers. For every hundred dollars a Nilsson, Vickers or Suther-land would earn in the affluent 1960s, the Beatles or Rolling Stones would be netting a thousand or more. In the early 1980s, when Domingo was earning something like a million dollars a year, Andrew Lloyd Webber, composer of *Jesus Christ Superstar*, *Evita*, *Cats* and other popular musicals, was at one time said to be getting a million a month.

Nor are today's top opera fees high in comparison with those paid in earlier times. Adelina Patti regularly received at least two to three thousand dollars a performance as long ago as the 1880s, when a violinist in the orchestra of the new Metropolitan Opera in New York was earning a hundred a month. As recently as the 1960s, after accumulated inflation rates of several hundred per cent and the spectacular rise of the tax-man, top fees were still in the region of the $3,000 earned by Patti—though the sum has more than doubled in the twenty years since.

Agents never tire of pointing out that nobody sings Aida or Tristan every day of the week, and few star singers can notch up more than about sixty opera performances in a year. Furthermore, where most people have an earning life of perhaps forty or forty-five years, a singer is exceptional who can stay at the top for twenty. Singing is one of the most precarious professions: if your voice goes, your career goes, and even so established a figure as Domingo could lose most of his earning capacity overnight and forever. Nevertheless, whether today's top operatic performance fee is $5,000 or $20,000 (and it could be either, depending upon a variety of circumstances), it is still an uncommonly handsome sum for an evening's work. If the role is unfamiliar and has to be learnt specially, if the production is new, if the house is not one of the world's major operatic show-places, the fee might be adjusted upwards accordingly. As long ago as 1975, Hamburg reportedly offered Domingo $8,000 for the honour of hosting his first *Otello*.

Opera inevitably remains therefore a costly business to mount and an expensive entertainment to attend. The major houses try to make ends meet by a combination of tactics. They attempt to contain contract negotiations, accommodating as far as they can the demands for better working conditions from staff, chorus, orchestra and principals while remaining tougher on questions of money. They raise box-office prices, particularly in the more expensive parts of the house, as high as they think the market will stand without the price becoming self-defeating. They persuade top singers to perform for what passes in the profession as a relatively modest fee and in return offer the opportunity for outstanding artistic achievement in congenial conditions. And they try to get local and national governments as well as private business and industry and even private individuals to donate whatever they can, if only on the grounds that a civilization will be remembered for its artistic achievements and that these redound to the credit of those who help to make them possible. But for all this juggling, the sheer economics of opera prevent many people from having easy access to an art they might otherwise enjoy. When you add the aesthetic and psychological considerations mentioned earlier, it is scarcely surprising that opera remains a controversial minority pursuit.

The miracle of modern times is that the minority has been growing appreciably larger. For all that opera is regularly taken to task for being an expensive, old-fashioned, élitist art inappropriate to an era devoted to egalitarian politics and bedevilled by economic recession, audiences for live opera have obstinately and consistently grown wherever it has been made available. In Britain there was no permanent professional opera company fifty years ago; in the 1980s there are some half a dozen, all normally playing to full houses. In the USA in the 1982–3 season there were altogether 13,462 performances of opera produced by over a thousand opera companies and workshops for a record total audience of 12.7 million. This growing audience has undoubtedly been stimulated and nurtured by the increasing availability of sound and video recordings of opera and of opera on television. But what people want more than anything else is access to the 'real thing'—live performances of good opera well done. Certainly, pressure for seats is enormous whenever a performer of the stature of Domingo is scheduled to appear at any of the world's great houses. Ticket prices are inevitably high and admission to the holy portals eventually vouchsafed only to a fraction of those who apply. But if you are one of the fortunate minority—what is the nature of the experience that awaits you? And what goes on before a Domingo performance is unveiled to the public?

Ernani at La Scala

The Mecca of Italian opera is the Teatro alla Scala, Milan, the oldest and many would say the greatest of the world's major opera houses. In some ways, and surprisingly in view of its unpretentious eighteenth-century exterior, it is also one of the biggest. If you are misled by its genteel external appearance, try walking round the building. You will gradually discover, as you stroll down the Via Giuseppe Verdi then left along the irregularly shaped Via Arrigo Boito and left again into the northern end of the Via Filodrammatici and eventually back into the Piazza della Scala, that the theatre and its various associated offices take up a substantial chunk of central Milan. The front façade may be somewhat diminutive by the standards of the great nineteenth- and twentieth-century opera houses, but the Scala stage, for example, is over one hundred feet deep, which means that the sets for a spectacular production like the 1982–3 *Ernani* can all be kept on stage, some on view and others hidden at the back, throughout a performance. In the huge oval-shaped auditorium no less than six horseshoe layers of seats are topped by a giant chandelier 550 feet above the orchestra stalls.

La Scala was built on what was once the site of a fourteenth-century church called Santa Maria alla Scala and opened, to a new opera by Salieri, in 1778. Throughout its two centuries of existence, La Scala has been at the heart of the operatic currents of its time and its proud history includes many world premières of works by Rossini, Bellini, Donizetti, Verdi and Puccini. This was the house where Caruso first made his name, where Callas and Gobbi gave many of their finest performances, where Toscanini and de Sabata ruled with magisterial authority. But of all the giants to have contributed to the legend of La Scala, the composers who have written for it and the singers and conductors who have performed there, none ranks larger than the Shakespeare of Italian opera, Giuseppe Verdi. Verdi and La Scala long shared the honours of appearing on obverse sides of the most common unit of Italian currency, the 1,000-lire note. It was in La Scala in the 1840s that several of Verdi's early works were first performed and then, after a gap of forty-odd years, La Scala put on the first performances of his two final masterpieces, those pinnacles of Italian operatic achievement, *Otello* and *Falstaff*. The main road alongside the theatre today bears the composer's name while pride of place in the Scala museum is held by a rich and moving collection of Verdiana. When Verdi lay dying in 1901 at the age of eighty-seven, traffic along the Via Manzoni where Verdi had his apartment in the Hotel di Milano (still there, a couple of hundred yards from La Scala) was diverted so as not to disturb the aged maestro. And at a memorial ceremony after the Grand Old Man had finally passed away the city of Milan virtually came to a halt as the thirty-three-year-old Toscanini conducted an open-air rendition of Verdi's great patriotic chorus, penned more than half a century before, 'Va pensiero sull'ali dorati'.

For all its grand scale, there remains at a Scala performance a sense of direct communication, almost of intimacy, between performers and public. As the lamps above and around the deep red and gold auditorium begin to fade and people move into their seats in the orchestra stalls or in one of the tiers of boxes, the effect is magical. The lights remain on in the boxes as the last to arrive find their seats, aided by ushers wearing black, high-necked uniforms and chains of office. Far above the proscenium arch, roughly in the position occupied by the bas-relief of Queen Victoria at Covent Garden, the famous white-on-black Scala clock (digital long before such things became fashionable, yet still part-Roman too) shows the time to be $\overset{5}{\text{VIII}}$ Performances rarely commence precisely on time. Eventually, the box lights fade too, the maestro comes to his place at the podium and, after the applause and the noise of the latecomers have subsided, or sometimes before, the orchestra strikes up the overture. Two thousand pairs of ears—for this is the total capacity the theatre can seat—listen with rapt attention, their owners already cooing audibly if what they hear pleases them, muttering at what does not. The '5' on the clock slips to the right giving way to the '10' and slowly the great curtains part—a Toscanini innovation, this; until his time as musical director the Scala had a curtain that was raised vertically, but Toscanini did not like the thought that the first thing audiences would see of his singers was their feet and then their knees before getting to their faces. The vast Scala stage presents a vivid picture to even the most distant viewer in the uppermost horseshoe, though a distorted one to many in its side boxes, and the oval shape of the auditorium ensures clarity of sound everywhere. If this is the Mecca of opera, the typical Scala audience expects direct communication from its current gods, and it invariably arrives, and hopes to leave, in a mood of excited devotion and uplift.

It is every opera singer's dream to appear at La Scala. For Plácido Domingo the dream came true on 7 December 1969, the opening night of the 1969–70 season when, still only twenty-eight, he made his début there in the title-role of Verdi's *Ernani*. Since then, La Scala has witnessed some of Domingo's greatest triumphs. Many talk with something approaching awe of his first Scala *Otello* under Carlos Kleiber and produced by Zeffirelli which opened the 1976–7 season and was televised live, the first live telecast of opera in Italy. 'That was the greatest performance I ever saw in my life,' says conductor Riccardo Chailly. 'If I were given the chance of witnessing just one performance of opera before I died, it would have to be that Scala *Otello*.' And now the 1982–3 Scala season is to be opened with Domingo, thirteen years to the day after his début, the date

Americans think of as Pearl Harbor Day but which to every Milanese is the name day of their patron saint, St Ambrogio. And again the opera is to be Verdi's *Ernani*.

The opera is based on Victor Hugo's 1830 play *Hernani*, a story of romantic love, honour and death set in Spain and at Charlemagne's tomb at Aix-la-Chapelle in 1519. Hugo's plot concerned three men—an elderly grandee called Silva; King Charles of Spain (the Emperor Charles V as he becomes); and a handsome young outlaw known as Hernani. All three are in love with the play's heroine, a hapless lady known as Doña Sol, herself, naturally, in love with the bandit.

The opportunities created by this set of circumstances for an imaginative operatic composer much taken by the conflicts between love and honour and between political and personal obligation were legion. Too legion, one might almost say, particularly once Hugo's play had been boiled down by Piave, Verdi's librettist, into the far briefer text required by the exigencies of opera. The result, certainly by the standards of the far subtler libretti Verdi was to set in later years, is a somewhat bombastic series of *grands tableaux* in which the various men declaim the purity of their love, the inviolability of their honour, and/or their preparedness to die and/or kill for both—while the lady (renamed Elvira in the opera) sings of her love for Ernani, whose hand she is variously offered, denied, offered again and finally, as he commits suicide to redeem an absurd pledge to Silva, denied. Throughout composition of the work, Verdi was urging Piave to tighten up the action here, sharpen the characters there, give this scene greater pace, that act greater structural unity. In *Rigoletto*, the other Hugo-based opera on which the two men were to collaborate, the message got through. In *Ernani*, the plot, the characters, the individual lines—all retain a degree of woodenness that even some of the most stirring of Verdi's early music cannot fully conceal.

If the plot and characters of *Ernani* are hard to accept, the opera is none the less notable for some wonderful, thrusting music and for the abundant evidence it contains of the ways in which Verdi was already feeling his way towards the greatness of later years. When King Carlo in *Ernani* reflects on the trials of kingship, for example, one is reminded of the great monologue of Philip (historically, this same

Charles V's son, King Philip II of Spain) in *Don Carlos*; both arias, incidentally, feature a cello solo accompaniment. The tenor–baritone–soprano trio in the second scene of *Ernani* pre-echoes that in Act I of *Il Trovatore*. And the trio that brings down the final curtain on *Ernani* has many similarities to the closing trio of *La Forza del Destino*.

In musical terms, *Ernani* is largely the alternating and interweaving of four principal characters and the consequent blending, in various permutations, of the soprano, tenor, baritone and bass voices. The chorus has a secondary role, no great patriotic surges or mass outpourings here, though there are sundry carousings, a great oath-taking scene and the like. But it is the four principals who make or break a performance of *Ernani* and for the new production to open the 1982–3 season at La Scala the opera is cast from strength.

The title part, the noble bandit who loves and is loved by the lady and who dies in her arms, could have been written for someone with the dark Spanish looks and voice of Plácido Domingo. During the latter stages of his run of London *Fanciullas* Domingo flew over to La Scala for preliminary rehearsals on two occasions, once for two days and again for just one. Now he and Marta set up home in Milan, except that between the opening night and Christmas three weeks later Plácido will make four trips to Paris to record the sound-track of *Carmen* for next year's film . . .

With Domingo in the cast is Renato Bruson, the reigning Verdi baritone, as Carlo. Bruson's smooth, beautiful, slightly plaintive-sounding voice makes him a natural for the great Verdi baritone parts, and if his vocal acting is a trifle lacking in bite or malice this should be no great liability in the role of Carlo, much of whose music is flowing legato and whose characteristic phrases tend to be those of regality, forgiveness and the like. For Silva the Scala has obtained the services of the great Bulgarian bass Nicolai Ghiaurov who also sang the part in Domingo's début production thirteen years ago. If Domingo has matured in the intervening years, Ghiaurov has mellowed. The voice may have lost something of the tremendous power of those years, but poor old Silva has little to express other than outraged dignity and honour and for these Ghiaurov's sombre mien and cavernous voice are ideally matched.

For Elvira La Scala have booked the eternally youthful soprano Mirella Freni, still looking and sounding almost as fresh as when she first became an international star two decades ago. The tall, gaunt Ghiaurov and the buxom, cheeky china-doll Freni have for some years been one of the great double acts on the international operatic circuit, which probably only goes to show that opposites make the best couples.

At the helm is that masterful Verdi conductor Riccardo Muti. Muti is not yet a name normally associated with La Scala. For years this house was the property of his great rival Claudio Abbado. For a decade Muti and Abbado have been the terrible twins of Italian opera, two outstanding talents both of whom have also made their mark far beyond the confines of the opera house. Each is in 1982 director of a major London orchestra—Abbado the London Symphony Orchestra, Muti the Philharmonia. Abbado has also had a distinguished career conducting the Vienna Philharmonic, while Muti is Ormandy's successor in Philadelphia. Each has an impressive string of recordings to his credit, Abbado mostly for Deutsche Grammophon, Muti mostly for EMI. Both are dark, handsome, and still on the young side as conductors go (Muti is forty-one). While Abbado was king of La Scala, Muti's main operatic activities in Italy were centred on his direction of the Maggio Musicale in Florence.

For some years Abbado was reasonably happy at La Scala and he brought the house high musical distinction. But he grew increasingly restive at what he felt to be managerial interference in matters that were properly his domain as artistic director and several times threatened to resign. If he could not make artistic policy unmolested by the bureaucrats, he said, he did not want to be held responsible for the results. Finally, in 1979, his resignation stuck, and although Abbado would continue as 'direttore dell'orchestra' the post of artistic director remains in December 1982 unfilled. Is Muti being groomed, or auditioned, as Abbado's successor? The first night of *Ernani* is, after all, to be the gala opening of the season. It is anybody's guess—though with both the Philharmonia and Philadelphia orchestras Muti has a lot on his plate for the time being. Indeed, in a much-publicized piece of press gossip a few weeks before, Muti was said to have been approached by Covent Garden as a possible successor to Sir Colin Davis in 1986 and to have turned the offer down.*

Slim, dapper, topped by a thick mop of jet black hair, Muti has a habit of throwing his head back and up, almost as though to add inches to his stature, so that a firm line is drawn from the top of his brow, down through his long, distinctive patrician nose, through his arms to the tip of his baton. A man whose rhythmic vitality is expressed by every bone in his body when on the rostrum, he commands his forces with immense authority.

Musically, then, the occasion bodes well. Verdi's score has power throughout, and here are four of the finest singers of the age, led by a brilliant conductor, to give it all they have got. The problem, as ever with *Ernani*, is how to produce the work for the stage. For if Verdi left a feast for Muti and his singers and orchestra, Piave bequeathed a thousand headaches for the producer—in this case Luca Ronconi. Ronconi has a distinguished record as a director of opera and has produced regularly at La Scala for the past eight years. He has also made a name for himself in theatre and television. If anybody should be able to make sense of *Ernani* it is he. The trouble is, he does not seem to take it seriously as drama, and his lack of conviction shows through in some outrageously risky ideas. In interviews he seems to suggest that, since the four principal roles are all irredeemably two-dimensional, it would be pointless trying to instil genuine character into essentially characterless creations; better to devote one's efforts into getting the overall settings and choreography right. It is a view, but one fraught with danger. Also, with a cast of the calibre of the one at his disposal, all capable of excellent acting when given careful direction, it is a prodigal waste of talent. Never mind; Ronconi's *Ernani* will at least look good.

As a matter of fact, it will look spectacualar. He and set designer Ezio Frigerio decide on a multi-level staging. In virtually every scene there will be steps up to, or down to, different levels of action. The whole central portion of the vast Scala stage is dug deep—like a jacuzzi, one wit describes it. The swimming pool effect is accentu-

* In 1983 it was announced that Muti was to leave the Philharmonia at the end of the year and his place be taken by another Italian, Giuseppe Sinopoli, and in 1984 that Muti was to take over (in 1986) as principal conductor of La Scala.

ated, indeed, by the silvery, reflecting surfaces with which much of the stage is covered. Directors like to make their stagings work, as they say, at various levels, and at least in a literal, physical sense this multi-stepped production will do so with a vengeance. Not only will it work *at* a number of levels, but differently, too, *from* various levels. If you watch this performance from the orchestra stalls, for example, you will see merely the heads and shoulders of characters standing or walking in the sunken part of the stage—but you will be rewarded by seeing the cannons that fire (complete with what appear to be bursts of talcum powder) from high in the flies in Act III. * If you sit in one of the tiers of boxes, perhaps halfway up on the right-hand side, you may have a good view of all the action in the jacuzzi (even of people who are not supposed to be visible to the audience) *and* of the cannons and even, perhaps, of the assorted characters who spend part of the evening acting as silent voyeurs from the wing lines. You will certainly have a good view of the silver Corinthian pillars on the far side of the stage that beautifully complement those that support the stage boxes on the other side of the Scala footlights. But unlike someone in a left-hand box, you will probably not see much of the huge cupboard door from which sundry gentlemen emerge like rabbits from a hat into Freni's bedroom in Act I, the vast altar before which she will stand an act later (and from which she will be carried like a Madonna on a litter down the steps of Ronconi's jacuzzi and precariously up the other side), † or the massive tomb of Charlemagne into which Bruson will descend in Act III. The sets are designed on the grand scale; the massive altarpiece looks as though it has been carved bodily out of St Peter's in Rome. Too bad no one spectator will be in a position to see everything director and designer have put into the production.

If there is no single place from which everything in the production can be properly seen, there is also no one period or style in which it appears to have been set. This is partly a product of Franca Squarciapino's sumptuous but incongruous costumes. Most of the silent voyeurs are in late nineteenth-century evening dress (the ladies

---

* An effect that was wisely omitted from later performances.

† This too did not survive into later performances in the run.

with a touch of Spanish), Freni's wedding dress is high-bosomed Empire, Ghiaurov's retainers wear frock coats, Bruson's at one point wear powdered wigs or cocked hats, while Domingo's costumes and retainers seem more or less consistently to fit into the supposed setting of Spain in 1519. Weaponry on display includes guns and cannons, swords and halberds. Most of the great chunks of scenery are detailed and realistic; but the multi-level silvery stage sides and surfaces seem symbolic-cum-futuristic. Beds and ballot boxes appear on lifts from nowhere in mid-scene, while down-to-earth practical modern chairs are moved unceremoniously by members of the cast.

Ronconi believes that *Ernani* takes place not in an historical time and place but in a sort of 'Spain of the Mind'. It is an imaginative idea and helps to explain, for example, some of the occasional Goya touches. Also: put together a bewildering variety of costumes, a handful of stupendous (and stupendously expensive) props, and above all—or below all—the multi-level sunken stage with all its variable silvery steps, bridge and parapets, and you have a recipe for one of the most visually stunning productions one could ever hope to see. Will it ultimately make sense of the drama of *Ernani*? Probably not. But then, would anything?

This production of *Ernani* was the talk of operatic circles for months prior to its actual opening. The musical casting was clearly outstanding and Ronconi was known to have courageous views about the staging. Not surprisingly, various people in the recording and video industries began to express interest. First to come in was the recording arm of the giant British-based electronic group Thorn-EMI. EMI Records, owner of the famous HMV and Angel labels, had wanted for some time to have a version of *Ernani* in its catalogue—the only versions currently available on disc were an RCA recording from 1967 with Carlo Bergonzi and Leontyne Price and a recent Hungaroton version under Gardelli with Giorgio Lamberti and Sylvia Sass. The EMI people had found difficulty scheduling sessions when all the members of their ideal cast could be assembled together. Here, it seemed, was the cast of one's dreams performing the very work not once but some half a dozen times. Why not record all the performances and issue the edited result?

This would be an unusual venture for EMI and its producer John Mordler. He had on rare occasions supervised recordings done live in the concert hall or opera house, but most of his work had been in the studio where one could plan sessions, do retakes, control for external noise and atmosphere, fix and refix microphones. Recordings of live performances may give a greater sense of musical continuity and can certainly contain more electricity than the more clinical results of the studio. It is, also, obviously preferable to record an opera in its correct sequence, something rarely possible given the scheduling complexities of studio recordings; if you were to record *Ernani* in the studio in its correct sequence, you would have to pay to keep an expensive singer like Domingo in town for days at a time while his colleagues recorded scenes in which the tenor does not appear.

There are, however, a host of disadvantages built into the recording of live performances. Basically, you have far less control over the sound you record. Your singers are moving about, and as their faces turn to and from your microphones the tone quality captured on tape is bound to vary. Also, microphones fixed along the footlights will pick up the sound of the singers as they walk along the stage. In this particular production there is a scene where, to the accompaniment of the quietest *pizzicato* string chords, a large chorus of conspirators has to clamber quietly on to various segments of Ronconi's multi-level staging in semi-darkness. As Mordler and his team begin to monitor the sound they are getting from the Scala stage during early rehearsals it is clear that the conspirators' footsteps are going to present them with a major problem. As rehearsals progress and the chorus become more thoroughly choreographed, the stage movements become quieter and more streamlined. But as cloaks and swords take the place of jeans and gym shoes, sound and space take on new dimensions of danger. At one rehearsal, the conspirators are given away by the great clatter caused when one careless member drops his sword. And at the dress rehearsal, another stumbles awkwardly in the half light off one of Ronconi's innumerable staircases, utters an agonized '*maledetta!*' which could have come straight from *Ernani* but happens not to, and is whisked off to hospital.

The greatest problem the EMI team have to face, though, will be audience reaction. The occasional distant cough does not matter too much, though if persistent it can be distracting. The microphones can all be placed so as to capture the musical performance in intimate detail but to exclude all but the most general audience ambience. And, of course, applause at the beginning and end of scenes can be left in or edited out at the producer's discretion. But an Italian audience at an expensive, prestigious production can be notoriously volatile and its reactions may not necessarily be restricted to the occasions when Mordler and his team are prepared to have them react. When on the first night Bruson gets a frog in his throat in Act II a loud tremor of disapproval sweeps right across the audience and before long he is cruelly booed. When he more than makes amends with a beautifully poised aria in Act III he is greeted by the most thunderous 'bravos' while the solo cello accompaniment is still playing. When Freni is raised in her Madonna-type litter, the audience rocks with a combination of fear, incredulity and hilarity. How can a recording be issued if this sort of reaction occurs at each performance? 'Oh, the audience will settle down,' says EMI classical records boss Peter Andry, almost as if to reassure himself.

In addition to being recorded by EMI, this production of *Ernani* is to be filmed for television and video distribution by NVC. Within its first two years of existence, the National Video Corporation has already more or less grown out of the first third of its title. Originally conceived as a purely British organization primarily engaged in recording and marketing British performances of opera and ballet, it now has contracts in half a dozen countries and is beginning to employ talent from across Europe and America. In November 1982, less than a month before the opening of *Ernani*, NVC tied up a five-year tripartite contract with La Scala whereby NVC would, in effect, have first refusal on video rights to its productions while Radiotelevisione Italiana (RAI) would also have rights to an initial broadcast. The contract was rather like that NVC had with Covent Garden and the BBC though in the case of La Scala there was no obligation for NVC to use RAI production expertise or equipment. Indeed, for the filming of *Ernani* Executive Producer Robin Scott assembled a production team which was headed by Danish television's star opera and ballet director, Preben Montell, and that included an award-winning ex-BBC lighting man called John Treays, a free-lance Swiss–Italian production co-ordinator named Manuela Crivelli, and as sound director, working in harmonious co-operation with his friends in the EMI team, ex-CBS classical record producer, Roy Emerson.

The NVC–Scala agreement was launched with great enthusiasm on all sides though Scott and his NVC colleagues knew that what they were embarking upon represented quite a challenge. To date no television recording had been able to capture a Scala production with sufficient visual clarity and audio fidelity to make for a marketable product. Moreover, the *Ernani* rehearsal schedule did not at first allow for any special TV rehearsals—though Scott and his colleagues were allowed to sit in on all the stage rehearsals and they also obtained Scala agreement to put TV lights on the pre-dress rehearsal. The original idea was that RAI would broadcast 'live' the second perform- ance of *Ernani* on 11 December and that the film of this televised performance would subsequently be marketed on video-cassette and disc. Later it was decided to scrap the live broadcast and instead film *two* performances, those of 14 and 18 December, and put the edited result on the air in Italy on Christmas Day.

Robin Scott and Preben Montell had visited Milan and the Scala workshops several weeks before the *Ernani* opening and from the outset realized that the Ronconi–Frigerio conception worked at so many physical levels that no amount of imaginative camera work could hope to capture it in its entirety. Once rehearsals began, hours were spent contemplating how best to enable cameras to penetrate the recesses of Ronconi's jacuzzi. Things were not made easier by the tradition, common in many European opera houses, of steep light- ing. Every drop of light in this Scala production would come from the stage side of the proscenium arch which would inevitably mean that much of the staging was very dark, and tops of heads got more light than faces. This sort of lighting might be to the taste of a theatre audience but was less likely to work well on television. As the early rehearsals got under way, indeed, Montell and Treays were frequently seen going into a huddle with the Scala's own lighting man to discuss how best to rescue this production from—literally —obscurity. Montell and Treays were to be in charge of lighting for the two video performances and were determined that their audiences would see not just hair and hats but also faces.

At the 'ante-general' rehearsal (nicknamed by one or two cynics among the NVC contingent the 'anti-general' rehearsal) Treays is allowed to try out his TV lighting. The rehearsal begins at 8 p.m. and goes on until nearly 1 a.m. the following morning. For Treays and the NVC team it proves an invaluable evening's work: for the first time everyone in the auditorium can see the detailed texture and colour of many hitherto shadowy props, costumes and people. Silver pedestals look silver, marble columns marble, while individual faces take on real character.

As the rehearsal schedule creeps up towards the first night, tension in and around the house increases appreciably. Security is tightened up as the Scala officials receive strict instructions to keep out everybody not directly connected with the production. Where Freni a week before was getting a laugh by prolonging a trill in her opening aria and pretending to run out of breath, she now gets irritated at off-stage noise and says so. Where the three principal men were each singing a week ago in casual clothes with the occasional hand in trouser pocket, now in costume they each make visibly greater efforts to breathe life into their respective stage characters. It is not easy and Ronconi does little to help them. Domingo's Ernani to the end tends to be a slightly stooping figure, wearing a stylized pained expression on his semi-visible face, buckling a little at the knees, fists clenched in a somewhat generalized gesture of resolution or defiance. Perhaps Domingo is worried about slipping on, or off, the silvery and step-laden stage surfaces. When the inevitable accident occurs and a chorus member does slip at the dress rehearsal and Domingo is asked if he saw what happened, he turns away and says, 'I'd rather not know.'

The opening night of the Scala season is a major event in the Milan calendar, perhaps the biggest of the year. It is awaited with all the more eagerness for the fact that it does not happen until December, three or four months after most of the other great opera houses of the world are already well launched into the season's offerings. Why does La Scala, like other Italian opera houses, start its season so much later than Vienna, Covent Garden or the Met? Why, come to that, does the opera season progress at such a leisurely pace—three or four 'dark' nights in a week quite often, symphony concerts dominating the schedules for much of the spring—even once it has begun?

There are a number of answers. Tradition has something to do with it. The opera has 'always' opened in December, people will tell you, as though that in itself were a reason for having no opera in October and November. Also, La Scala prides itself on its presentation of new productions, often five or six in a season, and these not only cost huge amounts of money but also demand a lot of time and space. During much of the 'dead' time, the Scala costume makers, scenery painters, lighting engineers and the like are busily preparing details of new productions for later in the season while in the absence of any full-size replica of the Scala stage the real thing has to be occupied for all major rehearsals. Once the Scala season does eventually get under way, new productions tend to follow one another in a fairly rapid sequence—*Ernani*, for instance, will be followed within less than a month by a new production of *Andrea Chénier* under Chailly—so the Scala staff are scarcely less hard-worked than those in major houses elsewhere. Could not La Scala make better use of the time, space and money at its disposal by putting on more revivals of previous productions? Surely if they brought back *Ernani, Chénier* and the rest the following year, perhaps with slightly weaker casts, they could still fill the theatre's 2,000 seats and with such a policy have fewer 'dark' nights?

Here artistic, financial, political and social considerations get uncomfortably interwoven. La Scala is conscious of its position as the most famous home of Italian opera. Musicians, music lovers, critics, impresarios from all over the operatic world look to La Scala to give a lead in operatic standards. Of course each season's offerings include a sprinkling of revivals. A select handful of outstanding productions become regular staples. But, say the Scala management, how could this theatre put on revivals of less than first-rate productions, or even of good productions with second-rate casts? People would surely say, '*This* is not what we come to La Scala to see!' At La Scala only the best will do. If you put on *Ernani* or *Chénier* with anything other than a top-rank cast, not only will you probably not fill those 2,000 seats but, worse, you will start getting complaints in the press and the corridors of power that you abuse your government grant. And if you cast good but less established singers, you may also be doing *them* a disservice by exposing them to La Scala when they are not yet ready for it personally and temperamentally. No. If La Scala is to continue to justify its exalted place in the operatic firmament and also in the eyes of those who hold the nation's purse-strings and who, despite recession and chronic economic crisis, regularly pay out huge sums to subsidize opera there, it is felt that the theatre must continue to concentrate on top singers in prestigious productions such as the new *Ernani*.

St Ambrogio's Day, 7 December 1982, is grey and drizzly in Milan but by early evening the Piazza della Scala is awash with light and festive atmosphere. It is also ringed by police and crammed with several thousand people all looking expectantly towards the theatre entrance. Every celebrity in town and many from outside are coming tonight. One newspaper says that Burt Lancaster will be there. Leaders of the operatic world come in droves. Lord and Lady Harewood arrive, and so does Birgit Nilsson. Piero Cappuccilli, the Carlo of the 1969 production of *Ernani*, turns up looking dapper in formal evening attire and is eagerly pointed out by the *cognoscenti*.

Far from the Milanese crowd and the arriving celebrities, tonight's cast get ready for the performance. Up above the television vans parked in the Via Verdi, up a narrow, wood-panelled plum-carpeted staircase from the room where Freni is being bedecked in her Elvira outfit, the men prepare themselves. Bruson warms up in his dressing-room with some arpeggios and goes through his first aria with a pianist, while outside a young man on the Scala staff hunts on the floor for a pearl that has fallen from the crown Bruson will wear in Act III. Ghiaurov walks up and down smiling his shy smile, elegant bathrobe covering smock and gaiters. Domingo is being made up and, as he sits barber-shop style looking into his dressing-room mirror, he gaily greets the reflections of friends and family that materialize periodically into his range of vision.

Down in the piazza, the two people arrive in whose honour, above all, the lights, the curious crowds and the ubiquitous police have assembled. They are Giovanni Spadolini, tall, rubicund, once (and doubtless future) Prime Minister of Italy, and the elfin, sprightly eighty-six-year-old President of the Republic, Sandro Pertini. Both men are originals, almost unique in modern Italian power politics not only for not being Christian Democrats (Spadolini is head of the small Republican Party, Pertini a lifelong Socialist whom Mussolini periodically imprisoned for his resolute anti-fascism), but also for being incorruptible men of culture and learning rather than career politicians. As the two men are ushered through the crowds into the Scala they are accompanied by a tremendous rush of television lighting men, cameramen, sound engineers, journalists of all shapes and sizes. Little Pertini is a practical man with an impish sense of humour and looks to match and he takes it all in his confident stride, quite unfazed by the rush and bustle, the lighting and the heat that accompany his entry. Many in the auditorium are bedecked in the most elegant evening wear. Spadolini and the President are content with lounge suits.

Once they are in the house and safely seated near the front of the orchestra stalls, the Scala officials have a terrible job trying to get all the assorted journalists back out of the auditorium again. One poor usher, resplendent in his black uniform and chain of authority, mops his brow with frustration as, like Friar Melitone in Verdi's *Forza*, he tries in vain to persuade a large and unwieldy crowd to obey his polite request that they behave in an orderly fashion. Will those without tickets to the performance *please* leave the house? However, once in it proves impossible to get them all out. Back, yes; out, no. One wants to film part of the first act of *Ernani* for his television station, another to take stills for his magazine. Some just like music, while several clearly relish the thought of getting free access to an evening's entertainment for which some people have paid an official price —from touts it could be double—of £100 a seat. For most it is impossible anyway to accede to Melitone's increasingly desperate request that they at least move back a few yards ('*Al dietro, al dietro, signori, al dietro ancora un metro e mezzo per favore!*') if only because of the solid wall of people in the entrance behind them pushing forward. He pulls a rope around the front of the malefactors and then herds them like cattle back his precious metre and a half. And there they stand, at back centre of the auditorium, uncomfortable but with a perfect view of the stage, Melitone muttering at and about them and they reciprocating in loud stage whispers, for the rest of the evening. Two thousand people? Tonight La Scala contains a couple of hundred more, all of them blocking the fire exit in a solid phalanx of tightly corralled humanity, and all of them thrilled to be there.

It proves to be a rowdy evening, even by local standards. Everyone knows, but nobody likes to acknowledge, that the *claque* still exists, that iniquitous system whereby some shark buys up blocks of tickets in the upper galleries and gets those to whom he gives them to scream applause at singers who pay for the privilege and boo those who do not. It is a shameful residue from the past and most singers are resigned to its existence and reluctantly pay something for the privilege of not being booed. But tonight is something else again. The evening opens propitiously enough. Muti whips his orchestra and chorus into electric form and Domingo gives a ravishing account of his opening aria which you do not have to be a *claqueur* to want to applaud. The first real shouting from the upper reaches begins after Freni's Act I aria when she disrobes, as Ronconi directed, in full view of the audience. 'Va via!'—get going—yells someone, apparently thinking he is at a football match, and Freni shrugs her shoulders ever so slightly as if to dissociate herself from what she is doing. Later, Bruson is booed, Freni laughed at, Bruson cheered. Each time, Muti ignores the hooligans and signals for play to resume. Muti himself reluctantly becomes the focus of one of the evening's biggest demonstrations when, just before the start of Act III, he is ostentatiously embraced by President Pertini. This sets off a tremendous roar of approval and Muti has difficulty getting the house silent so that the act can commence. Someone shouts out the name of Abbado and the whole raucous racket resumes. Muti is giving a magnificent performance this evening and Pertini with his unexpected action has displayed yet again his penchant for expressing in a simple gesture the feelings of those around him.

The final trio is beautifully done, Domingo duly expires in Freni's arms under the watchful eye of Ghiaurov, and the great Scala curtains swing back into position. All hell breaks loose. At the back of the house, the herd of standee journalists and hangers-on stampedes across its restraining rope, while the horde up above spares nobody its assorted animal yells of joy and wrath. It is all quite good-humoured and at first the overwhelming audience reaction is one of pleasure. Domingo in particular receives a great shout of approval like a footballer who has just scored a goal. Eventually out come the production team: Ronconi, Squarciapino, Frigerio. Poor Frigerio slips over banana-peel style and the whole place goes wild with *schadenfreude*. It was the production team that the galleries were most eagerly looking forward to booing and now they take their chance. Each time thereafter that the principal singers reappear at the footlights to exchange waves with their audience, they are greeted by the cry 'Ronconi! Ronconi! Ronconi!' Ronconi does not reappear.

'A little bit violent,' Domingo agrees, grinning, as he stands in the doorway of his dressing-room to greet his friends after the show. 'Yes, they were quite a lively lot!' Neither he nor his colleagues seem to have been too upset by the vociferous reaction to the performance. You expect a bit of this at opening nights at La Scala. Domingo embraces friends. There are Bob and Joan Cahen from San Francisco; he is a friend—and first-class photographer—of most of the great tenors of the past twenty years. Guillermo and Berta Martinez are here, too. Guillermo, an émigré from Castro's Cuba who has carved a successful business career for himself in Puerto Rico, has become one of Plácido's closest friends over the years and looks rather like him too; the two men have been confused by pressmen before now. Dr Marcel Prawy is here backstage; he is the genial and talkative *dramaturg of* of the Vienna State Opera and a great Domingo fan. Plácido chats to him in German, to his Paris agent Michel Glotz in French, to the various Scala hierarchs who appear in Italian, to Peter Andry of EMI in English. It is a large, wealthy, cosmopolitan crowd. Whatever the *claqueurs* in the Scala gallery may think, Domingo and his many friends have all had an excellent evening.

The New York Metropolitan

When you are Plácido Domingo you do not have a place you can really call home. Or rather you have a number—luxury houses or apartments in Barcelona, London, Vienna, Monte Carlo, New York—and you tend to commute between them. To Plácido it is almost immaterial where 'home' should be. He is never more than a few weeks in any one location and the sense of distance can be kept to a minimum thanks to the telephone and the jet plane. But while his boys were growing up the family needed a permanent base. And since from the start of his international career Plácido regularly sang in New York more often than in any other city, New York has for much of the past twenty years been, with Barcelona, the principal Domingo home.

In the early days it was a house in Teaneck, New Jersey, just across the Hudson. It was there, late one Saturday afternoon in September 1968, that Plácido, having just returned home from a long stage rehearsal of *Turandot*, picked up the phone and heard the voice of Rudolf Bing, General Manager of the Metropolitan Opera. 'Plácido,' said Bing in his quiet, authoritative Austrian tones, 'you have to go on tonight.' This was four days before Domingo was officially scheduled to make his Met début as Maurizio in Cilèa's opera *Adriana Lecouvreur*. 'Corelli has just called to say he's sick and can't sing Maurizio tonight,' said Bing. Franco Corelli, a wonderful tenor in the heroic mould, suffered badly from nerves and had a reputation for cancelling. 'Please come at once,' Bing added with just the right combination of insistence and courtesy.

Domingo was angry and did not believe that Corelli was really ill. Furthermore, since the *Turandot* rehearsal had been for the staging, he had not sung all day and the voice had not had a chance to limber up. The early Met arrivals were already ambling towards their seats. They had been told that Corelli was being replaced by the young Domingo and were asked to be patient as Domingo was at that very moment driving back into town and would be ready soon. On the way, at the wheel of his car, Domingo sang a few scales and arpeggios to warm up the voice. He tells amusing stories of the reactions of fellow drivers alongside him at traffic lights. One was on his way to

131

the Met and worried he would be late. 'Don't worry,' laughed Plácido as the light turned green, 'they won't start until I get there!'—and sped off down the avenue.

Many, and not just Americans, consider the New York Metropolitan the world's premier opera house. How does one judge these things? The Met is certainly one of the biggest. The new house, opened in 1966, has an overall audience capacity of nearly 4,000 people who face a proscenium stage picture fifty-four feet by fifty-four feet. In a typical season the Met gives some 270 performances of from sixteen to twenty different operas over a forty-week period—fifty of those performances given during the seven- or eight-week tour of various major cities all around the USA that the Met makes each spring and a further handful given—free—in the parks of New York City during the summer. Running the Met costs over seventy million dollars a year. Of this, close to two-thirds can normally be recouped from box-office receipts, much of the rest from private contributions small and large and very large, and a tiny fraction from federal, state and city government agencies. In a good year the system will just about break even. No other of the world's leading opera houses operates without substantial government subvention. Covent Garden, La Scala, Vienna or Munich would collapse if they had to rely for almost all their income on box-office and private contributions.

The Met was not the first in its field in New York. Indeed, it originated as a reaction by New York's *nouveaux riches* against the reigning opera house of the 1850s to 70s, the Academy of Music on Irving Place and 14th Street. All the great operas and singers could be heard at the Academy of Music, but not all of New York's high society could be seen there. The Academy accommodated only a small number of boxes, and anyone who was anyone *had* to have—that is, to own more or less in perpetuity—a box at the opera. As new industrial wealth poured into the thriving city during the post-Civil War 'Gilded Age', a number of the rich and famous and deprived banded together to establish a new, larger opera house, *their* opera house, a glittering place where the finest opera could be heard and the most expensive furs and tiaras seen. As society moved uptown so did the opera. The new house was accordingly built on 39th Street and Broadway, and if its yellow-brick exterior looked like an office block or factory, its opulent interior featured the all-important horseshoes containing a total of over a hundred boxes. The Metropolitan Opera, New York, opened with a season of Italian opera on 22 October 1883 with a gala performance in Italian of Gounod's *Faust*.

Several times the Met nearly closed. The building was said to be fireproof but much of its interior was gutted by a huge blaze in 1892. The trouble was that the building itself *was* fireproof and so there was nothing the stockholders could really do except undertake a costly interior renovation in time for the 1893–4 season. Between 1906 and 1909, the impresario Oscar Hammerstein (uncle of Richard Rodgers' famous lyricist) built a rival opera house down the road from the Met and hired some of the greatest singers of the day; the Met only survived the threat from Hammerstein by buying him out for a colossal sum. A quarter of a century later the gods made another attempt to close the Met, this time assuming the form not of Fire or Rivalry, but of Depression. In desperation, General Manager Gatti-Casazza asked everyone to take a drastic cut in salary. Everyone did except Gigli, who left the company.

The Old Met was a nineteenth-century building that survived too long into the twentieth. It had a wonderful, elegant, spacious auditorium. Designed on the classical European principle of a series of horseshoe-shaped levels, it gave singers and box-holders a wonderful rapport. It was a good house in which to sing and a superb house—if you were in a reasonably central box—from which to see and hear. But there were over 700 seats from which you could see only a fraction of the stage. I myself remember watching, for example, the left half of a *Lohengrin* and a *Così* and the right half of a *Cav* and *Pag* in the early 1960s, and standing through a wonderful *Turandot* designed by Cecil Beaton and not being able to see the upper part of the multi-level staging. If the auditorium had problems, they were nothing to those backstage. The house was bounded by the limits of a rectilinear New York City block and early on had outgrown the space available. Dressing-rooms were small and dingy, the stage machinery primitive to the point of being dangerous, and scenery and costumes had to be stored outside the building on Broadway and

Seventh Avenue under primitive and inadequate covering, a prey to Manhattan's variable weather. Risë Stevens once recalled to me singing Carmen at the Met in a dress sodden from a recent downpour.

The new Metropolitan Opera is the central and dominant building of an arts complex, the Lincoln Center, opened in the mid-1960s, that takes up four entire New York City blocks just west of Broadway between 62nd and 66th Streets. Opera thus moved uptown from 14th Street to 39th Street to 66th Street, paralleling the general uptown shift in the residential and cultural pattern of New York. The Lincoln Center houses not only the Met but also two theatres, the Juilliard School of Music, a Library of the Performing Arts, two concert halls and the New York City Opera. In the carefully sculpted aesthetic compatibility of a number of different but closely adjacent buildings, and in its generous uses of the spaces between, the Lincoln Center is a model of intelligent planning and the prototype for arts centres developed in many cities of America and elsewhere.

The Met's neighbour, the New York City Opera, was founded in the 1940s and for many years performed in the former Shriners' auditorium known as the City Center on West 55th Street. Under the direction of Julius Rudel the City Opera grew into an enterprising imaginative company often playing a bolder repertoire than the Met and uncovering a wide range of new American and foreign talent. It was at the NYCO that Plácido Domingo applied for an audition when he came to the United States in 1965. Rudel still recalls the stunning impression Domingo made on him even before he opened his mouth. 'If this man sings half as well as he looks we've got a real winner,' Rudel thought. And once Domingo began to sing Rudel immediately decided to engage him. Domingo sang one or two roles at the old 'Mecca Temple' on West 55th Street and when the time came for the NYCO to open in its new house at Lincoln Center it was partly with Domingo in mind that Rudel planned the opening night. The opera was the US première of *Don Rodrigo* by the Argentinian composer Alberto Ginastera, a large-scale work with literally hundreds of participants on stage and off and an orchestra containing no less than eighteen French horns and twelve trumpets, some deployed backstage and others in various parts of the auditorium. As Rudel recalls it, the title part—a handsome Visigoth king from eighth-century Spain—seemed almost to have been written with Domingo in mind. 'I immediately assigned this difficult part to Plácido—I might add, over the strong objections of some of my immediate staff who worried about his youth, his lack of experience, his "too lyrical voice", and so on and tried to persuade me to engage another tenor. Well, the opening night was a triumph and catapulted Plácido into immediate world recognition. The composer was present and moved to tears.'

Once Domingo was safely installed in Lincoln Center as the star tenor at the State Theater he inevitably had his sights fixed on the big building just across the plaza. And the people at the big building just as assuredly had their sights fixed intently on him.

The new Met is in many ways a traditional house. Architecturally, it is a large, marble rectangular cube fronted by five high, glass-filled arches. The outer pair of arches reveal (or in practice partly conceal) two huge original Chagalls on musical themes. Inside there is a large proscenium stage faced by rows of orchestra stalls and five curved tiers of seats. The seating and carpeting are of red velvet, the stage curtain old-gold damask, and the whole thing is topped by a great chandelier. But so pedestrian a description does scant justice to what some consider the finest opera house in the world.

For the general public the Met means the auditorium. You approach the vast inner sanctum through one of the layers of richly carpeted foyer, perhaps ascending the generously curved central staircase, maybe pausing for a drink of cool water from one of the inlaid marble fountains 'In Memory of Ezio Pinza'. It is worth a thought that while the walls of the Met, the programmes, even the seat backs all bear the names of benefactors without whose tax-deductible gifts none of this would have been possible, the free water is named after one of the great singers of the past.

The Met auditorium is enormous yet does not feel excessively so. Singers will tell you that in the old Met you had a much larger space to sing across. You did not. The length of the new auditorium is the same as the old, yet because it is wider it looks and feels more compact. Audiences, too, are not too discomfited or distracted by the size of the building in which they are seated; although the architects decided to maintain the curved, horseshoe structure of the traditional opera house auditorium, they still managed to contrive that up and behind the great centre of each horseshoe are row upon row of well-upholstered seats virtually all of which face reasonably squarely onto the stage. Everything is curved. Not just the tiers of seats and the exterior of the boxes, but the uprights and top beam framing the proscenium stage, the swirling, lotus-flower discs of gold leaf that embellish the ceiling, even the wavy Congolese rosewood walls that enclose the auditorium. Everywhere the sound is projected rather than absorbed. This is one of the secrets of the Met's bright acoustic. So bright is the acoustic in some parts of the house, indeed, that first-time visitors sometimes come away presuming the sound they have heard has been amplified.

Perhaps the most famous feature of the Met auditorium is its many small chandeliers, spiky little clusters of light, like so many fluorescent snowflakes delicately suspended from the ceiling far above. As the lights go down, the chandeliers go up. Literally. They are raised up past four tiers of seating so as not to impede anyone's vision of the stage, and they stay up throughout the performance. In the early days, Met audiences used to applaud this little piece of technological panache though nowadays they take it in their stride. What the public never sees is the even more remarkable sight of these crystal clusters being lowered into the semi-darkened auditorium before the audience is admitted—glistening spiders spinning themselves a web up which they will later escape in full view of nearly 4,000 people.

There are perhaps two things wrong with the auditorium. The first is the bizarre sculpture that hangs precariously above the spare, old-gold proscenium arch and looks like a length of computer print-out tape threaded through bent violin necks. A chastity belt, one friend of mine calls it. The second is that there are no proper side foyers or even exits and the entire audience has to get out through the back of the auditorium, which means that leaving after a performance can be a slow crush. But (unless there were a flash fire) these are small discomforts for an audience to endure in a house that is so good at its primary task.

Quite how good it is only those who work backstage can really know. For a start the Met has not one stage but five. On either side of and behind the main stage are three further full-sized stages on which entire sets can be pre-assembled to save time in scene changing. Thus, in the Met's *Tales of Hoffmann*, for example, Luther's tavern sinks down below ground before your very eyes, giving way to a vision of Spalanzani's massively complex nutty scientist living-room slowly rolling towards you from its pre-set position on the stage behind the stage. The stupendous multi-level Momus scene from Zeffirelli's $700,000 production of *Bohème*, with nearly 300 people in position, is rolled on to the main stage as Act I is rolled off, the transformation taking a cool four minutes. As for the fifth stage-sized stage, this is below ground at what is called C-level and it is down here that artists rehearse their parts and gradually become adjusted to the size and space within which they will soon be expected to perform.

Below, above and behind the auditorium, the Met is a maze of spaces small and large, the largest being for the construction, painting and storage of scenery, the smallest tending to be for the offices of the people who actually run the place. Right there at the Lincoln Center the Met makes many of its own sets, costumes and props, has its own wigmakers, swordmakers and the like, and an electrical department that oversees everything from the replacement of bulbs in the spidery chandeliers to the smooth running of Spalanzani's cornucopia of inventive jiggery-pokery in *Tales of Hoffmann*. As in every opera house the Met has more sets, costumes and props than it can store, and on the corridors of almost every floor backstage you will run into packing cases marked 'Ballo Act I' or 'Rosenkavalier Act II' or into racks containing assorted regal gowns and capes or street urchins' leggings and tunics. For, strange though it may sound of an opulent, modern, purpose-built house, the Met is already too small. Its five great arches were originally to have been seven and when economic realities forced the planners to reduce the breadth of the building it was foyer, storage and office space that were sacrificed. Thus, sets for Met productions not in the current repertoire, and even some that are, now have to be kept in various warehouses, notably one the size of an aeroplane hangar across the Hudson in Weehauken, New Jersey. And when a big production like

Bohème is revived a convoy of twenty-one trucks (in the old pre-Zeffirelli production it was five!) has to be loaded for the journey.

On the outer left-hand rim of the building, one narrow corridor above the next for some six floors, where you might have expected, say a series of emergency fire exits, are the executive offices of the Met. On the first floor in a tiny side room is the office of James Levine, 'Maestro Levine', as his secretary says when answering the phone, 'Jimmy' or 'Jim' to all in the house who work closely with him. With his rotund, bespectacled face topped by a mop of curly hair, it can only be a matter of time before the Met Gift Shop produces the Jimmy Levine Teddy Bear ('Give it a baton and its arms rise and fall in rhythm'). Levine is a consummate musician. Anybody who has successfully survived the rigorous supervision of the late George Szell, whose assistant he was in Cleveland during his twenties, must possess tremendous musical talent, a taste for relentless hard work, and when necessary a pretty thick skin.

Levine's energies are unflagging and when you look at his work schedule you can see that they need to be. Of all his qualities possibly the rarest in this age of the jet plane is the fact that he stays at his New York post right through the Met's eight-month season. He takes his job seriously, is in the house every day, and keeps a close watch on every production, performance and performer. He rehearses his principal singers at the piano himself and even accompanies some of them in song recitals, and each season conducts a good half of the total Met repertoire. Do not be misled by the bouncy, boyish appearance, the informality, the Mid-Western accent, the towel over the shoulder, the casual sweatshirts. Levine may be personally without pretension, but his authority in matters musical is total. He is still young enough to be the son of some of the singers and instrumentalists he conducts, but Levine is the boss, the Maestro.

A brilliant, effusive talker when the time is appropriate, Levine prefers, like all the best conductors, to say little when rehearsing his orchestra. Occasionally that rich, fruity voice will ask the celli to separate two phrases more clearly or the horns to play with a more consistent dynamic. But most of the message is transmitted by the stick, the arms, the body, the eyes. Not blessed by nature with the aristocratic good looks of a Giulini or the obvious personal charisma of a Solti, a Mehta or a Muti, Levine relies on sheer technique and musicianship to achieve the results he seeks. All this, plus his rare and greatly appreciated steadfastness in staying throughout the long Met season, has succeeded in enveloping Levine with the right combination of authority and accessibility needed in so sensitive a post. He sometimes gets accused of being so attached to the Met, indeed, that he does not bring to the house frequently enough some of the world's other great operatic conductors. His Lincoln Center neighbour, Zubin Mehta, conductor of the New York Philharmonic Orchestra, is not on the Met's roster of conductors. Nor are Muti or Abbado, Maazel or Kleiber or, of the older generation, Solti, Karajan or Giulini. These absences are not, of course, only because the conductors concerned have not been asked—for years it has taken wild horses to lure Karajan out of Berlin or Salzburg or Giulini back into opera at all. But some Met productions have received indifferent direction from the pit and part of the blame must presumably be laid at the door of the Music Director.

The Met is a big building. The Lincoln Center is a vast complex. At a rapid pace the Center takes ten minutes to walk around, fifteen if you are more leisurely about it. From Broadway it all looks beautiful and opulent, a series of well-spaced buildings of bright travertine marble, each with its own distinctive style yet each blending with the whole. From the Amsterdam Avenue side, however, you can pass by the Center and scarcely be aware of its existence. On the far side of the avenue are high-rise housing projects and a couple of schools. And on the Lincoln Center side a large marble monolith broken by the occasional car-park entry and, a few yards above street level, by a little row of inconspicuous rectangular windows rather like those on the side of a small plane. Hard to look out of, impossible to see in. These, though you would never guess it, are the windows of the principal artists' dressing-rooms at the Metropolitan Opera. If you could see up through those little windows, you might catch a glimpse of Joan Sutherland, Plácido Domingo or Sherrill Milnes, Renata Scotto, Martti Talvela or Luciano Pavarotti changing clothes, putting on make-up, singing scales, disappearing into a shower. The dressing-rooms are small, comfortable, all the same size and design. Each has a piano, shower and toilet (these facilities had to be shared in the old house), and in each the sometimes severe house air-conditioning is turned off.

The dressing-rooms are within easy access of the stage and easy for artists to reach from the Met's underground car-parks. But if you want to get to them from the auditorium after a performance to get the autograph of your favourite singer, you have to walk down a series of long, narrow corridors past the scrutiny of several levels of security, along another corridor lined with tall metal cabinets, and then, if a Sutherland or a Domingo is singing, there is a further security check as you are asked to line up and wait your turn. 'Anyone who wants to see any artist other than Mr Domingo come this way, please,' the guard will intone along the length of the line. 'All those who want to see Mr Domingo kindly wait here in single file.' And the line stretches round the corner and halfway back along the corridor with the metal lockers.

To get that far you have to be on someone's list. Every singer has a list of friends who have his or her permission to go backstage after the show. Met regulars who want to see, but are not friends of, the star get themselves put on the list of some relatively minor cast member whom they do know and thus get easy access backstage and can even jump the 'wait-in-line-here-for-Mr-Domingo' ritual. Or else they simply leave a note to the star saying they would like to be on his list and no singer, certainly not a gregarious character like Domingo who knows the value of good public relations, normally refuses such a request. At most opera houses, even the most determined groupies are condemned to wait outside the stage door until their hero is ready to leave. At the Met they can get in alongside the genuine friends if they are determined enough.

Right in? Not quite. For what tends to happen on a Domingo night is that the really close friends go straight to the Principal Tenor's dressing-room where Domingo will be changing out of his costume. Everybody else—and it can be 200 people or more—must wait. The crush to see Domingo (it is the same for Pavarotti or Sutherland) is such that the dressing-room is quite inadequate as a place in which to receive, and the adjacent Green Room is often used instead. A table and chair are set up as another type of performance commences.

'How nice to see you,' he will smile, and 'How are you?' as he scribbles his name across yet another copy of this evening's programme. Someone will deliver a little speech. 'I heard you in this same role when you made your début in such-and-such a house in nineteen-sixty-so-and-so.' 'Yes?' Domingo will answer summoning up as much interest as he can for the occasion. 'You were wonderful then, and you were even more wonderful now.' 'Why, thank you so much.' Another smile, another signature, another handshake or kiss, and the people still lining up along the metal cabinets shuffle forward a few feet closer to the packed Green Room.

Some of the more private of today's major singers hate this ritual and try to think of ways of avoiding or at least containing and restricting it. After all, a performance can take a great toll and it is not everyone who, after three or four hours of intensive music-making, wants to endure a further hour or two of hero-worship. Others obviously live on their adrenalin at the end of a performance, are still 'high' and will clearly take time to wind down. Domingo is one of them, excited by the admiration of the crowds, and as cannily aware as a good politician that big happy crowds are good for business. Everyone whose programme Domingo signs, whose hand he shakes, whose cheek he busses, is a reinforced admirer. He knows this and courts the backstage crowds accordingly. It is a good job he enjoys it so, for it has already taken up over 2,000 hours of his life.

By 1983 Domingo was approaching his 200th performance at the New York Metropolitan—more appearances there than at any other single house—and during the countdown to this latest statistical triumph his energies and enthusiasms seemed redoubled. During February and March, he was scheduled to sing a relentless string of performances that would include, in one particularly frantic period of just over a fortnight, no less than four different operas: the last of a run of *Giocondas* (this performance to be broadcast live), a *Bohème*, an *Adriana*, a further *Bohème*, and two days later the first of a run of eight performances of Verdi's *Don Carlo*.

La Gioconda, by the gentle, professorial Amilcare Ponchielli, written in the 1870s, is one of those works that, unlike its heroine, refuses to die. It is opera on the grand scale: long, large, with exciting and excitable choruses, no less than six principals (one for each voice type, each with an aria), a ballet—the famous Dance of the Hours —an impossible story of love, hatred, gratitude, revenge, destruction (of an entire ship in Act II) and death. Dramatically and emotionally overblown, hard to cast at full strength, and difficult for producer or conductor to hold together convincingly, *La Gioconda* is not one of the staples of the operatic repertoire. But when it is mounted well its surges of gloriously ingratiating music make it a work to treasure, and American audiences in particular always seem to have had a soft spot for it. Caruso, Gigli and Tucker sang the tenor role, Enzo, at the old Met, while Destinn, Ponselle, Milanov and Tebaldi were famous Met interpreters of the title-role. Gioconda was the part that first brought the young Maria Callas to attention. The 'Gioconda', by the way, has nothing to do with Leonardo's Mona Lisa but is a street singer in Venice at the time of the Inquisition, a girl whose nickname has a certain irony since she is given very little to smile about. Her blind mother is pilloried, she herself is in love with a man in love with someone else, and in the last act, having announced her intention in a marvellous aria, she commits suicide.

The Met production is suitably lavish, Beni Montresor's designs filling the huge playing area. The great arches of the Cathedral of St Mark dominate the long opening scene and can be seen twinkling across the lagoon from the ship moored alongside in Act II. The production features large crowds of sailors milling to and fro and great draperies framing the interiors for the third and fourth acts. Everything is done to enable the work to make an impact. So lavish is this production, indeed, that when the Met produced a poster of an artist's impression of the way the huge backstage area worked, it was a cross-section of the Met in mid-*Gioconda* that was chosen.

The Met, like most of the world's leading opera houses, uses a *stagione* system. That is, they will put on a short run of properly rehearsed performances of a particular work with a carefully chosen cast, and then the principals will go their separate ways as the next production is prepared for a run. Productions overlap, naturally, so that at any given time several productions are running their course. But after half a dozen *Giocondas* or *Tannhäusers* or whatever, these particular operas will be rested until a new, concentrated, rehearsed run of performances is scheduled. In the case of *La Gioconda*, Domingo and his principal colleagues—Hungarian soprano Eva Marton in the title-role, veteran American baritone Cornell MacNeil as the evil Barnaba, mezzo Mignon Dunn as Laura—had a cluster of performances in October 1982, and were booked to re-meet for three more in February 1983.

One of the October performances turned into one of those legendary evenings opera fans tell their grandchildren about. It was the last Domingo was booked to sing. He felt a cold coming, considered cancelling, and the people at the Met asked Carlo Bini, who was due to take over the role of Enzo a few days later, to make himself available. In the event, Domingo went on, began well despite his misgivings, technique seeming to carry him through, and Bini, relaxed and perhaps relieved, settled down in the audience to enjoy the performance. To Bini's consternation, word came in the first intermission that Domingo's cold was worse and he felt he would do himself harm if he continued to sing. He had three *Toscas* the following week in Chicago and, reluctantly, felt he had to bow out of the rest of this performance. Domingo is not known as a canceller, but he is known to have the most scrupulous regard for the health of his own voice, and everybody appreciated his decision. Everybody, that is, except the luckless Bini who had hurriedly to change into an unfamiliar costume and step straight into Act II. Bini had had no proper stage rehearsal and was obviously unsure of his movements. Within minutes of the opening of Act II the tenor has the highlight of the whole opera, the ravishingly beautiful and cruelly exposed aria 'Cielo e mar'. Bini had had no chance to vocalize, was obviously in no state to give a proper performance, and was received with a combination of mirth and disbelief. Things went from bad to worse. Mignon Dunn, trying to help Bini with his movements, held his hands tightly during their scene together, even to the point of moving his hands at one stage a little lower down her body. Sections of the audience could restrain themselves no longer. There was outright laughter, slow handclaps, and real fisticuffs from those in the audience who objected to the clapping and laughing. Eventually, conductor Giuseppe Patanè turned round and begged the audience at least to have respect for Ponchielli. For a while things calmed down—and then, after the third act, it was announced that Maestro Patanè was too ill and would have to withdraw from the rest of the performance. His blood pressure was apparently fluctuating dangerously, as whose would not under the circumstances. Further groans as staff conductor Eugene Kohn took on the unenviable task of guiding this ill-fated evening to its close . . .

American opera audiences are an expressive lot, though the usual complaint is not that they boo or giggle too much but that they applaud at all the wrong places. As the curtain goes up, the stage picture is often applauded regardless of the music thus obliterated. They will often clap as the star makes his or her first appearance—the applause and inevitable counter-demonstration of 'sh-sh–shs' thus effectively drowning out the star's opening phrases. They can also usually be relied upon to clap the moment the curtain begins to descend thus ensuring that the delicate harp and string passages at the end of the *Bohème* or *Otello* love duets, for instance, have yet to be heard. But booing is not unknown either. At the Met, where top seats can cost up to $65, anything appreciably less than excellence is understandably resented. Renata Scotto was booed for her wobbly Norma at the beginning of the 1981–2 season. And a season later poor Bini was booed (or was it Patané, or the Met management, or Domingo for having cancelled in mid-performance?) on 'the night of the two-tenor, two-conductor *Gioconda*'.

By the time Domingo returned to New York in early 1983 he had his Chicago *Toscas*, London *Fanciullas*, Milan *Ernanis*, recording of *Carmen* and the French version of *Don Carlos* and some Miami *Chéniers* all successfully under his belt. *La Gioconda* required little rehearsal and the first two performances went well. The third, the last, was scheduled for a Saturday matinée and was to be broadcast.

Lincoln's Birthday, 12 February 1983, and New York wakes up to a thick carpet of snow. The thickest, indeed, that anybody can remember for years. In the past twenty hours, twenty inches have been dumped on a city shivering in twenty-degree temperatures as though the heavens were attempting to compensate in one fell swoop for the unusually mild winter New Yorkers had been experiencing up until then. The day before, the 11th, Plácido Domingo had taken

Marta to Kennedy airport where she was to fly to Switzerland to see their boys. He would join her in Europe for a few hours after his broadcast *Gioconda* performance on the afternoon of the 12th, returning to New York in time for his next Met rehearsal on the morning of the 14th. Except that with the snowstorm at its height it took the Domingos' car over three hours to get to Kennedy where they discovered a blanketed and closed airport, and another three to crawl back again into a still, quiet, white-carpeted Manhattan.

'The Blizzard of '83', as the newspapers instantly dubbed it, was in fact the worst New York had experienced for nearly forty years. The meteorologists had seen it coming, and by the time it was spent it had blanketed the whole Eastern seaboard from Virginia up into Canada. Millions of dollars of damage was done; two million alone were spent getting the streets of New York passable again. Buses stopped. So did subways. An intrepid few taxi drivers put on snow tyres and slithered up and down the main thoroughfares. One diapered toddler fell from a seventh-storey window and was reportedly unharmed as he landed in a snowdrift seven feet deep.

As the skies turned eventually from dark grey to bright blue and the piles of fresh snow covering the Lincoln Center plaza began to glisten in the sunlight, the snow-bound Met, with its five great arches, looked like a multi-headed white beetle crawling over the arctic plains. Inside, under its protective crust of marble, conversation drifted gradually back to opera. Everybody in the East might be preoccupied with the blizzard and its picturesque but inconvenient aftermath, but this very afternoon there was a performance of *La Gioconda*, to be broadcast live across the nation.

People walked miles across the city to get to the Met that day. One couple walked clear up eastern New Jersey, across the George Washington Bridge and halfway down Broadway before finding a taxi prepared to take them down to Lincoln Center. Some people got there, but late, and missed an act or two. Everyone was decked out in thick down coats and boots.

The performance went well. Domingo, so reliable and so easy to take for granted, was in stunning form. At his first appearance, as Enzo sees Gioconda's blind mother cruelly taunted as a witch and erupts with anger, he was electrifying, investing Enzo's opening

145

phrases with the kind of grandeur normally associated with *Otello*, while his 'Cielo e mar' was sung with piercing beauty of tone and elegance of phrasing. It has been said that among his other virtues, Domingo is the most exciting 'finisher' in the business in the sense that his phrases and individual high notes never tail off but end with a clip—the full steam, as it were, being maintained until the final millisecond. And thus it was on this day in a performance heard not only by an almost full house but heard, too, by millions across the nation. Eva Marton gave a larger-than-life portrayal of the title-role that revealed her as an international star of the first magnitude. Never mind the occasional chesty gulps and breathy gasps in the lower register or the glottal stops as she reached for higher notes; this was grand opera at its grandest and the crowd at the Met loved her big, open voice and her large, expansive, truly operatic personality.

The performance was a great success, the crowds flocked backstage afterwards as usual, and the backstage staff in their sweaters and thick snow-proof boots removed St Mark's Cathedral and Enzo's ship and replaced them with the rooftops of bohemian Paris. Domingo was frustrated at not being able to go off to Europe for those precious few hours with his boys, but Marta was here with him, and it would do Quiet Sunday no harm to live up to his name for once. There was, after all, a lot of work to do on Monday.

Four different rehearsals in four different locations, to be precise. At 10.30 on Monday morning 14 February, St Valentine's Day, a day for love but also associated in American minds with a massacre, Domingo was due in the Met Orchestra Room to run through Act I of *La Bohème*. By 12.45 he was to appear on the Main Stage where Levine was rehearsing the huge *auto-da-fé* scene from *Don Carlo* until 2 p.m. From 3.15 until 5.30 Domingo would be rehearsing Act I of *Carlo* on the C-level stage. And at 5.30 he had to find his way to Studio 210 for a *Bohème* piano rehearsal with Levine.

This was broadly the pattern of Domingo's life throughout February. There were days when three different operas had to be rehearsed, some where the scheduling was so tight that he might have to be in the Orchestra Room from 11–11.30, on the Main Stage from 11.30–2 p.m., and on the C-level stage rehearsing something else from 3–6 p.m. Office hours are rarely so rigid and so programmed. And in most offices you do not have to stand up, dress up, make up, act and every now and then burst into song. The only days on which Domingo did not have rehearsals were Sundays and performance days. There was no nonsense about letting him rest the day before a performance. The day before his first scheduled *Bohème*, for example, the Met house timetable shows Domingo rehearsing *Don Carlo* Act II Scene II and then Scene I all morning until 2.30 p.m. and the day after having a three-and-a-half-hour rehearsal of the opening three scenes of *Carlo* followed by a scheduled (but later cancelled) piano rehearsal of *Adriana Lecouvreur*.

By the time the first of Domingo's pair of *Bohèmes* comes around, he feels he has the makings of a possible cold. He considers cancelling. The last thing he wants—the last thing he ever wants again—is a repeat of last autumn's *Gioconda* when he went on and then cancelled in mid-performance. Better to cancel, if cancel you must, as far ahead as possible to give the management a chance to prepare a proper substitute. As a matter of fact, the scheduled Mimì, Teresa Stratas, has done just that. People talk of her as a passionate, somewhat neurasthenic lady said to be obsessed with suffering and death, qualities that certainly come through as Domingo's intense and moving partner in the recently completed Zeffirelli movie of *La Traviata*. Stratas's official cover, Linda Zoghby, has known for a week that she instead of Stratas will be going on as Mimì and when the time comes she is ready.

In the event, Domingo decides he will sing but confides to those closest to him that he will hold back somewhat and rely on technique to see him through. If he gives all he has he may give a memorable performance but will be in no condition to work through the next few days of gruelling *Don Carlo* rehearsals. Once up there on stage in that superb Zeffirelli production of *Bohème*, however, with a packed and enthusiastic house, there is no holding back. As Act I unfurls, all the familiar features of a Domingo *Bohème* are revealed. The infectious playfulness of the early scenes with his bohemian companions; the authentic look of concern as he refreshes Mimì's brow; the casual and spontaneous glance out of the window at the moonlit night as he reaches the words '*ma per fortuna è una notte di luna*' in his aria; the liltingly reached and superbly sustained high note (B, not C, as the aria is transposed down a semitone) a minute or two later; the peck on Mimì's cheek after '*curioso*'; and the long, gentle, harmonized final note of the first act as he and the excellent Zoghby walk off together.

As the evening progresses, moments of great power are unleashed too—notably a positively roof-shattering top B at the end of the ensemble following Musetta's waltz in Act II. And if Domingo has an incipient cold it does not seem to affect his breath-control, which is constantly adjusted to maximize the musical and dramatic impact. Two small examples: at moments of heightened emotional intensity in both the Act I duet with Mimì and the Act III dialogue with Marcello, Puccini writes a dramatic musical 'lift'—a stirring new phrase beginning a few notes higher than the end of that which preceded it. Most tenors normally and reasonably take a breath before these outbursts and in both instances Puccini clearly permits them to do so. But Domingo's combination of vocal and pulmonary resources enable him to sustain the flow of sound uninterrupted and thus heighten the emotional effect just as Puccini, by literally raising the note, the key, the volume, intends. I recall exactly these details when I first heard Domingo sing *Bohème* nine years earlier.

No performance of opera is ever perfect and, in addition to one or two weak links in the chain of casting, Domingo shows the occasional tell-tale sign of the tickle that had been worrying him earlier in the day. The softer sections with Mimì towards the end of Act III fall awkwardly for the tenor on the *passaggio*, the break between the natural chest and head registers, and Domingo's normally smooth gear-shift sounds a little less well oiled than usual on this occasion. Once or twice Levine's spirited direction leaves the singers drowned by an over-enthusiastic orchestra. But all in all it is a superb performance and afterwards the crowd goes wild. From the upper reaches Domingo is showered by the Met equivalent of ticker-tape—hundreds of bits of torn programmes fluttering down into the orchestra pit and onto the stage. A terrible mess for the Met cleaners to clean, but a spectacular visible tribute for a great singer to receive after a highly-acclaimed performance.

Domingo would probably not have chosen *Adriana Lecouvreur* as his début opera at the Met in 1968. It was only in the repertoire at all because one of Bing's *prime donne*, Renata Tebaldi, had begged him to mount it for her five years before (against his better judgement, he said later) and now, towards the end of her career, he gave her a final run of performances. Written at the very beginning of this century by Francesco Cilèa, it resembles its great contemporary *Tosca* in some ways. Both are Italian works in, but not entirely of, the *verismo* tradition and both are about the life, love and eventual death of a great woman of the stage. Both (like *Manon Lescaut* and *Andrea Chénier*, two further stable-mates) are set in earlier times, *Adriana* in the 1730s, *Tosca* in 1800. In both the soprano loves the tenor and is unsuccessfully pursued by the baritone. There are musical resemblances, too. In both (again as in *Lescaut* and *Chénier*) there are a handful of fine set-piece arias separated by through-composed atmospheric music-drama as well as passages that deliberately pastiche earlier musical styles. As in Meyerbeer's *L'Africaine*, the heroine of *Adriana* dies an unlikely death by breathing in the poisoned perfume of a plant. And as in a much earlier work, Donizetti's *Maria Stuarda*, the moment of highest drama comes with the confrontation between two angry women, Adriana and her rival for Maurizio's love, the passionate Amneris-type Princess de Bouillon.

Where does all this leave the tenor? Off the stage a lot of the time or, during one scene at the Met production, standing stock still watching a somewhat tedious ballet. Still, he does have a gentle, expansive aria and duet in Act I, a powerful outpouring to the Princess (the aria 'L'anima ho stanca') in Act II, and a beautiful final duet with Adriana as she approaches death. It is not an easy opera for the tenor; his role is musically and dramatically far less significant than that of the soprano playing the title-role, while the contralto playing the Princess can dominate some of the most striking scenes. Stepping into an existing production in mid-run for a single performance is not easy either, and on 22 February 1983 Domingo does not sound entirely at his most relaxed in his early scenes with Renata Scotto, a vocally and dramatically somewhat histrionic Adriana. The lovely descending phrase 'Bella tu sei, tu sei gioconda' that recurs through Maurizio's early utterances is delivered with beautifully restrained *cantilena*, but the sound is once or twice slightly edgy. As usual, however, Domingo's performance peaks at just the right place—in this instance the Act II aria to the Princess. 'L'anima ho stanca' (My spirit is weary) is brief, weighty, infinitely sad. Domingo sings it as though he believes every word of it and gets the sort of ovation that in earlier, less disciplined days would have been rewarded with an encore.

At the end of the act Domingo does not join his colleagues at the curtain call and the intermission seems to go on longer than usual. As the members of the audience drink their water in memory of Ezio Pinza or (if members of the Metropolitan Opera Guild) their champagne in the elegant Eleanor Belmont Room, rumours fly fast. Domingo is sick; they're bringing on Neil Shicoff. Or Bini. Domingo has had a tiff with Scotto. He thought he was off form and did not deserve a curtain call. Some say Domingo has been seen leaving the building. In costume . . .

When Act III does eventually get under way Domingo is present and apparently in perfectly good voice and humour as he sings to the Prince de Bouillon's guests Maurizio's description of his latest military adventures. By the next interval, word of what has really been going on spreads rapidly through the house. Domingo *did* leave the building in costume. He went across the plaza to the adjacent State Theater where a gala musical evening was being filmed for the Public Broadcasting Service to be screened on TV a month later as part of a PBS fund-raising exercise. *Everyone* was appearing —Mirella Freni, Nicolai Ghiaurov, Grace Bumbry, Sherrill Milnes, with orchestra conducted and piano accompaniment played by James Levine. Not the sort of thing Plácido Domingo likes to miss. Hostess Beverly Sills was just delivering an elegant little speech to the effect that unfortunately some artists whom she would have liked to have on the show were unavailable tonight, such as her good friend Plácido Domingo who was engaged in a performance at the Met, when who should walk onto the set, in costume, than that self same Plácido Domingo. He flashes the audience a broad grin, says that having fifteen years before left the New York State Theater to go to the Met he is particularly happy tonight to retrace his steps, and adds that, since encores are forbidden at the Met, he would like to give this second audience a rendition of the aria he delivered over the way ten minutes before. 'L'anima ho stanca', Mark II. The Domingo *'anima'* shows no sign of being 'stanca' as he then bounds back to the Met to carry on with the next act of Adriana.

The performance ends beautifully. The final scene, as Adriana expires slowly in Maurizio's arms after sniffing the deadly flower, is ravishing, Domingo singing at his most seductive, Scotto at her most persuasive. Backstage an admirer presents Domingo with a tall, slender flower—but a voice in the crowd jokingly warns him, 'Don't sniff it or you'll snuff it!'

Later that night, after the plaudits, the ticker-tape, the hundreds of autographs and handshakes, the kisses and the congratulations, Domingo eventually makes for a select restaurant across town where a small group of his closest friends awaits him. They have all enjoyed Adriana earlier in the evening and by the time he arrives are enjoying an excellent Chinese supper as well. Domingo, radiant with the success of his evening and perhaps a little proud of having carried off his quick theatre-hop with such bravado, is in an expansive mood. 'People often ask me if I am nervous before performances,' he says. 'Fifteen years ago when I first sang at the Met, the whole thing was sprung on me so suddenly that I had no time to be nervous. But today, I tell you, I was really nervous!' He had not exactly looked it. 'No, but you know I was worried people might say, "Fifteen years ago this fellow stepped into this opera at very short notice and—well, he was actually pretty good. But today, when he has had time to prepare properly . . ."' Domingo pulls a long face and his friends collapse with laughter. By now it is well past 2 o'clock and even Domingo admits he is beginning to feel tired. 'Il corpo ho stanco' he sighs to Marta with a smile, as Lauren Bacall, Joe Dash of CBS Records, Marianne and Gerard Semon (his New York agents), Berta and Guillermo Martinez and others slowly take their leave after a wonderful evening.

At the following morning's Don Carlo rehearsal call Domingo is absent. Not because he has had a late night, but because he has slipped off to Europe by Concorde to attend the Paris première of his Traviata movie . . .

There are operas that can make an impact even if inadequately cast or produced. Gatti-Casazza thought Rigoletto, Traviata, Lohengrin and *Faust* came under this category; middle Verdi, for which he had the greatest admiration, 'can even be done with dogs' and survive! Other operas—Gatti singles out *Otello*, *Tristan*, *Meistersinger* and *Carmen* as examples—simply have to be done well or not at all, and most would surely put *Don Carlos* in this category.

Originally written for the Paris Opéra (hence its French libretto and the French form of its original title) it was frequently revised by Verdi in his later years. Passages were added, others temporarily suppressed. There is probably no one 'authentic' version of the work, though the 1983 Met revival (except for its use of an Italian text and title) probably gets as close as any. The entire opening scene in the Forest of Fontainebleau, essential if the later music and plot are to hold together, is given in short form or even omitted in some productions but given its full weight at the Met. The temptation to edit is understandable. But the very scale of the work's ambition and the nobility of its sentiments demand expansive utterance. There can be no Reader's Digest *Don Carlos*.

At one level the opera is about love and jealousy: the love between Carlos, son of King Philip II of Spain and the young Elizabeth de Valois who for reasons of state becomes Philip's wife; and the jealousy of Princess Eboli, whose love for Carlos is unreciprocated. It is also, more than any other of Verdi's operas, about politics: specifically, the clash between the forces of liberalism (Carlos and his friend Rodrigo, Marquis of Posa, who believe Spain should give freedom to the people of the Low Countries) and those of authoritarianism (Philip and, even more so, the Grand Inquisitor). The opera contains scenes of tender intimacy, of mistaken identity, of love and of anger. The King and the two ladies have arias among the most expressive in the operatic literature while the Carlos–Rodrigo friendship duet is equalled only by that from Verdi's own *Forza del Destino*. *Don Carlos* contains in its central *auto-da-fé* scene a spectacle on a scale with the Grand March scene from *Aida*, while it also includes mystical elements that can chill the blood—a celestial voice welcoming the souls of the martyrs to heaven; the reincarnation of the Emperor Charles V calling his grandson Carlos to his bosom at the opera's end.

Don Carlos holds a special place in the affections of many opera goers. Until relatively recently it was given, even in its various truncated versions, only infrequently. Then after World War II it gradually began to come into its own. Rudolf Bing made it the inaugural work of his period as General Manager at the Met in 1950. And when Covent Garden celebrated the centenary of the present theatre in 1958 it did so with a production of *Don Carlos* by Luchino Visconti, with a cast including Vickers, Gobbi, Christoff, Barbieri and Gré Brouwenstijn under the baton of Giulini, that came to be regarded as a touchstone of the greatest heights of which operatic performance is capable.

The 1983 revival of the 1979 Met production aims scarcely less high. The magnificent sets—rich dark blacks and browns, old-gold walls that look like extensions of the great arch of the Met stage itself, curved and filigreed Moorish arches, elegant monastic screens and grilles and columns, great flickering fireplaces, fountains, tall, elegant cypress trees—all have been refurbished, and John Dexter is on hand to re-think every detail of his production. In its casting, too, the Met has given notice that an outstanding run of performances is to be expected. In addition to Domingo as Carlo, the Met has assembled Mirella Freni as Elisabetta, Nicolai Ghiaurov as King Philip, Grace Bumbry as Eboli and veteran Canadian baritone Louis Quilico as Rodrigo. Quilico is a regular Met performer, not perhaps as penetrating or as noble in the part as his predecessor Sherrill Milnes but still capable of rich, round top notes when required. Bumbry, black and beautiful, is one of the great stars of modern opera. With her feline good looks, mesmeric stage presence and a voice capable of encompassing a huge range of notes and modes and moods, she is ideally cast as the passionate, jealous Princess Eboli. As for Freni and Ghiaurov, both lucky to be alive after a recent car crash, they too are the right people in the right roles, and it would be unthinkable these days to cast the one in such an opera without the other. Freni has not sung at the Met except as part of a visiting Scala company for some fifteen years and is sure of a tremendous reception. And as Ghiaurov has been one of the great interpreters of the role of King Philip for twenty years now, what he may be beginning to lose vocally is compensated for by his years of experience in the part.

The countdown to *Carlo* is hectic. During the first half of

February, Levine and Dexter work with the cast in various locations in the bowels of the Met. Domingo is fairly assiduous in attending these sessions though naturally he has no *Carlo* rehearsals on days on which he is giving a performance. He rehearses *Carlo* and *Bohème* on either side of his *Giocondas*, *Carlo* and *Adriana* around his first *Bohème* on the 17th, and from then on it is *Carlo* on the Main Stage almost every day until the dress rehearsal on the 25th.

The morning after Domingo's *Bohème* he arrives at the Met to find nineteenth-century Paris transformed into sixteenth-century Fontainebleau, the knotty, snowy trees of David Reppa's forest clearing. For this occasion everybody is listed on the Met call sheet, including off-stage band, chorus, extra chorus, supers and animals. On the stroke of 11 a.m. James Levine raises his baton and the first stage rehearsal of the first scene begins. Pě-*namm*, pě-*namm*: that typical Verdi grace note that gives this opera so much of its unique character. The Met curtain rises (for most other productions a dividing curtain is used) to reveal a rectangular drop featuring stylized heraldic patterns. When this rises in its turn it reveals a chorus of French peasants bewailing the wars that have afflicted their land. Soon, the crowds part as Elisabetta appears, preceded by four Irish wolfhounds and a man on horseback. The Met menagerie is at full stretch these days; only last night the horse was bringing on Musetta's carriage in *Bohème* while this season's other offerings include the *Rosenkavalier* dog, the *Hansel and Gretel* cat, and a big donkey for *Barbiere* and a small one for *Bohème*.

Dexter would have liked Elisabetta to arrive on horseback. But Freni, perhaps still mindful of the precariousness of Ronconi's Madonna effect in the Scala *Ernani*, to say nothing of her recent car crash, would prefer to make her entry on foot with the horseman preceding her. She comes immediately to the front of the stage and sings out in full voice—a miraculously rich and round voice for one so petite. She is made to appear even more petite by the heavily hooped gown she is wearing. Among this crowd, Domingo looks distinctly unorthodox as he emerges wearing, of all things, a grey suit, white shirt and tie. Levine stops the orchestra and asks Mirella to step forward. When she does, pretending to trip over her skirts as she approaches the edge of the stage, Levine introduces her with a few

Central Park, New York, June 1981: Domingo acknowledges the
applause of some 250,000 people at the Met's free, open-air *Tosca*

Sherrill Milnes, Renata Scotto and Domingo in Central Park,
New York, June 1981, after the rehearsal of *Tosca*

Domingo in the CBS recording studio, August 1982. Left to right: Lee
Holdridge, Rosemary Okun, Milton Okun, recording engineer Mike
Ross, Plácido Domingo

Domingo as Don Carlo over the murdered body of his friend Rodrigo (Louis Quilico) at the Metropolitan Opera, New York, March 1983

Kiri Te Kanawa and Domingo (in his Act III cloak) rehearsing
Manon Lescaut at Covent Garden, April 1983

Domingo, Sir John Tooley and the Queen Mother at the first night of
Manon Lescaut at Covent Garden, May 1983

Marilyn Zschau arrives on the scene to rescue
Domingo from hanging. A rehearsal of *La
Fanciulla del West*, Madrid, June 1983

Domingo's father and mother, the Queen and King of Spain, Marta
and Plácido Domingo during the interval of *Fanciulla*, Madrid, June
1983

Domingo in his Don José costume talking to the youngsters assembled in the Cinema Merced in Ronda, July 1983

Domingo off-duty in Ronda during the filming of *Carmen*

Domingo rehearsing the Orchestre National de France, Paris,
October 1983, prior to *Le Grand Echiquier*

Curtain call after *Die Fledermaus* at Covent Garden, 31 December
1983 Left to right: Kiri Te Kanawa, Hermann Prey, Domingo,
Benjamin Luxon

Domingo in Vienna on his 43rd birthday,
with his sons Alvaro (*left*) and Placi (*right*),
and Austrian football star Hans Krankl

After the first night of *Carmen* in Vienna, January 1984.
The photo includes Ruggero Raimondi and Franco Zeffirelli (top left),
Lorin Maazel (top middle), Faith Esham (top, second from right,
in blonde wig), Domingo and Agnes Baltsa (centre, front)

warm words of welcome and the musicians in the pit tap their music stands appreciatively. Domingo, who has scarcely been off the Met stage these past twenty days, steps forward and asks plaintively: 'Jimmy, how come you don't introduce *me?*'

During the first interval, as the Forest of Fontainebleau is removed and the Monastery of St Iuste instated, the soloists go backstage. Freni relaxes, and doubtless worries, as everyone else at the Met worries, whether the bout of 'flu Ghiaurov is suffering will soon be over. Bumbry chats to friends as she makes sure her magnificent dark green costume fits properly—and Domingo makes a long-distance call about details of a recording contract and then rushes off for a quick television interview about the charity concert in Washington he is to give early in March. Hence perhaps the suit and tie. Miraculously, he appears in the Monastery of St Iuste twenty minutes later, on cue, in costume, and looking and sounding as though he does not have another thought in the world other than the rehearsal of this scene in this opera. The truth is, he probably doesn't. This is one of his great strengths, a capacity to devote all his concentration to the job in hand and exclude all other things from his mind until he has time to deal with them properly.

Each day, as the various scenes are rehearsed, the screw tightens. While Ghiaurov is recovering from 'flu his place is taken by the tall, black, elegant American bass Simon Estes who plays the friar in the Giulini recording of the opera. One day, Ghiaurov is back but Bumbry is sick. She has woken up with a tickle in her throat and is worried she will do herself damage if she sings. It is agreed that she can simply mouth the words and rhythms but would she please not miss the rehearsal. Grace agrees. Next day, Domingo is angered to see photographers in the house. People are always trying to publish rehearsal pictures as though they were photos of the real thing, he complains, or even reporting on a singer's 'performance' on the basis of the way he sang at rehearsal. One of the photographers is tactless enough to say to Domingo that they 'don't need' him. Domingo, understandably put out, leaves the house. It is only when it is explained to him that a *New York Times* feature article is being prepared about the Met animals and that they need a photo of Freni with the wolfhounds that he agrees to return.

For the final dress rehearsal, an invited audience is present—a mixed blessing for, although it is useful to have some reaction to a production in the final stages of rehearsal, it is very difficult—or so Domingo at any rate feels—to hold back and save your voice when hundreds of strangers are present and full of high expectations. If you do not sing out properly, particularly if your colleagues do, some in the audience will surely spread the word that your voice is not what it was. If you *do* sing, you may spend too much of your vocal capital—especially dangerous if you happen to have a performance of *La Bohème* to give the very next day. At the *Carlo* dress rehearsal, accordingly, Domingo has an announcement made that in view of his performance tomorrow he will conserve his voice today. And for once the adrenalin of the occasion does not take over and he does, indeed, sing almost the whole dress rehearsal in half voice. The high notes are taken falsetto or an octave down, while only the gentler passages in the middle of the range are voiced in anything like the normal fashion. The elegance, the phrasing, the buckling at the knees, the toss of the head, are all there. But only in one scene, the penultimate scene with Quilico as Rodrigo, a section that had perhaps been less thoroughly rehearsed than the rest, does Domingo give any indication of the vocal powers normally at his command.

The dress rehearsal of this unusually long and demanding opera—longer than almost any other work in the standard repertoire outside Wagner—carries on until nearly four o'clock in the afternoon. It goes well and the production shows every promise of being a great success. Freni and Ghiaurov, Bumbry and Quilico can rest for three days. Domingo, visibly tired, goes home to try and build up his energies for the following evening's *Bohème*.

In the night he awakens feeling giddy and sick. His throat is raw and his brow spotted with perspiration. He reaches for the telephone and calls Paul Garner. Paul is in a sleepy daze and cannot for the moment focus on where he is. He glances at his watch. Five o'clock. In the morning. In New York. Plácido is on the phone saying that he is sick and cannot sing today. 'Yes, Plácido; of course. I'll let them know,' says Paul—and hangs up and tries to get some more sleep. He fails because he fears he has a very busy day ahead. The unscrambling involved when Domingo cancels a performance is unpleasant and time-consuming. Not only must the Met management be informed, of course, at the earliest reasonable time, but so must Domingo's agents and each of the sixteen or so people who were coming to the performance as Domingo's guests, and the Met box office which can now re-allocate those tickets. A lot of Paul's time and energy will inevitably have to be devoted to convincing people who do not believe that Domingo can really be too ill to sing.

Domingo was not imagining things at five o'clock in the morning. It appears he has picked up an infection which develops into tonsillitis. His place in *Bohème* is taken by Giuliano Ciannella, who does a creditable job. And on the opening night of *Don Carlo* the title part is to be sung by Ermanno Mauro, a regular Met tenor, a man with a somewhat stiff vocal manner but under normal circumstances perfectly acceptable. When word spreads that Domingo is sick there is a frantic attempt to unload tickets among the touts who frequent the Met and expensive seats are available, if you know where to look, at knock-down prices.

'Mauro only knows the role in French.' All opera houses are rumour-factories but none more so than on the opening night when the star is sick. 'Domingo's not really ill, just saving himself for his concert in Washington.' 'Did you hear,' asks one eager young lady of her companion, 'that Domingo stormed out of the dress rehearsal because there were photographers there? And his voice was in terrible shape—perhaps that's why he left.'

Thus Dame Rumour holds court in the foyers before the performance. But all her insinuations are forgotten, or re-allocated to the back of the consciousness, as Levine lifts his baton in the darkened auditorium and the lower strings beat out their powerful opening motif: pĕ-*namm*, pĕ-*namm*, pĕ-*namm*. Freni gets a tremendous hand when she first appears, and Mauro sings his Fontainebleau arietta—in Italian, of course—gracefully enough to give promise of a perfectly respectable performance. As the evening progresses it becomes clear that Freni is in the most spectacular form, while Bumbry, pulling out all the vocal and dramatic stops she knows, is at times a serious rival not only for the love of Carlo but also for that of the huge and enthusiastic Met audience. Will the later addition of

Domingo add a further touch of inspiration, as the *New York Times* man hopes? Well, yes, it will. But *Carlo* with a substitute Carlo is not *Hamlet* without the Prince and a happy crowd is sent home after four hours of glorious music drama.

Manon Lescaut at Covent Garden

You could walk past some opera houses like the old Met or the Chicago Lyric and scarcely guess you had done so. Others—Bayreuth, Paris, Sydney—positively command attention. The Royal Opera House, Covent Garden, stands somewhere in the middle. Like La Scala, Covent Garden has a handsome if slightly understated exterior that cannot be observed except from fairly close proximity. The front of the house, facing east across Bow Street to the police station and magistrates' court, is grand enough with its Greek-style portico and six Corinthian columns of Portland stone. But Bow Street is little more than a narrow side street, just as it was a century and a half ago, before the erection of the theatre, when the predecessors of London's police were known as 'Bow Street Runners'. And Floral Street, which runs along the length of the opera house on the north side, past the amphitheatre entrance and on beyond the stage door, is a mere alleyway—or so it sometimes seems to the overnight scene-shifters who have to struggle with their huge flats in its confined spaces. The opera house itself, containing one of the most beautiful of theatrical auditoria, has pitifully inadequate space for anything else. Despite the addition of decent dressing- and rehearsal-rooms opened in 1982, the administrative offices are mostly over the road in a maze of rooms huddling between Bow Street and the parallel Long Acre. From Restoration times until the 1970s, 'Covent Garden' to most people meant London's principal fruit, flower and vegetable market rather than an opera house. And after the removal of the market to its new site at Nine Elms on the south bank of the Thames, the Covent Garden area went through a remarkable and unanticipated renaissance so that now, the magnificent and extended opera house notwithstanding, it is mostly for the italianate piazza with its stylish cafés, open stalls selling art work, and its street musicians and entertainers that visitors come to the district.

Most of London's theatres lie further west than Covent Garden, in and around Piccadilly or what has come to be known as the 'West End'. But London moved westward comparatively late in its history and Edward Barry's opera house, opened in 1858, was the third theatre on a site that once formed the gardens of a convent. The first theatre was opened in 1732 so it was decided that the 1982–3 season would be celebrated as a 250th anniversary. The best way for the Royal Opera House to celebrate would naturally be by presenting outstanding productions and performances. In a normal season, the management like to put on at least three or four new productions of both opera and ballet. By this criterion the 250th season is sadly far from normal. Money is always a problem for an opera house and Covent Garden management never tire of pointing out how much they achieve on a small state subsidy. But this year proves even worse than usual. During the first few months of 1982, all three of Covent Garden's normal sources of income look bleak. Box-office takings are down. (So are those of other London theatres; people blame the Falklands war which allegedly kept people at home glued to their TV sets.) Prime Minister Thatcher, having earlier sacked her enlightened Arts Minister Norman St John-Stevas, permitted his successor to make noises suggesting a reduced grant in real terms to the Arts Council and its principal regular beneficiaries. And in the absence of American-style tax concessions any increases in the level of private subsidy to opera and ballet seem out of the question.

Making long-term plans against this sort of background can be demoralizing for opera managements and as the 250th anniversary season approaches Sir John Tooley and his team at Covent Garden see one well-laid plan after another evaporate. The long-awaited new production of *Andrea Chénier*, for example, has to be shelved for the second time, and the press, understandably enough, ask about money wasted on aborted projects. Eventually, Tooley and his chairman, Sir Claus Moser, have the melancholy task of announcing that the special anniversary season will feature a grand total of two new productions each of ballet and opera—the lowest number since the early 1950s when Covent Garden first got going on a year-round basis. The two new operas are to be Handel's *Semele* and Puccini's *Manon Lescaut*. *Semele* is a product of the time and place that produced the first Covent Garden theatre, and in due course John Copley's colourful production, starring Valerie Masterson and Robert Tear, creates an appropriately festive atmosphere. *Manon Lescaut*, based on the novel by the Abbé Prévost also dating from the early 1730s, is to star Plácido Domingo and Kiri Te Kanawa, and to be conducted by the latest comet out of Italy, Giuseppe Sinopoli. And the producer? Piero Faggioni.

Faggioni is everybody's image of the archetypal artist, a man of brilliantly imaginative ideas and impossibly mercurial temperament. A man of many parts, Faggioni is also a designer (the Bregenz *Otello* designs were largely his), a former actor, and something of a television director too when the opportunity presents itself. Indeed, his belief in his own prowess as a TV director was partly responsible for the fracas that developed at Covent Garden during the television rehearsals of *Fanciulla* last November.

Rumour and counter-rumour sweep through the opera world after *Manon Lescaut* has been officially announced. Will Covent Garden really have Faggioni back to work there? Will he demand as much money as last time? Who will be his designer? And—for the BBC and NVC are not about to miss a production with this cast—which television producer will the BBC assign to work alongside him? This last question is answered first. There is no way John Vernon could work with Faggioni again and Humphrey Burton agrees to take on the job. He knows the principals well and is an experienced hand at televised opera. As for the rest of the Faggioni questions, most remain unanswered, for his relations with Covent Garden become so strained that the two part company. The final divorce occurs dangerously late. Less than two months before the opening night of *Manon Lescaut*, the Royal Opera House announces that Faggioni's designs have proved too large to fit properly on to and off from the Covent Garden stage and that, under the circumstances, it is going to prove necessary to borrow a production from elsewhere.

The press rumbles on again about taxpayers' money, while Tooley insists that very little had in fact been spent as Faggioni's sets and costumes have been stopped before work on constructing them commenced. While Tooley is applauded for his proper sense of financial responsibility, observers find it hard to accept that the building of sets and 200 costumes should not even have *begun* a mere eight weeks from opening night . . .

'They're going to use the Coliseum's sets for Massenet's *Manon*,' says one semi-serious Long Acre wiseacre, 'but with the *Walküre* rock for Act IV.' Some point to Scottish Opera's excellent current production of *Manon Lescaut* by John Cox. Eventually, it is from Hamburg that salvation comes, in the form of a production by Götz Friedrich originally mounted in 1979. It is not at first clear that all the principals will agree to stay. Domingo is rumoured to be particularly close to Faggioni, Te Kanawa to be disheartened at the prospect of working with Friedrich, Sinopoli obdurate about conducting only new productions. Then, one by one, everybody involved lets it be known that they will agree to stay involved. As a matter of fact, Domingo had starred with Eva Marton in the 1979 Hamburg production and his familiarity with it is a point in its favour, as is the fact that Friedrich had been principal opera producer at Covent Garden in the 1970s and is keen to do whatever he can to help his old house in its moment of need. Indeed, Friedrich has even managed to clear a crowded diary so as to be able to come over to London and direct some of the rehearsals himself.

It is a source of wonderment that many opera productions ever see the light of day. In this particular instance, it will be little short of a miracle if everything were to slot into place in time. With little more than a month to go, the huge Hamburg sets are dispatched to London, costumes are re-made or adapted, and a full schedule of daily music and production rehearsals lined up for principals who are jetting in from various parts of the operatic world.

Manon Lescaut is the opera that really established Puccini's reputation. Until then he had been one of many young Italian composers struggling to find an individual voice and emerge from under the towering presence of Verdi. *Manon Lescaut* was first produced in Turin in February 1893 just eight days before the world première in Milan of Verdi's last opera, *Falstaff*. Within a short time prescient observers, George Bernard Shaw among them, said that at last they thought they knew the identity of Verdi's successor.

Something in Puccini's psyche seemed to like to have someone else against whom to compete. His interest in writing *La Bohème* appears to have been stimulated by the knowledge that his friend Leoncavallo, composer of *Pagliacci*, was working on an opera on the same theme, while one attraction of the libretto of *Tosca* was the fact that it had been inveigled by his publisher Giulio Ricordi from another composer. In the case of *Manon Lescaut*, the competition had already made its case, so to speak, in the very considerable form of Massenet's recent opera *Manon*, a work in many ways closer to both the story and spirit of the Prévost novel than anything Puccini was likely to achieve. This much Puccini was prepared to acknowledge. Indeed, one of the many ways in which he made life difficult for the succession of librettists who worked with him on *Manon Lescaut* was that he was repeatedly suggesting ways in which, even at the expense of plot or character, they might try and distinguish his work from Massenet's. He probably need not have bothered with these matters of detail for, as he himself said, 'Massenet feels it as a Frenchman, with the powder and the minuets; I shall feel it as an Italian, with desperate passion.'

Passion there is in abundance in *Manon Lescaut* and one can easily see in the retrospect of Puccini's later works the irresistible appeal of this story of an innocent young girl, torn between her romantic love for the dashing Renato des Grieux and the material attractions of life with her middle-aged protector—a girl who eventually dies, sick and frail, in the arms of her lover. She is the soul sister of Mimì, Butterfly and Liù, though Puccini has given her great Tosca-like outpourings of pride, passion and grief as well. As for des Grieux, he is the typical tenor hero of romantic opera, the 'good guy' who, having fallen in love with the girl at first sight, follows her, literally, to the ends of the earth rather than lose her. It is a difficult part for the tenor. Dramatically he has to convince an audience of the sagacity of a young man who gives up so much for the love of so irresolute (not to mention avaricious) a girl, while musically much of the tenor line lies uncomfortably high and is punctuated by frequent outbursts requiring the utmost vocal reserves. The two principal tenor arias appear in Act I, but woe betide the singer who spends too early all the coin in his vocal purse. The greatest concentration of effort for the tenor is required towards the end of the later acts, so *Manon Lescaut* is an unusually hard work to pace.

Domingo has sung the opera many times and recorded it with Caballé in 1971–2. In early 1980 a much acclaimed New York Met performance with Domingo and Renata Scotto was televised live around much of the operatic world. Des Grieux is, for all that, a young man's role and by later in 1980 Domingo was telling friends he was considering dropping it from his repertoire. Then a series of exhilarating performances in Munich with conductor Riccardo Chailly persuaded him to re-think—and the result is that he is now engaged to perform the role for the first time at Covent Garden. The opera is not often available to British audiences and with Domingo and Te Kanawa in the cast every seat for every performance is sold, and could have been sold eight or ten times over, shortly after postal booking opens.

Immediately after Easter, a full month before the opening, Kiri Te Kanawa goes into intensive rehearsals at Covent Garden. Domingo, who knows the work intimately and recalls much of Götz Friedrich's Hamburg staging, arrives a week later, going to the Royal Opera House straight from a twelve-hour overnight flight from California. For most of the next three weeks he is at the house five or six days a week, usually from 10 a.m. until five or six in the afternoon. But he has also lined up a further array of activities for himself while he is in London—two Sunday evening concerts at the new Barbican Centre, and, during the final run-up to the *Manon Lescaut* opening, a series of evening recording sessions with Milton Okun and Lee Holdridge.

The first of the Barbican concerts is a platform performance of *La Gioconda*, promoted by Denny Dayviss and Alan Sievewright. Dayviss and Sievewright are an extraordinary pair, nineteenth-century-style impresarios capable of thinking big operatic thoughts and bringing them to fruition, risk-takers with an impressive record of presenting concert performances of the grandest operas with the grandest singers. In 1969 they helped set up a concert version of *La Gioconda* with Elena Suliotis and Sherrill Milnes—the first, and until 1983 the last, professional performance of the work in London since Covent Garden did it with Rosa Ponselle back in 1929.

Gioconda is scheduled to take place just two days after Domingo arrives in London from California. Plenty of time to get adjusted to the new time zone and climate, do some solid work on *Manon Lescaut* at Covent Garden, and get into shape for the Barbican. He will join in *Gioconda* rehearsals, of course; but perhaps not on his first day in London . . .

There are not many places Domingo sings that are new to him but the Barbican is one of them. The Sunday rehearsal begins at ten but it is an hour later before Domingo arrives—just before conductor Anton Guadagno and the London Symphony Orchestra reach the tenor's big aria. Orchestra, chorus and the other soloists are given an early coffee break as Domingo saunters in looking like the genial proprietor of an Italian or Spanish restaurant or gown business, or perhaps a former football player whose muscles are beginning to go to fat. His large frame is loosely attired in a light brown suit, the jacket flapping above baggy trousers. Hands in ample pockets, head lolling forwards, a chubby grin on his face, his walk small-stepped and his feet facing slightly outwards, Domingo's body language is deceptive. One of the great interpretative artists of the century? This man gives every appearance of having nothing to do today except perhaps enjoy a lazy day of good food, wine and company with perhaps a nice doze in the afternoon.

In fact, of course, this almost excessively casual-looking gentleman has a great deal on his mind. Tonight's concert will be widely reported. The seats are expensive but sold out. It is not only Domingo's first *Gioconda* in London and only the second professional performance of the work here for over half a century but also the centenary of the work's first performance in Britain. Covent Garden's Sir John Tooley will be in the audience tonight, and if things go well everyone will be pressing for the work to be produced on the opera stage. *Gioconda* remains the only major work in Domingo's repertoire he has not recorded. (RCA set up a recording some years ago, then withdrew and paid everybody off; to date Domingo has still not cashed in the cheque—you never know, maybe they'll change their minds . . .) Perhaps the record companies, whose representatives will also be liberally sprinkled among this evening's audience, might reconsider if *Gioconda* were to show promise of getting a firm place on London's musical map.

Domingo has more immediate things on his mind too. Notably to assess the nature of the Barbican acoustic. The boxed-in knotty pine platform feels at first somewhat too enclosed. But that may be no bad thing if the box projects the sound powerfully and clearly out into the audience. Also, because the hall is wide and the three tiers of seats curved at the sides and raked, there is a greater intimacy of communication here than in a smaller auditorium like the long, rectilinear Queen Elizabeth Hall on London's South Bank, let alone the QEH's big sister, the adjacent Royal Festival Hall. Architects and acousticians will tell you that all the wood in the Barbican Hall helps the sound, that the reverberation time compares favourably with such acoustically outstanding halls as the Amsterdam Concertgebouw or the Vienna Musikvereinsaal. But architects and acousticians do not have to sing there. Domingo has heard that from part of the hall some resonances tend to get lost. How will the top of his voice come across? After the interval he goes onto the platform, runs through 'Cielo e mar' and the subsequent duet with Barbara Conrad at half-pressure, letting the great voice off the leash, as it were, every now and then for a run. Then he comes off the platform and places himself in various parts of the hall, his face now firmly set. It is as though the fat had turned straight back into muscle. No longer does he remotely resemble a jolly Latin restaurateur but an artist knowing that this evening, as on every evening he sings in public, his reputation will once more, and this time in unfamiliar surroundings, be on the line.

On the Saturday it was spring in London. One of those beautiful, warm, mellow days that make the whole dreary English winter worth enduring. But that was yesterday. Today, winter has returned, cold, grey, rainy. During the day God relents but little and as the evening performance approaches the heavens are merciless.

The Barbican is not the obvious place to make for on a damp London evening. Indeed, the impossibility of even being able to *find* the Barbican was a standing joke for long after the Centre was opened. Unlike most arts centres, it has no grand façade, no spectacular main entrance, affords no great vista to passers-by, and has no artists' entrance. Once inside you are immediately confronted by a concrete-encrusted assault course; an array of levels, lifts, pictorial instructions, sloping balustrades that can dizzy the head and spirits of the most determined culture vulture. You enter at what you presume to be street level but the arrows tell you, if you are not bewildered by the sheer multiplicity of them, that tickets for tonight's performance are on sale two floors down at level Three and for future performances at an altogether different ticket office two flights up at level Seven. There is no clock anywhere to be seen. It is all a bit like the sort of classy airport terminal building some latter-day Kafka might have invented.

Despite all its inevitable problems, there is much in the Barbican Centre to admire. The principal theatre is a great improvement on the Aldwych where the Royal Shakespeare Company performed for twenty years and the quality of RSC productions in its new home has been consistently high. Also, despite disappointing attendance at many of its most attractive events, the concert hall itself is generally pronounced a success and on this particular night, notwithstanding the persistent drizzle and the high seat prices, the Centre's multi-level foyer is buzzing. The well-travelled through time and space expatiate to those with more limited operatic experience about performances of *La Gioconda* they have seen, while those in more contemplative mood read quietly that Domingo is a 'phenomenon among tenors' and that Ghena Dimitrova, who sings the title role tonight, is 'one of the most highly regarded and sought-after singers in the world today'. A long queue of people develops hoping against all reasonable hope for returned tickets. They can at least purchase by way of compensation the handsome but expensive programme book, complete with no less than seven photographs of Plácido Domingo.

Inside the hall the crowd settles. In the orchestra, behind the strings but placed on a dais as though intentionally to obscure the sight-lines between conductor and wind players, is a row of white Louis XV-style chairs. It is there that everybody's attention is fixed, almost to the point of not noticing the arrival of Maestro Guadagno. Guadagno bows his stiff, wooden puppet bow to the audience, raises his baton, and is about to bring in the front row celli when from the far side door there emerges a little group of dignified and well-dressed ladies and gentlemen, tonight's soloists. Or at least some of them. The large black-haired lady in the long russet gown is Dimitrova. The middle-aged blonde in a blue dress is Elizabeth Bainbridge; she sings the role of Gioconda's blind mother, La Cieca, this evening, just as she did in the 1969 Suliotis-Milnes performance of this opera. The dark lady in the pale gown is Barbara Conrad; gone is the gum-chewing, finger-cracking All-American persona of this morning and in its place a handsome black woman in the Verrett/Bumbry mould. The women are followed by several men in white tie and tails led by Piero Cappuccilli, small, dapper, capable of a far bigger and more commanding sound than his appearance would initially suggest. Plácido Domingo is not among them. He is delaying his entry until the music and drama require his presence.

The soloists get their round of applause and sit on the Louis Quinze chairs. Guadagno raises his baton again, cello bows hover above strings for the second time—and this time the performance begins. Cappuccilli performs a few preliminary passages with characteristic brio—and pulls off his white tie, preferring to sing with his neck unconstricted. Bainbridge as La Cieca sings her gentle lilting phrases to her daughter, and as Dimitrova responds a *frisson* goes through the crowd—for here is a voice, never before heard in England, with greatness in it. The chorus, at the urging of Cappuccilli's wonderfully malevolent Barnaba, start taunting La Cieca and the orchestra rises to fever pitch. The side door opens and there, scurrying up onto the platform timing his opening cue to perfection, is Domingo. '*Assassini!*' he sings, rising with ease above the orchestra and momentarily dominating the proceedings.

In white tie and tails Domingo looks exactly like the image of him used in the Rolex watch ads and reproduced, among all the other ads and publicity pictures, in tonight's programme book. Which is to say that he looks tall, dark, serious—and somehow constricted. Perhaps he too should pull off his tie. As he sings he moves not just his body but also his position on the platform. Sometimes he sings to the character to whom, as Enzo, his words are addressed. Often, he seems to be projecting his sound deliberately towards different spaces in the Barbican Hall as though feeling out the acoustic and experimenting with different ways of riding it successfully. At times, his tone seems to lack body—unlike Cappuccilli, with his more 'open' sound and his preparedness to let his tone and even his pitch spread occasionally in the interest of size of impact. It is as though Domingo, by constantly 'covering' his sound so tastefully, is depriving his listeners of some of the impact they expect. He seems to be reining himself in more than usual. In his aria, such a show-stopper when he performed it at the New York Met a few weeks earlier, he sings the last bars of the first stanza (*'o sogni d'or'*) in a risky half voice, and the big note at the end is chopped uncomfortably short as though he did not want to give the audience too much of a good thing. Is he uncomfortable with the acoustic? Or just plain tired?

Domingo's singing is never less than beautiful throughout and, as the London *Times* reviewer was to say later, Domingo even at half stretch is preferable to other contemporary tenors at full stretch. But it is not Domingo who takes this particular evening by storm. That honour goes to Ghena Dimitrova whose large, versatile *spinto*-dramatic soprano is a revelation. Anybody who can sing like that *must* be asked back, and soon. Yes, says Sir John Tooley to persistent questioners after the show is over, as a matter of fact Dimitrova is booked to sing at Covent Garden in the 1984–5 season. As Turandot.

Exactly a week later Domingo is again to sing at the Barbican. It is a long time since he gave two concert performances in eight days but, as with every such occasion, this one too is special—a charity performance of operatic arias and duets for which he, soprano Luciana Serra, baritone Thomas Allen and conductor Robin Stapleton have donated their services to the Society of the Order of St John, the international ambulance, medical and first-aid organization.

If you can find your way not just *to* the Barbican Centre but *into* the complex, an even harder task on a Sunday morning when its only public entrances are closed, and make for the concert hall, you will on this particular occasion come across an uncommon sight: the English Chamber Orchestra, a highly select ensemble accustomed primarily to the refined atmosphere of Bach and Handel, Haydn and Mozart, sight-reading its way through such richly textured works as Verdi's overture to *La Forza del Destino* and the great, sad, heavy intermezzo from Puccini's *Manon Lescaut*. If the LSO a week ago found Ponchielli unfamiliar, this is nothing to this morning's encounter—the one and only rehearsal the English Chamber Orchestra is having for tonight's gala concert.

In charge is Robin Stapleton. His tall, slim body flows with the music, his baton almost an extension of his expressive fingers, and his unexpectedly deep, slightly cockney voice helps create for the musicians in front of him a useful no-nonsense atmosphere. The last section of the *Forza* overture has a difficult passage in which the strings have to play a variation of the big tune in fast triple notes; one slow run-through and this passage is safely under the belt. The Puccini is not *pesante* enough at first. The *Barber of Seville* parts contain a corruption and half the orchestra play G flat and the rest G natural . . .

Domingo arrives. Not without difficulty. Luciana Serra has never been here before and does not speak much English. Everybody hopes she will make it. Serra is not yet especially well known to London, except perhaps as the sensational doll Olympia in Covent Garden's *Tales of Hoffmann* with Domingo a couple of years before, a performance that is now gaining wide currency on video-cassette. More recently she was an enormous success in an otherwise dull revival of Bellini's *Sonnambula* and right now is winning excellent reviews playing opposite Geraint Evans in *Don Pasquale*. Serra has a funny, cheeky look, a curved nose and big round jaw—and huge round eyes that pop out of her head whenever she wants to look coy. Which in the music lined up for today is a lot of the time.

Thomas Allen is a more familiar figure. Tall, rugged, handsome, with a shock of light brown hair and vestiges of a Durham accent, he has become one of the most popular of Britain's top operatic performers in recent years. In the right work, *Pelléas*, for instance, or in the title-role of Britten's *Billy Budd*, Tom Allen is an artist of major international standing. He is currently rehearsing *Manon Lescaut* with Domingo at Covent Garden, a colleague he first sang with years ago as Schaunard to Domingo's Rodolfo in *La Bohème*. Tom Allen is a seasoned Barbican hand and gave a successful solo recital in the hall last autumn. He will certainly find his way in.

Domingo wanders into the hall wearing another of his expensive, loose-fitting suits. He chats amiably with Sir Claus Moser, with various St John dignitaries, with the leader of the Israel Chamber

Orchestra who is here as a guest. The body language is relaxed, lazy, slovenly almost as he slouches off to vocalize a little.

After the players have had a coffee break, the singers run through their numbers as Robin Stapleton tries against the odds to familiarize the orchestra with not only the notes but also the style of what they are playing. Domingo sings towards the players rather than out into the hall, willing them along, as it were, with Robin, almost acting as a second conductor. Luciana Serra turns up wearing green corduroy trousers and a comfortable Missoni-style cardigan, her copious blonde hair pinned in place by a pair of sun glasses perched atop, and throws off the most sensationally embellished version of Rosina's 'Una voce poco fa' from the *Barber of Seville* heard in London for many years.

The rehearsal ends late, just in time for any who wish to watch the Met *Don Carlo* all afternoon on Channel Four. Domingo watches some, is pleased with most of what he sees, is a little uneasy watching himself deliver a slightly stilted commentary between acts, then takes a nap.

At the Barbican that evening the anticipated audience of opera lovers is augmented by an army of girls in the uniform of St John's Brigade, plus a larger than usual contingent of dowagers in evening dress and, as guest of honour, Princess Alice the Duchess of Gloucester. Tonight the knotty pine box stage is embellished with large black and white symbols representing the Order of St John and that regular patron of the ECO, the National Westminster Bank.

On its single rehearsal the ECO plays the *Forza* overture with exemplary precision and panache. Tom Allen sings Valentin's aria from *Faust*, and then Domingo bustles on, arms swinging, a big smile on his face. No longer the stiff image on the Rolex watch ads, his movements seem altogether freer, his face sunnier than a week before. The orchestra slips into the strange harmonies with which Puccini sets the atmosphere for 'Recondita armonia' and Domingo gives an account of this air from *Tosca* that has the audience gasping. He must have performed this piece two or three hundred times, yet never can he have given it more heart-swelling beauty.

The evening catches fire and by the end nobody in the audience is prepared to leave. After Robin Stapleton and his three singers have trooped on and off the platform many times responding to applause, he reappears with only Domingo and Tom Allen. Domingo addresses the audience. 'Your Royal Highness, ladies and gentlemen,' he says with a broad grin. 'Since there are three of us singing tonight but only two of us on the platform, it will be obvious that there will be two encores!' There is a burst of applause as people enjoy the logic. 'First, we will sing the duet from the last act of *La Bohème*. And then, for the second encore, there will be something I'm sure you'll recognize as soon as you hear it. And by the way,' he adds, 'since by then we will have done an awful lot of singing tonight, we would like to invite you to join in with us!'

After the *Bohème* duet, Tom Allen's place on the platform is taken by Luciana Serra. She and Domingo stand close together pretending they do not know what is coming—and smile with feigned relief as the orchestra strikes up the 'Libiamo' from *La Traviata*. And when it comes to the choral variation Domingo beckons to the audience to join in, cups his ear as though to demand more volume, and makes as if to conduct the huge and happy crowd. London concert audiences do not often give standing ovations, but tonight the impulse to stand carries all British reserve before it. 'What an exciting evening!' someone says to Domingo next morning during a break in *Manon Lescaut* rehearsals at Covent Garden. No, he demurs, saying that excitement implies insecurity, the overcoming of risks. 'I'd rather say it was so *relaxing*!' Hard to believe when you consider the energy he had thrown into the evening. But one sees what he meant.

Much of the rehearsing for *Manon Lescaut* takes place in the back extension of the Royal Opera House, production rehearsals in particular being scheduled in the large new stage-sized opera studio with great arched windows overlooking James Street. Until the summer of 1982 virtually all preliminary production rehearsals took place in an old former cinema in the Commercial Road in London's East End, miles from Covent Garden. The luxury of a full-sized rehearsal studio *in situ* is still hard for old hands to believe. It is here that Wolfgang Bücker, Götz Friedrich's principal assistant now as in 1979 when this production first opened in Hamburg, takes the cast through their scenes. He is a slight, balding young man with glasses who speaks excellent if highly accented English of which Kiri Te Kanawa does a very funny imitation, to Wolfgang's own good-natured amusement.

Act III of *Manon Lescaut* takes place at the quayside at Le Havre. Manon, in company with a long line of prostitutes, is herded on to a ship for deportation to New Orleans. Des Grieux tries in vain to prevent her going and then, distraught at the prospect of losing her for ever, successfully begs the captain to let him go too. 'OK, so ve go now from ze begeening,' Wolfgang says, clutching Götz Friedrich's 1979 production book. 'Ah, ze begeening!' says Kiri as she climbs in her blue sweater and black tracksuit pants up to perch temporarily on top of a cupboard. Domingo, incongruous in shirt, tie and trousers covered by cloak and ill-fitting tricorne hat which points jauntily upwards, moves over to her with the music, then stands with an equally bizarre-looking Thomas Allen (who plays Manon's brother) as the roll-call of prostitutes commences. 'Rosetta'—and out from behind Kiri's cupboard towards the 'ship' the other side of the stage comes an actress, hired specially for this production, looking as slinky as she can. Next 'Madelon' swivels across the stage, wearing jeans and a denim cap. Manon/Kiri appears next from behind the cupboard, all coy and demure, then 'Ninetta' who is pushed roughly to the ground by a 'soldier' also in jeans but carrying a musket. The girl who, in this production, is to bare her bottom insolently at the soldiers, does not do so at this stage of rehearsals. Soon, the scene is reached where des Grieux tries forcibly to prevent Manon embarking. The skirmish looks phoney and Wolfgang wants it redone.

'Wouldn't it be better if I were to try and push my way towards the ship?' Plácido suggests. 'Then someone could restrain me and push me back.' It is a good idea, consistent with des Grieux' motivation and mental state at that moment, and it would add credibility to his great outburst 'Guardate, pazzo son!' which immediately follows. They try the scene this way and, after Domingo is shoved and has shaken off his assailant, he sings the 'Pazzo son' in full voice.

There is a lull as Wolfgang wants to go over some details with the prostitutes and soldiers. Kiri is in skittish mood. She waves to her husband who is sitting on a nearby table reading the paper—and promptly disappears inside Plácido's voluminous cloak. Plácido, eyeing the long line of rather attractive 'prostitutes', thinks with a chuckle what a time of it des Grieux is going to have once he gets on that ship. No wonder he was so keen to be allowed on . . .

It is back to 'ze begeening' again and everybody takes up position. Kiri on top of her cupboard lies on her back and does a series of very creditable limbering-up exercises, kicking her long legs one after the other high above her head. She is still having trouble remembering some of her words and musical phrases but accepts prompting and production willingly and is obviously fun to work with. A few days later, when she and Plácido are on stage in the main auditorium rehearsing their intense duet towards the end of Act II and are stopped for some extraneous reason, she adapts Puccini's opening phrases into an *ad hoc* rendition of 'Tea for Two'.

Stage rehearsals are an altogether different affair from those in the studio, for here you have the real space, the real sets, the real auditorium to play to. And, in the final week, the real orchestra with Sinopoli at the helm. Giuseppe Sinopoli has been in evidence throughout the rehearsal period with his Bizet-like dark, bushy hair, thick glasses and shaggy beard, and his somewhat tentative English but unmistakably commanding musical authority. It was he who took charge of all the early piano rehearsals with the principals, shaping every bar and mouthing every lead, and he would often be present in the background during Wolfgang's production rehearsals too. When music and production begin to come together with the full orchestra in the final week, Sinopoli grows naturally to fill the larger role all this co-ordination requires. He is a master musician to his eloquent, restless fingertips, a composer of serious avant-garde music, and this very week he is announced as successor to Riccardo Muti as principal conductor of the Philharmonia Orchestra.

Watch Sinopoli rehearsing an orchestra and you see a punctilious musical sculptor at work. No detail of tempo or texture is left to chance—'That F sharp should be slightly more flat,' he admonishes his strings at one sensitive point in the *Manon Lescaut* intermezzo—yet the result is an intensely communicated whole. One morning, after a full rehearsal of Acts I and II, Sinopoli asks the chorus (who thought they could go off for a lunch break) to assemble on stage in whatever costumes they happen to be wearing so that he can coax them through the rhythmic difficulties of Act III. The chorus are not at their happiest; they had hoped to get extra rehearsal sessions and overtime pay for *Manon Lescaut*, but this was turned down by the Covent Garden management, and their chorus master, John McCarthy, is teetering on the edge of resignation. In addition to rehearsing *Manon Lescaut* the chorus is also currently having to relearn Wagner's massive *Die Meistersinger*. Still, if the Maestro wants them on stage at 1.30 p.m. to work through their part in Act III they have to be there. Sinopoli is relentless in his attempt to get things right and has the chorus speak through one particularly difficult section to make sure the rhythm is spot on. Then he has them sing through the scene, and as they do so Domingo appears at the side of the stage and sings his part alongside theirs to help them along. It is a trying time and Sinopoli's keen ear lets nothing go by that is ragged. But once the various corners have been successfully turned he thanks them—and says they will not now be needed until the next day. The chorus are taken by surprise and respond with a spontaneous burst of applause.

Götz Friedrich is as good as his word and supervises rehearsals himself as often as he can get to London. The piano dress rehearsal is in effect his last major opportunity to have the cast to himself and to tighten up all the production details. On this particular day the orchestra is ensconced with the Royal Opera's Music Director, Sir Colin Davis, in the theatre's Crush Bar working on *Meistersinger*. Yesterday and tomorrow they have *Manon Lescaut* rehearsals, last night and tonight performances of *Don Pasquale* and Poulenc's *Dialogues of the Carmelites*. Never let it be said that the life of these orchestral musicians is dull or routine; nor is that of the people who plan the rehearsal schedules of a busy opera house. There *has* to be a piano dress rehearsal of *Manon Lescaut* and the orchestra *has* to have these *Meistersinger* sessions with Colin Davis. That the pieces of the operatic jig-saw puzzle usually come together as effectually as they do is a source of perpetual wonderment to the outsider and chronic anxiety to those responsible.

By and large Friedrich likes what he sees at the 'piano dress'. The Brechtian screen projections that precede each act are lopsided and Götz wonders whether there is a drunkard in the house. And that dance in Act I—couldn't some of the dancers take their eyes off the conductor so as to give their movements more freedom? During the first scene change Friedrich and Sinopoli stand together and chat in German. The BBC's Humphrey Burton is in the auditorium too, wearing a cardigan that looks like a television colour-card; he starts a conversation with Götz in excellent German and is answered in equally resolute English. Friedrich asks Domingo if he has a stiff neck. 'No, why?' Götz is not completely happy with the high-necked cravat Plácido is wearing and thinks it looks a bit like a bandage. Domingo agrees it needs adjustment, but adds that it will help hide his incipient double chin!

Sir John Tooley slips into the auditorium for a while. Earlier in the week some of the cast expressed anxiety that the 'Friends of Covent Garden' are to be allowed in for the dress rehearsal on Saturday. People always come and then report on what they saw as though it were a performance. Could not the Friends be kept away on this occasion? Te Kanawa in particular is nervous about being judged before she is ready. She knows she has not yet got the full measure of the part she has to sing in public within a week and is feeling under considerable pressure. Tooley takes the point and promises that no press will be admitted to the dress rehearsal and that the Friends will be told, even more explicitly than usual, that what they are witnessing is a rehearsal and *not* a performance.

The piano dress rehearsal progresses well, Götz Friedrich occasionally asking for brief scenes to be redone and rehearsing curtain calls at the end of acts. For this production he uses a huge drop-curtain painted like a Watteau sky in place of the usual Covent Garden velvet drapes. It is onto this drop that a sentence or two is projected setting each scene (except when the show is filmed for television), and in front of this drop that the principals have to walk, out of a little doorway on stage left and back through another the other side, when taking their individual bows. It is a little like a puppet theatre, or perhaps one of those old-fashioned weather vanes. But it keeps the eighteenth-century feeling of the production despite the mid-nineteenth-century scale of the stage and auditorium.

After the second act there is a break for about an hour, ample time for the sets to be changed from a Paris interior to the quayside at Le

Havre, adequate time, too, for a quick sandwich and a cup of coffee. During this break I happened to be standing outside the Stage Door and could hear the *Meistersinger* Nightwatchman being rehearsed in his small but haunting role in a studio overlooking Floral Street. Half an hour later it was the turn of the *Manon Lescaut* Lamplighter, one of Puccini's many apparent nods to Wagner in this score. The Lamplighter, the prostitutes and soldiers, the crowd and the sea-captain are all now in costume, and Domingo's 'Pazzo son' is delivered against a realistic set of the Havre quayside, complete with the prow of a ship onto which, with the piano tinkling out the reprise of the Big Tune, he rushes, ecstatic, at the end of the act.

In the 1730s a transatlantic voyage took months. Here at Covent Garden it must be accomplished in minutes while the scene-shifters hurriedly stretch an all-purpose 'rocky desert' tarpaulin over the stage and Kiri and Plácido get their arms and faces dirty and climb into their Act IV rags in preparation for Manon's death 'near the border of New Orleans'. Plácido doesn't think Kiri's costume is tattered enough and gives it a series of good-natured tugs. He himself is exposing a lot of manly brawn and sporting an instantly-acquired three-days' growth of beard, courtesy of Covent Garden's efficient make-up department. Act IV is dramatically static—'We do a lot of rolling around on the floor,' Plácido explains cheerfully—but musically it is desperately intense. The problem is how to maintain the intensity and prevent its deteriorating into sentimentality. It does not look bad though it is not yet fully credible. When Kiri falls onto the desert tarpaulin she must not be seen to bounce as on a waterbed; when Plácido looks desperately into the far distance he must somehow act with body and voice like a man who knows all he lives for is doomed. It is coming along well. And there are in any case two full orchestral rehearsals to go . . .

During the final week of *Manon Lescaut* rehearsals everybody is expected at the opera house each day, the principals for full three-hour sessions virtually every morning and afternoon. For three of those final days, however, Domingo, after spending five or six hours on his feet, in costume or part-costume, and periodically having to sing, has also scheduled for himself a series of evening recording sessions with Milton Okun. For this album Domingo has chosen territory that feels particularly close to home. Although Plácido does not visit South or Central America as often as he would like he still feels roots firmly planted there. His parents and his sister and her family all live in Mexico, while probably his closest friends, Berta and Guillermo Martinez, live in Puerto Rico. When Plácido and his Latin friends and family relax it is often to music like that of Ernesto Lecuona, the Havana-born composer active between the wars.

For every one person familiar with the name of Lecuona, thousands know his compositions. Ask who wrote 'Damisela Encantadora' (even if you call it 'It's No Secret that I Love You'), 'Canto Karabali' ('Jungle Drums') or the musical score of the Vera-Ellen/Cesar Romero movie *Carnival in Costa Rica*, and you will probably receive blank stares. But hum 'Andalucía' (which Vic Damone used to sing as 'The Breeze and I') or 'Malagueña' (a well-known Connie Francis and Caterina Valente number some years ago) and you will get knowing nods from most people of a certain vintage. So it was a logical step for Domingo to consider recording some of these pieces. Logical, too, for Domingo and Okun to call once again on Lee Holdridge to do most of the arrangements. Lee spent his first fifteen years in Costa Rica and is the perfect person to create a modern, American-style, middle-of-the-road accompaniment appropriate to these popular Latin compositions.

Studio sessions and dates in diaries were fixed long before anybody knew for sure what would be recorded. Would Plácido use the studio time to round off an uncompleted album of Neapolitan songs started some years before? There was talk in CBS circles of an album of modern Spanish guitar concertos with Plácido conducting, also of an album of operetta songs à la Tauber, then of an Offenbach disc with Plácido conducting and singing. Perilously close to the studio dates, the decision was made: Plácido would record an album of Lecuona. Milton Okun went into action, obtained the compositions and lyrics, alerted Lee Holdridge and got copies to him. In Los Angeles, while Lee was still working on the arrangements, Plácido recorded some of the songs with a five-man rhythm section. In London, he heard Lee's orchestrations for the first time (so did Lee, who literally finished them on the plane coming over) and recorded all the rest of the songs.

The orchestra this time was a section of the Royal Philharmonic, once Beecham's pride and joy, today struggling financially like all self-governing London orchestras and glad to get lucrative work. This morning they were recording with Andrew Lloyd Webber and tomorrow they have sessions with Yehudi Menuhin. Tonight and for the next few evenings it is Domingo and Lecuona. The RPO players are not unfamiliar with middle-of-the-road pop; this is the orchestra that made a much-needed pile of gold with Louis Clark's 'Hooked on Classics'.

Lee Holdridge has arranged 'Malagueña' and 'Andalucía' as a linked medley. These are probably the best-known of all the Lecuona compositions and there is a nice musical contrast between them. Plácido, who has been rehearsing at Covent Garden all day, turns up at the studio in the early evening refreshed by a shower, a light meal and a ten-minute cat-nap in the car on the way over, and is clearly keen to get down to work. As Lee takes the orchestra through its paces Plácido sight-reads his way through the vocal line Milton hands him. After a brief discussion about tempi it is decided to try a take of the first half of the medley, 'Malagueña'.

This kind of music must be performed with no rigidities of tempo, indeed Lee has specifically marked one important passage in Plácido's score 'ad libitum', and it will be a while before orchestra and singer are each performing with the requisite looseness of style while yet staying together. As Plácido's acquaintance with Lee's arrangement increases, the hands come out of the pockets, the body begins to sway, the arms to stretch out before him, and art imperceptibly takes over from technique. 'How are his words?' asks Milt as he swivels round to Marta Domingo who is sitting in on this session. Plácido is always anxious about his pronunciation—but this after all is Spanish. And Latin American Spanish at that. As a matter of fact there are some minor problems. That word *'inconstancia'* for example; it is not easy to say in mid-song; far harder, say, than its Italian equivalent *'incostanza'*. Plácido jokes that he has forgotten how to sing his own language.

He has a more serious concern. 'Why are we doing "Malagueña" and "Andalucía" as a medley?' he asks. 'They are both so beautiful, and both reasonably long. But together aren't they a bit *too* long? I think maybe it would be better to make them two different tracks.' He wonders whether there might not be a possibility of issuing 'Malagueña' as a single. 'In which case, wouldn't it make sense to keep it separate?' Good point. Lee adapts the bridge passage between the two songs and Plácido goes back into his cubicle to do the new 'Malagueña' ending.

'Andalucia' at first proves the harder of the separated twins to perform satisfactorily. A lovely, flowing waltz, everybody in the studio is soon swaying to its catchy rhythm. But for Plácido it begins uncomfortably low and his voice sounds husky and unfocused. 'I think I would like to sing that second phrase an octave higher. It will give the feeling that the song is taking off.' Milt at first demurs as he fears this might reduce the impact of the higher section that follows, but Plácido tries it anyway and incontestably sounds better. He also feels that the whole song drags a little and that Lee should push the tempo along at certain passages. By the third take the song begins to acquire a momentum, coming to life like the bones in Ezekiel's dream. Domingo, no longer husky or phlegmy, is now more at home with the *tessitura*, the tempo, the whole style of the piece. 'This is so exciting!' he exclaims, as he almost dances back into his booth for a fourth and fifth take, his voice seemingly acquiring greater beauty and power as he enters his eleventh and then his twelfth hour of largely uninterrupted work.

Each day the schedule is similar—*Manon Lescaut* rehearsals all morning and afternoon, sessions with Milt, Lee and the RPO in the evening. One day, Domingo is excused *Manon Lescaut* in the afternoon as he has two important press interviews to give. This would leave him with three or four free hours. 'Great,' he exclaims, and thinks about taking in the England v. Hungary football match at Wembley. The evening proves grim and rainy and he decides after all not to expose himself to the inclement British weather, but none the less turns up at the studio looking like the football fan he is in jaunty scarf and peaked cap.

Each of the Lecuona songs provides its own problems and eventual rewards. With one a phone call to Mexico is necessary to check details of the lyric. With another, Plácido finds his vocal line unconvincing and goes off quietly with the original score for twenty minutes to figure out the details for himself at a piano. One evening the orchestra record their last piece without him so that they can be dismissed early; Plácido then has as long as it takes to get his own contribution right. At the final studio session he has no plans to sing, merely to hear the balance between his pre-recorded voice and Lee's arrangements. But all evening he is visibly craving to get into the action, his fists constantly opening and shutting, his left leg periodically twitching like a horse ready for the race. By about 10.30 p.m. he can restrain himself no longer and goes into his booth to give Milt a further version of 'La Comparsa'. It is close to midnight before Teresa Cole of CBS pops a champagne bottle to toast the new album.

The *Manon Lescaut* opening has been chosen as Annual Gala night with the Queen Mother in attendance as an added attraction. Prices are pushed up to the limits to raise money for the Royal Opera House Benevolent Fund and Development Appeal but that only serves to make tickets more sought after. Every *Manon Lescaut* night is sold out, but this night is more sold out than all other nights. The inevitable huddle of hopefuls congregates in the shadows of Floral Street and when a rare spare ticket does materialize it is instantly swallowed up for four or five times its already high nominal value. It is rather like the old sidewalks of Pigalle save that the people doing the soliciting are those wishing to part with money rather than those hoping to acquire it. Round the front of the house, meanwhile, a small crowd attracts a larger crowd who crane necks and flash cameras as the ascending hierarchy of the nation's social and cultural élite turns up in its formal finery. Inside the entry foyer, young men in cutaway eighteenth-century costume take and break the larger-than-usual tickets, and the customary pre-performance sardine crush is subtly but effectively dispersed well in time for the arrival of tonight's guest of honour.

To the minute, the great crested plum-coloured Rolls rounds the corner and sails down Bow Street to the red-carpeted entrance of the Royal Opera House. The crowd, by now several hundred strong, applauds as the Queen Mother emerges, followed by her companion for the evening, the doyen of the Royal Ballet, Sir Frederick Ashton, and is greeted by the ROH chairman, Sir Claus Moser. Directly opposite, a handful of police keep an indolent eye on the proceedings, some at the curbside, the rest inside Bow Street station sitting comfortably in front of a closed-circuit television screen.

Inevitably perhaps, the performances of *Manon Lescaut* are not of quite the quality the crush for tickets might have warranted. Kiri Te Kanawa's Manon seems to some emotionally uncertain and subdued, particularly earlier in the run, while Sinopoli's indisputably dramatic reading occasionally generates almost too much electricity and sheer decibelage for the singers he is accompanying. Domingo's des Grieux is carefully paced, a little withdrawn at first, both Act I arias being held well in check, then by degrees increasingly passionate and desperate as the evening progresses, achieving the highest praise from the critics and the most vociferous plaudits from the public. To some who witness the production, it is a matter for congratulation that the Royal Opera House was able to mount so good a show at all given the much-publicized attendant difficulties. To others, Covent Garden's problems with this production are somehow symptomatic of a deeper malaise—why risk putting so much faith, not to mention money, into the occasional 'prestige' production rather than spread resources more evenly? It is easy to carp, and the production is far from perfect. But most of it looks and sounds good, and it gains in cohesion and overall impact as the run progresses.

Only the first night was officially billed as a 'gala', but a special atmosphere of excitement, and some tension, is perceptible outside and inside the house at each performance. This, for better or worse, is the big prestige production of the season, the one critics and public have been particularly awaiting and which everybody wants to see. It is also, naturally, the one above all that caused an early gleam in the eye of the National Video Corporation.

In some important ways the video and television people have something of a lucky break with the change of production even if it did not seem like it at first. The sets and many of the basic costumes from the Friedrich production by Günther Schneider–Siemssen and Aliute Meczies are attractive, fairly traditional—and already in existence. Friedrich, moreover, would re-produce a show that had worked successfully several years before and, unlike Faggioni with

Fanciulla, not try to *re*-re-produce it when the time came to work on the telecast.

In a sense that time arrives as soon as Friedrich's production rehearsals reach the main auditorium, for throughout these sessions during the final week or so before the opening the BBC's Humphrey Burton sits at a desk in the stalls watching the stage action, making notes in his copy of the score, testing the light from various angles, considering possible shots for each scene. At the dress rehearsal he has permission to shoot a video of the whole show and is able to work on this frame by frame with his colleagues as a next step in preparation for the real thing. The camera crew all come to the third performance of *Manon Lescaut,* which they greatly enjoy. This is the only time they will be able to look up at the stage, though they will spend another twenty or more working hours in the theatre over the next few days. Sunday, 15 May, is put aside for blocking. That is to say, every shot and every camera angle must be fixed during the course of what will inevitably be a very long working day. On the Monday the company will run through the whole show for Burton's seven cameras, and the performance on the Tuesday night will be filmed.

The Sunday call is from 11 a.m. (11.30 for soloists) until eight or nine at night. Everybody is expected except the orchestra— principals, chorus, scene-shifters, make-up artist, wardrobe staff, lighting technicians, assistant stage managers, production assistants, music staff—the lot. In the pit, the head of Covent Garden's Music Department, John Barker, brings down his baton and brings in one of the Royal Opera's many first-rate *répétiteurs* on the piano. Friedrich's painted drop curtain goes up revealing the square in Amiens, and Humphrey Burton watches the action on various monitor screens in his scanner van outside the ornate Floral Hall in Bow Street.

The opening scene is mostly for chorus and for the first half-hour or so the principals' parts are sung by members of the chorus placed temporarily alongside Barker in the pit. Domingo arrives, waves at a camera and says hello to Humphrey, and takes over from an excellent chorus tenor. They reach the point at which the coach arrives and out of it come Tom Allen in costume as Lescaut, Forbes Robinson in costume as Geronte—and Romayne Grigorova, Ballet Mistress of the Royal Ballet, who is standing in for Kiri, clad in blue jacket and skirt, improbably holding Manon's pre-gladstonian Gladstone bag. This scene, like every scene, has to be done again: the coach, it seems, is obscured by the chorus. Götz Friedrich, contravening every imaginable rule by smoking constantly, sorts out the stage grouping satisfactorily and goes back to his production desk at the back of the stalls. Second time around the scene already looks much better on the TV monitors, though it is still Romayne who emerges from the coach.

Plácido is wearing his dark, contemplative look this morning. In the past few days he has been signing records at a shop in Kingston-upon-Thames, appearing on BBC television talking about his video-recordings and the newly released CBS album 'My Life for a Song', taking an hour of phone calls and singing an ad-libbed duet with Howard Keel on BBC Radio Two with Radio-Personality-of-the-Year Gloria Hunniford, hopping over to Rome for a costume fitting for the *Carmen* film, and visiting his son Joe's photography exhibition in Northampton. Maybe he is tired. Or perhaps he is permanently acting the part of the shy, moody student he is portraying. In any event, his fists are clenching and opening, his leg twitching, and when he is not actually required on stage he is constantly moving around the auditorium, seeking out and talking animatedly to Sinopoli, Tooley, Friedrich, Robin Scott, whomever. Domingo is

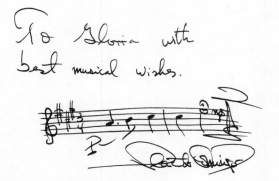

Domingo's signature in Gloria Hunniford's BBC guest book. After the initial 'P' he has written the musical equivalents of 'la', 'ci', 'do', a second 'do', 'mi' – and then the letters 'ngo'

never very good at sitting or standing still for any great length of time, but he had better get used to it as he has another eight and a half hours of it ahead of him today.

By the third time the coach arrives and delivers Romayne Lescaut it becomes clear what is bothering Plácido this morning. Where is Kiri, he wants to know? Is she coming, or what? When she does eventually arrive, she looks weak and pale and has the chorus soprano in the pit continue to sing for her while she merely goes through the moves. Kiri has not been well. The whole production has been a considerable ordeal for her, and a ten-hour television rehearsal would not exactly be her number one choice for a way of relaxing between performances.

Act I takes thirty-five minutes to perform but two and three-quarter hours to rehearse for television. Act II takes slightly longer to run, but lacking complicated chorus movements is supposedly slightly less arduous to block. Nevertheless, it poses its own problems. Should the chandelier be visible on T V or not? How many times should Forbes Robinson spin around before falling on the sofa? Do the shiny doors reflect too much light as they open and shut? At what precise point will Plácido fling Kiri's jewels away from him? Kiri looks positively regal in her Act II gown and though she is still scarcely voicing her part she begins to regain some of her accustomed bounce. She and Tom Allen play with Manon's fake jewellery, Tom placing an elaborate necklace across his stomach like a weighty chain of office and strutting around like a pompous provincial mayor. Kiri lies back on her sofa and wishes she were wearing jeans.

There is a break between acts during which assorted eighteenth-century prostitutes, naval captains, sturdy citizens of Paris and Le Havre, plus a few from twentieth-century London, converge upon the Covent Garden canteen. A man in powdered wig and jeans sips a lager, a couple of tarts wearing wide panniered skirts munch their sausage-and-two-veg and one accidentally drops a pea down her receptive cleavage. Domingo meanwhile is in his dressing-room giving a couple of interviews (one in English, one in Spanish)—and being filmed doing so under extra-bright and extra-hot lighting. On his table is a large, open, layered make-up box rather like a sewing basket, on the peg his black, yellow and brown Christian Dior dressing-gown, and on a series of hangers his costumes, act by act, from the elegant blue coat of Act I to the carefully wrought tatters of Act IV.

The opening of Act III, now as on that day three long weeks ago in the opera studio, begins with Tom and Plácido in cloaks and tricorne hats, only now they are in full costume and have the ship looming up over them and on the far side a derelict quayside house with a high, barred window. At the back is a lighthouse, the top half of which is invisible to those in the amphitheatre, and the gentle lapping water of Le Havre, which cannot be seen from most of the stalls. 'Pazienza ancor' Tom sings to Plácido with evident feeling. You have only another two or three hours to go . . .

The long day begins to seem infinite, unbounded by the normal rules of time and space, like an interminable intercontinental air flight. On stage they get as far as the procession of the prostitutes and then Humphrey Burton, just like Wolfgang Bücker in the rehearsal studio, has them go back to the beginning of the scene again. Several times they rehearse the moment at which Tom taps his sword on the high railing enclosing the little window, and each time Kiri's bedraggled face peers out wearing various Manonesque expressions. Once, as Tom repeats his gentle knocking, Kiri looks out, sneers, and says 'Sorry, luv, she's not 'ere!' She can be very funny, and her rough and ready humour helps prevent time from dragging. Humphrey has Plácido stand beneath Kiri's window for several minutes, reaching up for her hand. Various camera shots are tried as, doubtless, is the patience of the two principals. Plácido and Kiri pass the time doing a little Romeo and Juliet number, and Plácido comes out with a burst of Romeo's aria 'Ah, lève-toi, soleil' from the Gounod opera.

Four times the prostitutes have to parade across the stage, four processions of wiggling busts and buttocks, of spits and cat-fights. Four times Georgetta reveals her naked rump to the shocked crowd and soldiers. Will Humphrey show this in close-up? Plácido wonders. And four times Plácido throws all his body, though only a fraction of his voice, into the great outburst at the end of the act.

The last act acquires a degree of verisimilitude rarely matched in actual performance inasmuch as Kiri and Plácido can never be quite as weary in performance as they are now. Their cries of despair as

Manon and des Grieux, as they roll around on their desert-coloured canvas and polystyrene rocks are even more heart-wrenchingly realistic than usual, if only half-voiced. 'Thirst devours me,' Manon cries in desperation as she feels the end drawing near. 'Cut,' cries Humphrey's floor-manager, and the end is evidently not as near as she had thought. Kiri lies flat on her back, only revived by a welcome plastic cup thoughtfully provided by one of the assistant producers. Plácido and Kiri sit and sip and think what a hoot it would be if drinks always magically appeared at this very moment in the drama. The cups are put aside, Manon's agonies resume, and it is 9.15 before she dies for the third and final time.

By the end of a long and tiring day there seems little or nothing that the complex technology at Humphrey Burton's disposal would not be able to cope with. And in any case the Monday run-through (with some stand-ins for principals) should sort things out. The performance to be recorded is the fourth of five and everybody should be well and truly run in, but not yet stale, by then. And just in case of problems the BBC will issue little slips to warn seat-holders that an occasional re-take or two may be necessary at the end of an act.

One of nature's iron laws is that it is always the unforeseen that occurs. For the filmed performance, and at no other, the ball the children play with in Act I rolls rapidly down towards the orchestra, saved only by a quick-witted child near the footlights; one of the musicians making a brief stage appearance in Act II drops his bow which visibly cracks in half, while one of the extravagantly-accoutred madrigal singers inadvertantly drops, and leaves behind, her white floppy hat; and in Act IV as Plácido tries to lower Kiri gently on to the ground, the hair from her long loose wig catches almost inseparably round a button on his shirt so that for a full half minute their poignant clutchings take on an added dimension of desperation. Nevertheless, the only re-takes required are, in fact, musical ones—the chorus was not quite together when the Act I coach arrived, the celli were flat at the introduction to Kiri's Act II aria as were two of the solo strings in the opening of the Intermezzo. The audience watches bemused as Kiri, tartan shawl over her Act III whore's dress, clowns with a succession of polystyrene coffee mugs, and Tom Allen, Forbes Robinson and the chorus lounge about in front of the Act III set good-humouredly re-singing the brief excerpts Sinopoli demands. If there was anything in Plácido's performance that he or Sinopoli or Humphrey Burton were not satisfied with, it is hard to imagine what it might have been.

People often talk of this or that performance of opera as having been seen or heard by more people on earth than any other, and it is unwise to tangle with such intangible statistics. However, the Covent Garden *Manon Lescaut* is destined for a place of sorts in the record books as the first opera to be broadcast in its entirety by the World Service of the BBC. If you live in Hungary, Korea or Saudi Arabia, in Botswana, Bolivia or Bangladesh, you may hear *Manon Lescaut* on your short-wave radio. Not all in one go, as the exigencies of the world's various time zones and relay stations mean that only an act or two can be broadcast to any one area on any one occasion, but the whole opera to the whole world none the less. The BBC's Sarah Dunant interviews Domingo about *Manon Lescaut* and warns him he will be talking to millions who know nothing at all about opera. He takes the point, and describes as simply as he can the story and also the nature of his particular role. This is a wonderfully tuneful opera, he insists, and mentions some of the highlights. Then his eyes twinkle as he leans forward to Sarah. 'You know,' he says, 'the main tune in *Manon Lescaut* is really one of the most famous ever composed because, many years after it was written by Puccini, it seems to have become one of the main inspirations of—you know what?—*Star Wars!*'

Rivals

Is there anything in Domingo's astonishing career so far that he regrets? He thinks for a while and then says yes, there is. He dislikes the unnecessary backbiting, the rivalries, the jealousies to which his profession seems particularly prone. Is Domingo talking about the supposed rivalry between himself and Pavarotti? He is reluctant to talk publicly about Pavarotti except in the broadest terms and has often said that the world of opera is quite large enough for two or ten or twenty or fifty good tenors and he does not see why the press should have constantly tried to provoke a rivalry between them. However much Domingo, or Pavarotti for that matter, may dissociate himself from the idea of rivalry, however, the fact remains that for years the two of them were set up as a sort of prize fight and the result was the greatest operatic spectator sport since Callas and Tebaldi were rallying their respective troops in Milan and Rome a quarter of a century before.

The careers of the two men have curious parallels—curious because, on the face of it, the differences are far greater. Pavarotti is Italian, Domingo Spanish but raised in Mexico. Pavarotti is more than five years older than Domingo, a long time in the active life of a singer. Pavarotti's early operatic experience was in provincial Italy, graduating through places like Glyndebourne, Dublin and Australia to Covent Garden, while Domingo cut his operatic teeth in Mexico, Israel and then, via Hamburg and elsewhere in middle Europe, gained his first real recognition in the USA. Vocally, Pavarotti has a high, lyric tenor ideally suited to Bellini, Donizetti and early-to-

188

middle Verdi, and except for *Bohème* and *Tosca* has infrequently ventured outside this domain; Domingo's natural repertoire starts where Pavarotti's tends to tail off, in mid-nineteenth-century Italian opera, and includes a vast amount else besides, including most major works from the French repertoire. Pavarotti has sung some thirty-odd roles, Domingo close to eighty. Pavarotti's most famous part, certainly one that helped shoot him to fame at Covent Garden and later at the Metropolitan, was that of Tonio in Donizetti's light and frothy *La Fille du Régiment*, while Domingo's will surely continue to be one of the heaviest and most sombre roles in the whole of Italian opera, the title part in Verdi's *Otello*. Pavarotti's entire recording career has been as a virtually exclusive artist for Decca (or London as they are known in the USA), while Domingo tried exclusivity to RCA for a few years but eventually abandoned it in favour of the free-lance life.

Yet for all these differences, consider the parallels. The two men made their débuts at the New York Metropolitan Opera within a few weeks of each other in the autumn of 1968, Domingo in September in *Adriana Lecouvreur* and Pavarotti in November in *Bohème*. Within a few years each was finding his way onto the television chat shows, opening the Met or Scala season, and recording an album of popular religious songs (which both of them did in 1976). Pavarotti has sung with Frank Sinatra, Domingo with John Denver. Pavarotti was the star of the Met's biggest show, its free *Rigoletto* in Central Park in June 1980; a year later the opening night of the Met's 'Opera in the Park' featured Domingo in *Tosca*. Domingo is the father of three sons, Pavarotti of three daughters. Domingo's parents were *zarzuela* singers, his mother particularly well-known; Pavarotti's father was a talented amateur tenor who might have made a professional career if circumstances had been different. 'Domingo sings to please his mother, Pavarotti his father,' says one well-known colleague of both whose wit perhaps exceeds her sagacity. Each man has said that he does not care for those silly 'world's greatest tenor' labels that the press, particularly in America, insist on sticking on them, and each has pronounced, safely and predictably enough, that the world's greatest tenor was in any case Caruso. Each has become a multi-million-dollar international business and a household name in all parts of the developed world, while each has always maintained that his prime allegiance is to his art.

It would be nice to think that the world of opera is immune from the excessive partisanships that tend to characterize the world of spectator sport, nice but inaccurate. Pavarotti and Domingo are simply the latest victims—or beneficiaries, for they are both—of a pattern that has recurred throughout the history of the art. In his Memoirs, Beniamino Gigli recounts how 'with grim amusement' he read two advertisements that appeared in the New York press on the same day in the 1920s a few years after the death of Caruso. One said, 'Gigli, the world's greatest tenor, will sing at a benefit recital for the Italian Hospital on Sunday afternoon, February 19th.' The other said, 'Martinelli, the world's greatest tenor, will sing at a benefit recital for the Relief Society for the Aged at the Waldorf Astoria Hotel on February 26th.' Gigli's voice was one of the most effortlessly mellifluous voices the world has ever heard, Martinelli's one of the noblest. And people at the time also had the pleasure and privilege of hearing, among others, Pertile, Fleta, Crimi, Melchior and Schipa. But as Gigli added ruefully, 'Impresarios have a fondness for publicity-catching labels.'

They still have. Whoever invented the title of Pavarotti's solo album 'King of the High Cs' deserves a medal of a sort. Certainly, it was Pavarotti's glorious ease with the high notes that won him his early popular fame. But the 'King of the High Cs' implied more. There was the buccaneering image, the suggestion of swagger and swag, that played its part in endearing Pavarotti to a public not yet familiar with him. And above all, of course, there was the suggestion that he was Numero Uno, the King. It was many years before Newsweek would finally dub Domingo on its cover the 'King of the Opera'.

Once Pavarotti had conquered the American public he made the New York Metropolitan his base. He sang elsewhere, of course, but the Met was 'home'. He also hired as his agent the astute, some would say ruthless, Herbert Breslin. Breslin had had a lot of experience managing some of the biggest stars and Pavarotti willingly put himself into his hands. The results soon became apparent. Pavarotti was everywhere. In addition to opera appearances he was also giving solo recitals all over the United States and elsewhere. Gradually a public image took shape. American audiences got used to seeing his burly shape emerge on to the concert platform, arms raised in the style of a prizefighter or the victorious General de Gaulle, his large fluttering white handkerchief—'my security blanket' Pavarotti called it—held in one hand. Within a few years Pavarotti was also appearing on all the big television chat shows in the USA and on the cover of the big-circulation weeklies, riding a horse at the head of New York's Columbus Day Parade, advertising American Express cards on TV or Blackglama Furs, singing at the Academy Award ceremony, pictured in the glossies sweeping up the snow in the winter or playing tennis with John McEnroe in the summer.

Pavarotti stuck with Breslin and as a recording artist stayed with Decca/London. His fidelity paid off. To him and to them. 'Today,' one bitter-sweet Pavarotti-watcher told me, 'Luciano has only to burp and Decca would record it—and they would sell a million copies!'

Domingo's career has been different. In one sense he has done less than Pavarotti in that he does not give frequent concerts. But the amount of operatic work Domingo has taken on puts virtually everyone else's efforts into the shade. His repertoire is larger than any other major recent tenor except perhaps Nicolai Gedda, and instead of tying himself primarily to one opera house or even country Domingo has continued incessantly to water most of his favourite patches virtually every year, seeming to attempt the herculean task of letting all his admirers wherever opera is produced see him sooner or later in almost all his major roles.

Like Pavarotti, Domingo has learnt the publicity value of appearing on television chat shows, of allowing his name and face to be used for advertising commercial products, of doing what the publicity people call 'PAs' or Public Appearances signing records and photos, and of starring in television variety specials. Pavarotti and Domingo may both protest that they dislike the rivalry that has been set up between them but it strains credulity to be told that neither has deliberately contributed to it. Domingo's agents can list a string of 'coincidences' that suggest that many of the tactics employed in this particular fight would not pass muster in the boxing ring: several times, for example, Domingo opened in an important new production only to find that some glossy publication in the same city just happened to be running a major feature on Pavarotti at that very moment. On one occasion the programmes for a Domingo perform-ance contained a large ad for Pavarotti's record company provo-catively announcing their man to be 'the world's greatest tenor'. Domingo, normally a man to keep his cool, insisted that the offending ad be removed from the programmes or he would refuse to sing. It was removed.

Publicity is, or should be, a means to various ends. Like enabling the public to know when something is available to them, and making more money for the product publicized. The more publicized Pavarotti became, the more he could charge for his concerts and opera performances, and the more copies of his records Decca/ London could sell. And if the supposed rivalry with Domingo for top place in the global tenor stakes kept his name before the public —particularly the wealthy, record-buying American public—so much the better. It would do him more good than it would Domingo, because it was from the Pavarotti camp that the pre-emptive strikes always seemed to emanate and Domingo either had to be seen to acquiesce in the statement that Pavarotti was Numero Uno or else to counterattack after the initial deed was done and incur the inevitable accusation of sour grapes. Furthermore, the more brazen publicity statements about Pavarotti tended to appear in his chosen patch, the rich and publicity-conscious USA, whereas Domingo tended to spend three-quarters of his time on his travels through the less materially-and-publicity-minded parts of the musical world.

Eventually Domingo began to fight back. It was not a conscious decision nor one reached at a single, blinding moment of rage or truth. Rather, it was a combination of converging decisions all of which in themselves had to do with other things. As the Barcelona Liceo went through a rocky passage, for instance, and Domingo found himself turning down opportunities of singing there, it made sense to move the principal family home, at least for the time being, back from Barcelona to New York. At about the same time, Milton Okun's pursuit of Domingo began to show signs of success and Domingo was soon launched on his new career as a popular singer of primarily American songs. Meanwhile, Domingo had recently switched publicity agents in both London and New York and in both cities was soon the recipient of a great deal of favourable media attention. For these and other reasons, Domingo found himself in these years spending more time than before in that very fulcrum of the 'Pavarotti–Domingo' controversy, New York.

The Domingo counterattack was swift, powerful, effective—and at first perhaps overdone. Domingo now feels he may have over-reacted when, for instance, Kurt Herbert Adler, boss of the San Francisco Opera, said in public that he thought Pavarotti the greatest tenor in the world and Domingo refused for a time to sing there. The incident with the Pavarotti ads in the Domingo programmes, similarly, produced anger in Domingo which was understandable at the time but which he now feels it might have been wiser to restrain. But the more positive aspects—the visible presence in New York including a growing number of performances at the Met, the pop records, the TV appearances and Rolex watch ads—mostly did Domingo a power of good and led to a self-perpetuating snowball of favourable publicity that still continues. Events, furthermore, seemed to play into Domingo's hands as Pavarotti received a poor reception for some performances during this period and cancelled others, and made a much-heralded but little-praised commercial movie called *Yes Giorgio!*

Both men were frequently featured in the glossy magazines and on television, with variable results. Pavarotti did an embarrassing TV show in which sundry famous friends passed through his happy home in Modena; Domingo took on a live TV homage to Caruso in which he was clearly nervous and below his best. The catalogue of what were essentially publicity appearances by Domingo at this time lengthened considerably, and not only in the USA. He managed to fly into Paris, for example, at considerable personal inconvenience, on the morning of President Mitterrand's inauguration, bone up on the words of the 'Marseillaise', and later in the day give a splendid account of the anthem ('with all the fire of a committed socialist!' said one incredulous bystander) to tens of thousands of spectators and of course countless millions of televiewers. It is hard to resist opportunities like this when they come your way, the chance of being fêted by President Mitterrand, the Pope or the Queen Mother, or watched by

millions as you hand out Oscars on worldwide TV, play football with
Maximilian Schell, Kevin Keegan or Hans Krankl, or exchange
wisecracks and songs with Carol Burnett or Miss Piggy. All publicity
is said to be good publicity and both Pavarotti and Domingo have
succeeded, as perhaps no other opera singer has since Callas, in
becoming household names. Some observers feel they have also paid
a price, that each has sometimes courted publicity for its own sake or
to upstage the other and that, in any case, these activities are not
consistent with the dignity required of a serious artist.

Perhaps. But a more fundamental question is whether all these
activities have eaten into the artistic capacities of the two men. Have
the operatic performances suffered? Has the publicity served the art or
vice versa? Certainly, both men have sometimes squeezed publicity
appearances into already overcrowded calendars, and as a result had
to perform on one side of the Atlantic too soon after arriving from the
other. Pavarotti's much-publicized vocal and personal problems in
the early 1980s were attributed by some knowing critics to the
inexorable rule that the higher you believe you can fly the harder you
will inevitably fall. But one must also acknowledge, for example, the
courage with which Pavarotti agreed to step out of his normal
repertoire and sing, extremely well, Mozart's *Idomeneo* at the Met.
Domingo, too, after twice turning down the opportunity of recording
the difficult part of Aeneas in Berlioz' *Les Troyens*, finally accepted
the challenge by agreeing to do the role on stage at the opening of the
Met's Centennial season. Both men are blessed with powerful
constitutions and nerves of steel, quite apart from their formidable
artistic capacities.

But it is the artist who ultimately counts. Certainly, it is in the
opera house that Domingo would ultimately want to be judged, as
Hoffmann, José, Otello, Cavaradossi, Dick Johnson, des Grieux and
the rest. If he did not continue to portray these characters to his own
very exacting standards, he would not consider he warranted the kind
of publicity he now commands wherever he goes. And in this he is
surely right. When his powers as an operatic performer begin to
wane, as they inevitably will, one might legitimately ask how far
Domingo's extra-curricular activities have taken their toll, or
whether, on the contrary, they might even have helped sustain the

impetus of his artistic energy. But at the moment the question is purely academic, for the powers are, as I write, largely unimpaired and, in their combination, probably unparalleled.

ACT IV
<u>El Domingo</u>

Tosca in Barcelona

Think of all the operas that, between them, more or less form the
staple repertoire of the world's opera houses, perhaps the top twenty-
five or thirty. Take away all those that mostly take place in the country
from which the composer came. Then list those remaining by
country of location. I would be surprised if this list were not topped by
Spain. Consider the masterpieces that have been set there: *Le Nozze
di Figaro, Don Giovanni, Fidelio, Il Barbiere di Siviglia, Il
Trovatore, Don Carlos, La Forza del Destino*, and of course that most
quintessentially Spanish of all operas, *Carmen*. 'Spain the home of
opera?' scoffed a friend, pointing out easily enough that most opera
houses go years, decades, without mounting a work by any of Spain's
thimbleful of opera composers. But the number of works located in
Spain gives at least a cosmetic validity to the claim.

More substantially, so does the number of outstanding Spanish
opera singers who have bestrode the international operatic stage in
recent decades. To take just the tenors, there have been not only
Domingo but also Alfredo Kraus, José Carreras, Jaime (or 'Giacomo')
Aragall and Dalmacio González. When you add, among the
women, such resounding names as Victoria de los Angeles, Pilar
Lorengar, Montserrat Caballé and Teresa Berganza, it is clear that
Spain has contributed mightily to the world's enjoyment of opera in
our time.

Discuss all this in Barcelona, discuss almost any aspect of music or
art or literature in Barcelona, and you will soon be told that what you
are talking about is primarily not a Spanish but a Catalan

phenomenon. Carreras is a Catalan. So is Aragall. Dalmacio González used to work on the Barcelona metro system until his singing career took precedence. De los Angeles and Caballé are Catalans. And if any doubt should remain about the operatic eminence of Catalonia, a quick tour of Spain's opera houses would confirm that by every imaginable standard the country's principal operatic standard-bearer is the Barcelona theatre known to the world as the Liceo, but to Catalans, proud of their newly reactivated right to use their own language, as the Gran Teatre del Liceu.

Domingo is one of the few major Spanish figures in the operatic world who is not a Catalan. He was born in Madrid and raised in Mexico, while his parents were popular *zarzuela* artists—a form of musical entertainment native to Castile and central Spain rather than Catalonia. A man of essentially cosmopolitan tastes and interests, Domingo has never made any secret of his background or pretended to bogus local roots or tastes. It is, on the other hand, a matter of historical fact that he and his family long maintained their principal home in Barcelona and he is even on record in a Madrid newspaper as claiming the Barcelona Club de Futbol his favourite soccer team. Thus, Domingo has over the years become something of a Catalan by adoption and has sung frequently at the Liceo ever since his début there in 1966.

The casual visitor to Barcelona may be surprised to hear that there is an opera house in the city at all, let alone the principal one in Spain. Not that the Liceo has anything less than a superbly central position, fronting right on to Barcelona's busiest and most popular streets, the mile-long Ramblas. But the Ramblas contain a great many other and more obvious features, from the big banks, the American hamburger joints, and the Mercado de San José near the top just off the huge Plaça de Catalunya, down to the whores, the bullring and the port overlooked by Christopher Columbus on his pedestal at the bottom. The Ramblas are in fact a succession of wide, straight shopping streets divided in the middle. The broad central reserve contains a plethora of open-air cafés, sellers of exotic birds and beasts, pavement artists, actors and jugglers and, once the evenings begin to lengthen, half the population of Catalonia. Strolling up and down the Ramblas is a pastime verging on an obsession.

You walk along the Ramblas before dinner to work up an appetite, after dinner to help digest your meal.

In the lower part of the Ramblas, the periodic turn-offs to the left as you face the port take you into the exotic maze of narrow lanes that form Barcelona's ancient Barrio Gótico, the core of what remains of mediaeval Barcelona. Halfway down the Ramblas to the right is a tiny street called the Carrer de St Pau, one of the many in this district in which cafés offering 'boccadillos' nestle intimately with a sex shop here, a jewellery or jeans shop blaring hot rock there. St Pau is a half-turn really, a Y-fork, and it intersects the adjacent building sharply. The turning is easy to miss, and the modestly-fronted building thus diagonally foreshortened even easier. And yet this is one of the oldest, grandest and, inside, one of the biggest opera houses in Europe.

If you could walk down past the Liceo without noticing you were passing an opera house, there is no mistake once you enter. You may possibly think that the cool, deep foyer with the checker-board tiled floor through the rich blue velvet drapes belongs to some government building, though the fact that the guardians at the doorway look friendly, wear dark blue jackets emblazoned with an ornate letter 'L' and not military uniforms, and carry no visible guns at their hips should dispel that thought. The foyer contains elaborate clusters of lamps and the walls are hung with the palest of blue silk. Go up the carpeted central staircase, or one of the shallower ones on either side, and you reach further foyers, the precincts of what begins to materialize as a huge and elaborately ornate amphitheatre. You do not approach the auditorium directly from the back as with virtually every other opera house, nor even at a symmetrical right angle but, somewhat disorientingly, from roughly the back left-hand corner. For this monumental nineteenth-century opera house, some think the grandest of them all, had to be squeezed by its original architects to fit the uncomfortable place provided for it by Barcelona's already existing street plan. If you fit a huge horseshoe-shaped opera house into a V-shaped street corner, there is a geometric inevitability to the odd angle at which patrons will have to enter.

The Barcelona Liceo is in the tradition of the great nineteenth-century opera houses, first built on monastic land confiscated by the government in the late 1840s, then reconstructed after a catastrophic fire fourteen years later. It dates, therefore, from very roughly the same era as the San Carlo in Naples and London's Covent Garden, is a couple of generations younger than La Scala, a couple of decades older than Bayreuth or the original New York Met. Like all these except Bayreuth, it is built in a great oval, and contains all the familiar features of good, reverberant acoustics and, from a sizeable number of seats, poor sight-lines. The Liceo must be one of the most ornate of all houses. There is no square foot of wall or ceiling that does not contain some degree of embellishment or art work, and the man who painted the elaborate ceiling would surely, if alive today in the age of electricity, ask the management to keep the auditorium lamps down a watt or two, not only to reduce the oppressive heat but also so that patrons could see through the radiance of the lighting more clearly to his creations far above.

If the physicality of the Liceo auditorium speaks evocatively of former times, there are further reminders. Within what one must, to use an inappropriate twentieth-centurism, call the Liceo complex, are also housed not only the Barcelona Conservatoire of Music, but also the ornate and exclusive Liceo Club. You do not have to be a music lover to join. All that is required is that you be rich enough to afford membership, influential and popular enough with your peers to be nominated and backed—and a gentleman. No ladies need apply. The Club consists of a series of elaborate late-nineteenth-century rooms decorated in the modernist Catalan style made famous by Gaudí, and contains among other exquisite features a set of delicate wall-panel paintings by Ramon Casas. It is as though the Athenaeum were a Siamese twin of Covent Garden, or Washington's Century Club an annex of the New York Met.

Catalonia's sense of separateness from the rest of Spain has never disappeared despite periodic attempts to stamp it out. With the passing of Franco in 1975, it became possible once again for the proud spirit of Catalonia to rise from its network of subterranean cultural and political aspirations. Soon the democratic government in Madrid agreed to a degree of Catalan self-rule with the establishment of a new provincial 'Generalitat'; Catalan became an official language and some legislative autonomy was granted. The

Generalitat of Catalonia was from the outset anxious to promote Catalan art and culture and a series of events was put in train, one of the eventual objects of which was to put regular opera of high quality back on the map in Barcelona.

It was only in 1980 after the eventual death of the Liceo's long-serving intendant that a new consortium was set up representing in equal shares the City of Barcelona, the Generalitat of Catalonia and the owners of the Liceo. At the head of the new consortium was Luis Portabella, founder of the city's principal music-giving organization 'Pro Musica'. As soon as Portabella's appointment was confirmed and the new regime installed, the consortium got down to the job of getting Barcelona's opera onto a proper footing. The Liceo orchestra and chorus would be radically overhauled and realistic fees offered not just to visiting singers but also to producers, designers, conductors and so on. The consortium would put on an annual season of perhaps thirteen or fourteen works, most in productions borrowed from one or the other of Europe's leading opera houses, each presented with top soloists for three or four performances. Then, in May and June, after a brief respite, there would be a short 'Festival' promoted by 'Pro Musica' in which, with luck, the operatic heights would be scaled.

The 1983 spring Festival of Opera, the third under the new regime, is to consist of two Italian productions, *Il Trovatore* and *Tosca*, both borrowed from La Scala, and, in the centenary year of the death of Wagner, *Tannhäuser* from Vienna and *Parsifal* from Hamburg. The three *Tosca* performances are fixed for late May and will star Plácido Domingo, Carol Neblett and Silvano Carroli—all under the baton of Romano Gandolfi, chorus-master of La Scala, and permanent-conductor-elect at the Liceo.

For some years in the late 1970s, Domingo's name was absent from the roster at the Liceo. Some said this was because Liceo standards were low and Domingo did not wish to appear in inferior productions. Others suggested darkly that he would not sing there unless offered his normal full fee—or that he had been accepting a cut-price fee only to discover that the management were paying a higher sum to another tenor. Whatever the reason, several years went by without Domingo singing at the Liceo. Under the new con-sortium, however, with the promise henceforth of regular seasons of high-quality opera, Domingo signed up again. In 1982 he was down to sing a pair of *Bohèmes*—in between which Carreras was booked to do a performance of the same opera. The pressure for tickets for the Domingo performances was tremendous, lubricated, doubtless, by the enormous popularity in Spain of his recently released album of tangos. People fought for places in the queue for inexpensive tickets. When the time came, however, Domingo appeared to rush in and out of town for his appearances—he was filming *La Traviata* elsewhere at the time—and was not at his best, while Carreras, who had previously been off form but on this occasion sang superbly, undoubtedly won most of the available laurels. Carreras was widely regarded, like Caballé, as a local hero, a Catalan loyal to his origins who, although an international star, found time to give of his best in his homeland. When Domingo returned to the Liceo in 1983, therefore, it was with the feeling that he had some leeway to make up, a slightly bitter taste to exorcize, and he was determined to throw himself into his three *Tosca* performances with especial gusto.

Tosca is one of the tiny handful of maybe a dozen or fifteen works that no opera house on earth can long be without; a success with audiences everywhere, a superb opera for the performers to sing, and relatively inexpensive to mount. To some with fastidious tastes, *Tosca* is too melodramatic, perhaps even the 'shabby little shocker' one critic once called it. Certainly Puccini's setting of Sardou's play, a famous vehicle for Sarah Bernhardt, is so much larger than life that it can be difficult truly to identify and to smile and suffer with the characters, to get under the skin of the painter Mario Cavaradossi and his mistress, the singer Floria Tosca, or really to hate the irredeemably villainous chief of police, the Baron Scarpia. But there is more to this work than mere melodrama. First produced in 1900, the action takes place in Rome a century earlier during the Napoleonic wars. Thus, Cavaradossi is not only an artist but a free-thinking liberal believing in the Rights of Man, while Scarpia, a natural autocrat of the most bloodthirsty kind, inevitably lusts after Cavaradossi's mistress. The lady at the centre of this politico-sexual tug of war, Tosca, is the reigning diva of Rome, impulsive, passionate, loving and hating individuals rather than causes, wholeheartedly, if jealously, devoted to her painter, prepared to run every risk for life and love. At its simplest, this is the story of a woman who becomes the tangible sexual prize in a power struggle. The two men stand at opposite corners of the political spectrum and Tosca, possessed by the one and coveted by the other, is the prize. Neither wins. Or, rather, all three are losers. Scarpia has Cavaradossi tortured and gives orders for him to be shot, and is himself stabbed to death by Tosca who, in the last minutes of the opera, flings herself off the battlements of Rome's Castel Sant'Angelo.

Musically as well as dramatically, *Tosca* makes a direct appeal with its powerful, surging tunes, its passionate love music, the great chords representing the evil Scarpia, and three of the most famous arias ever written, one for the soprano and two for the tenor, one in each of the opera's three acts. For the performers it is good to sing and quite short. Scarpia dies at the end of Act II while Cavaradossi has a total of perhaps twenty minutes or so of music to sing. The chorus is required only briefly and most members can go home after Act I. The only unusual musical features in *Tosca* are the various bells and the off-stage shepherd boy at the beginning of Act III. Blood and guts, sex, politics, violent death—and wave after wave of powerful and immediately appealing music—*Tosca* has them all. Little wonder that it is one of the most frequently produced and widely attended of all operatic works. Little wonder, too, that the role of Cavaradossi is one in which all the great tenors have excelled—Caruso and Gigli and, in our own day, Pavarotti, Aragall, Carreras and Domingo. It is the role Domingo has sung more often than any other.

This production, like most performed at the Liceo, is borrowed, in this case from La Scala, where it was first mounted in 1979, with Domingo as Cavaradossi. Produced by Nicola Benois and designed by Piero Faggioni it made a great impression when it first appeared. Imported productions can have drawbacks—one of the Liceo's biggest headaches during the 1983 Opera Festival is that the production to follow *Tosca*, the Vienna *Tannhäuser*, has to be given without sets as the trucks transporting these across Europe have been immobilized by anti-Spanish demonstrations by French agricultural workers north of the Pyrenees. There are artistic problems that can arise with imported productions, too, designs or lighting plans that fit the conventions acceptable to one audience and not to another.

Moreover, the Liceo system scarcely ever admits of a revival, so if you happen to miss the Scala *Tosca* or the Hamburg *Parsifal* or whatever it may be, you are unlikely to get another chance to see it. And while many of the principals are often international celebrities already familiar with their parts, think of the locally recruited chorus, who have to learn ten or more different operas in a season for a mere three performances of each. Some operas always have to be included precisely because they do *not* have large chorus parts. Still, it is not a bad system, enables the subscribing public at least to savour a lot of operas and some of the world's finest singers and productions, and has certainly helped to return Barcelona's Gran Teatro del Liceo closer to the centre of the operatic map.

The Scala *Tosca*, as you might expect of one designed by Faggioni, looks superb. Faggioni himself has been in Barcelona to supervise the production, and it shows his imaginative hand throughout. The large gestures are there: the removal of a giant sail-like cloth and the folding back of Cavaradossi's huge easel and its supporting scaffolding to reveal the vast church interior with real incense—you could smell it at the back of the auditorium—towards the end of Act I; the sight of Cavaradossi being carried on bodily by his sepulchral and long-shadowed torturers in Act II as though they were pall-bearers and he already dead. Nor were the small details ignored. Scarpia loses Tosca's hand in Act I as he tries to kiss it—but gets it back with alacrity as he then offers her the Attavanti fan; the sheer height from which Tosca leaps to her death in the last act is simply but magnificently suggested by a carefully placed cut-out of the upper part of the dome of St Peter's.

Domingo must surely have sung this opera more often than anyone else alive, but there is a wonderful freshness of response in his performances. When he sings the semitone 'lift' in the Act I love duet without pausing for breath at the words *'occhio all'amor soave'* it is as though he had been carried away by the ardour of the moment, while in Act II his feverish grabbing and holding aloft of a tattered tricolor as he gathers his remaining strength for a stupendous 'Vittoria! Vittoria!' causes a perceptible tremor of emotion throughout the packed Liceo audience. Whatever Domingo's faults a year ago, he can do no wrong now. In Act III, the applause after 'E lucevan le stelle' bursts like a thunderclap, graduates into a sustained roar, and eventually metamorphoses into a regular clap-clap-clap-clap-clap that is only brought to an end, after a full three minutes, when Gandolfi points to the clarinet to begin the aria again.

All three performances were received with similar rapture. One or two of the local critics, however, suggested after the first night that Cavaradossi is an 'easy' role for the tenor and that much of Domingo's applause came because of who he is rather than how he sang. This stung Domingo into giving a press interview in which he riposted that he would return to sing in Barcelona 'for as long as the public wish me to do so'.

Tosca, a three-acter, is not long as operas go, and is usually over, intervals and all, in three hours or so. At the Liceo it took four, partly because of the encore in Act III, and partly because Faggioni's tremendous sets took forty minutes or more to change. The performances began at 9 p.m. At midnight Act III was being set. By about 12.30 a.m. the audience was wallowing in an orgy of applause after the first version of 'E lucevan le stelle', and the final curtain went down at about 12.45 a.m. The applause each night was tumultuous. Well after one o'clock, Domingo was embracing his wife, his parents, his friends on the Liceo stage behind the curtain as the bravos continued. 'Come on, Cah-rol,' he would call cheerily to his co-star as he and Neblett went out for yet another call, and then in Italian to Carroli's wife, 'Can you get Silvano?' Eventually, Silvano, long since 'dead' in his role of Scarpia, and now dressed in a lounge suit, would emerge from his dressing-room and join Plácido and Carol as the excited rump of the night's vast audience got a chance of hurling yet one more burst of applause, of flowers, of whoops of delight. Thirty or forty minutes later still, after the auditorium had been cleared and the safety curtain lowered for the night, Domingo, showered and changed, would descend into the theatre foyer to a further burst of applause and sign his way through yet another throng of admirers, writing his name on this person's programme, that person's record, somebody else's publicity photo of him. The crush was unpleasant and there was no semblance of an orderly line. The time was 2 a.m., 2.30 perhaps. Never mind. Every customer would be served. Indeed, there was the added bonus that he would probably shorten his signature and merely write his first name for them. He does this to save time and his writing wrist, but recipients can take it as a sign of personal friendliness if they wish. In the shadows of the foyer patiently sat his wife, his parents, his uncle, one of his sons, his agents, his friends. By his side, feeding photos to him to sign, discreetly taking the gifts that were proffered, looking for signs of trouble to forestall, stood the infinitely patient and carefully inconspicuous figure of Paul Garner.

Domingo was in exuberant mood on these occasions. On the night of the final performance of *Tosca* he agreed to go on to a party thrown by friends of long standing. Next morning he had to make a flying visit to Ronda in Andalusia in the south of Spain to check on the house he would be occupying during the forthcoming summer of filming there—and then back that evening to Madrid. Since he would get no sleep for a day or two anyway, he said agreeably to his hosts, why not pass a few hours in congenial company . . .

Fanciulla in Madrid

Much of Madrid consists of huge, wide, tree-lined boulevards, something in the style of Paris, dominated by monumental late-nineteenth-century architecture. The Old City, however, still largely preserved from the ravages of time and warfare, with its narrow cobbled streets, dark stand-up bars and occasional regal squares, nestles comfortably in the mile or two between the colossal Palacio Real to the west and the equally massive but more welcoming Retiro Park to the east. If you stroll through the leafy Retiro eastwards away from the centre of town, up past the boating lake and out on the far side, you will find yourself in the broad, divided Calle de Ibiza, with its cafés, its newspaper stands and, at the far end, a big modern medical complex. The elderly sit on benches under the trees in the central reserve just as they did forty years ago, while the youngsters, now as then, play their precarious games in and out of doorways, darting this side and that of the divided avenue. The Domingos lived at number 34, up in the apartment block on the corner of the Calle

Fernan de Gonzalez. Since 1978, that apartment block has proudly displayed a large marble plaque proclaiming the site to have been the birthplace of 'El Tenor Plácido Domingo'. Not many people get a birthplace plaque in their native city while they are alive, much less when they are only thirty-seven years old. Domingo's celebrity in Madrid is immense. In June 1983 he is in town for a run of performances of Puccini's *La Fanciulla del West* at the Teatro de la Zarzuela, and everywhere he goes he is watched and pursued by crowds of admirers.

Some opera houses are conspicuous spots on the map of their cities and some have entire districts or at least metro stations named after them. In Madrid, however, a taxi or metro ride to 'Opera' may land you where you had not intended to go. The elegant Teatro Real, across from the majestic Royal Palace, has housed Madrid's Conservatoire of Music and periodic symphony concerts, but no opera has been staged there since the 1920s, though there are constant rumours that the place is going to be refurbished. If it is opera you want, then it is to the 'Teatro de la Zarzuela' that you should direct your taxi-driver. He may not know the place. *Zarzuela*, after all, the quintessentially Spanish form of light opera, is not everybody's favourite entertainment these days, and this particular theatre is in a tiny, sleepy side street, the Calle de Jovellanos, that links two only very slightly less sleepy side streets, the cross-bar in a rather obscure letter 'H'.

If the streets alongside the Teatro de la Zarzuela are obscure, its position in Madrid is not. For a start, the theatre is just behind the Cortes, the Spanish parliament building. The theatre forms the central point, moreover, of a triangle formed by three of Madrid's most fashionable thoroughfares: the Calle de Alcala, the Carrera de San Jeronimo, and the Paseo del Prado. Look at the map of Madrid and find its most spacious landmarks. If you draw a line between the Puerta del Sol, the Plaza Canovas del Castillo and the huge Cibeles fountain you will find you have precisely enclosed the spot in which the Teatro de la Zarzuela nestles, known by relatively few in Madrid, yet close to everyone and everything.

The Teatro de la Zarzuela is an attractive house, built in characteristic nineteenth-century horseshoe-and-chandelier style, perfectly adequate for the popular musicals it has mostly staged though far less well equipped for opera. Plácido Domingo first sang here in a 1970 production of *La Gioconda* and has put time by to sing here every year since. In the 1930s and 1940s his parents used to sing *zarzuela* in this theatre. They always get special pleasure from their son's Madrid appearances and are here in June 1983 to watch him rehearse and perform *Fanciulla*.

Fanciulla is the seventh of this year's eight opera productions at the Teatro de la Zarzuela, sandwiched between *Falstaff*, with Juan Pons, and *Semiramide*, starring Caballé. The entire season is run under the auspices of the Spanish Ministry of Culture, financed by them, the theatre staff appointees of the Ministry. To its credit, the theatre management has regularly made a point of trying to commission young producers and designers for some productions, and the team in charge of *Fanciulla*, for example, producer Emilio Sagi and his designer Julio Galan, are an exceptionally talented young pair who look barely out of college—'I am thirty-four,' says the slim, moustachioed Emilio, 'but I think Plácido thinks I am even younger!' It was not until the summer of 1982 that it was agreed to put *Fanciulla* into the 1983 schedule, and only then that Emilio, who had just won his spurs with an excellent *Don Pasquale*, was invited to direct.

Emilio and Julio are both from Oviedo in the north of Spain and neither was brought up on a regular diet of top-class opera. Emilio had studied in London and been to Covent Garden a few times, but this new commission set his head spinning. He had seen the opera once before at Covent Garden in 1977 and made a point of visiting London in November 1982 to see the Faggioni production again and to discuss the opera with Domingo. A few minutes of small talk established that Emilio's uncle had sung *zarzuela* with Plácido's parents. A bond was set up immediately. Domingo advised Emilio to get to know the text inside out, and to prepare a realistic show and not to attempt anything too symbolic or avant-garde. There are operas that can benefit from imaginative and unusual production, others that require to be taken realistically. *Fanciulla*, said Plácido, comes pretty firmly under this second category.

The Teatro de la Zarzuela is not Covent Garden and there was no way Emilio Sagi could or would want to emulate the lavish complexity of the Faggioni production. *Fanciulla*, after all, is about simple people living an impecunious existence and Emilio felt it required a production in which their physical and emotional environment, too, was simple, bold and clear. Emilio set to work with a will, familiarized himself thoroughly with all aspects of the opera, and, with plenty of leeway, discussed the details with Julio.

In any opera production, a great deal has to be left to the last few days. It is only when sets and soloists, orchestra, chorus and costumes all come together that you can begin to see whether things will really work out. This is especially true in a house like the Teatro de la Zarzuela which only has space for one opera production at a time. While Plácido was singing *Tosca* in Barcelona, Emilio and Julio were poised to go, the initial designs long since in the hands of the workshop building the sets. *Falstaff* had its successful run of four performances and then, the following day, the Fat Man moved out and the Girl of the Golden West began to move in.

And did not fit. A frantic five days remain and Emilio, Julio and their technical staff work round the clock to get the pieces of scenery to fit each other and the theatre stage. As for the theatre orchestra, fresh from *Falstaff*, they now try to come to grips with Puccini's far more loosely-reined, almost impressionistic score under the also somewhat loosely-reined direction of Emerson Buckley, for many years director of the Miami Opera. The elderly, goateed Maestro is given to dressing in memorable outfits; at rehearsal he favours a succession of opera-imprinted T-shirts (the 'Turandot' rehearsal went better than the 'Mefistofele'), while for more formal wear he inclines towards Colonel Sanders-type string ties. Each afternoon and evening during the rehearsals for *Fanciulla*, if you had happened to wander in through the stage door of the Teatro de la Zarzuela, along a grubby corridor covered with bits of Christmas trees and chunks of varnished logs, and into the darkened theatre, you would have seen a group of amiable Spaniards, plus the odd Italian, sitting around on a semi-circle of chairs on the edge of the stage surrounded by increasingly cohesive increments of nineteenth-century California, being taken through their paces. On and at the back of the stage, more logs are being set in place, varnished, polished, painted with snow. A large plywood wall, carefully marked 'FANCHULA' (if the opera were spelt correctly, the Spanish stage hands might call it 'Fanthyulya'), is turned slowly round during one rehearsal to reveal the interior of Minnie's hut. And, day by day, the men in the semi-circle of chairs imperceptibly take on something of the mien of the characters they are playing. Even Plácido Domingo, usually dressed carefully in shirt and tie, appears towards the end of the rehearsal period wearing a cutaway leather jacket.

Fifteen men and a girl. That's the alternative title to this piece, someone suggests. There are two girls, actually, the second being Minnie's Indian servant who appears briefly in Act II. But there is one main girl, *the* Girl of the Golden West after whom the opera is named. In this production the Girl is Marilyn Zschau. We last met her briefly when she sang Minnie in the Covent Garden production in November 1982 before Carol Neblett's return. Marilyn is one of those tough, beautiful if slightly battle-worn Americans like Carol Neblett who are ideal for the role. With her attractive, unconventional pale blue denim pantsuit or white smock over sandals and her thick shock of blonde-red hair, Marilyn is the very antithesis of the traditional prima donna. Furs, jewels and hairdos? Yes, if necessary. But she is happier lying on a sofa reading a book on Gestalt therapy, or going off on a cycling or back-packing holiday. Many opera singers are blessed with generously proportioned mouths, but few permit themselves to laugh as uproariously as Marilyn does with hers, and when she laughs her wide, translucent, almond-shaped eyes laugh as well. This is a giving, open person who enjoys life, gives as much as she gets from it, and throws herself with full gusto into whatever part life or art require of her.

Which is just as well when you consider the enormous demands of the role of Minnie. Minnie has to scale the musical heights, sound as tender as Mimì and as indomitable as Turandot, she is on stage for a lot of the opera and, as Marilyn puts it, there's an awful lot of running about to do. You do not just stand there and sing, as a Turandot can usually do; every phrase you sing requires visible motivation and appropriate action while everybody else's requires a reaction. If you cannot dominate the stage with the wide range of emotions and moods the part requires—authority, piety, tenderness, ruthless resolution—*and* sing loud and long and beautifully all evening, do not take on Minnie. You will lose.

Marilyn Zschau knows this. Vocally, she may not have the most purely mellifluous soprano voice in the world or, for that matter, the richest chest notes. But she possesses a secure instrument right through its large tonal and dynamic range and, so essential in some of the great exposed moments in this opera, an especially ringing top. Dramatically, she does not stint and puts everything she knows into each action, each move. For the Madrid *Fanciulla* she has to break a bottle to stave off the advances of Sheriff Rance, played by Ettore Nova. At one rehearsal she does this with such vigour that pieces of glass scatter over the orchestra and the music scudders to an angry halt. A week before *Fanciulla* opened she bruised her thigh in a minor cycling accident in Madrid on her new folding bicycle, and there is no doubt that people who throw themselves so vehemently into all they do can sometimes have accidents. No doubt either that any opera house with a Marilyn Zschau on stage will not be dull for long.

Rehearsals are intense and multi-purpose. There is no time or space in this house for separate musical and production rehearsals. As Emerson Buckley works through the score each day with his orchestra and singers, Emilio Sagi gradually gets the cast to act through the motions of the production—while the hardware gets sawed, planed, hammered, nailed and painted behind them. Singers are normally averse to the presence of sawdust around them, but there is simply no margin for such sensitivities here. There is a big job to do, and it must be done with as much zeal, good humour and sheer professionalism as everyone has at his or her command.

Domingo, back from his flying trip to Ronda and installed in Madrid's Ritz Hotel, walks his way through things fairly easily. When he is not himself singing, he is chatting to everyone in the cast, giving Marilyn a kiss, asking Emilio how things are coming along, edging his way across the darkened auditorium to chat with his parents or his uncle. He saves his singing voice, but rarely seems to rest his speaking voice for long. The other soloists sing out much of the time, even Marilyn with her big, open top notes. She acts her part to the limit that any given stage of rehearsal permits. At one point, when they reach Minnie's dramatic Act III entry, Marilyn comes running on in her blue pantsuit and tasselled scarf brandishing a gun at the others so realistically that some of them, while grinning at her splendid Calamity Jane act, instinctively duck for cover. This is after all the Broken Bottle girl, the lady who is said to be accident prone . . .

Two days before the opening everybody at last gets an opportunity to rehearse in costume. Marilyn's wig, she says, gives her something of an 'Alice' look, and she is promptly misunderstood as having in some way compared herself with Callas. Plácido wears the trousers and *'gilet'* of the London production but also a splendid new coat Julio has designed for him. Even now, not every aspect of the production is ready, and the orchestra will probably never feel really comfortable with what they are expected to do. Still, a rehearsal is not a performance and the piece is beginning to take on real cohesion. One further rehearsal is scheduled for the following day, but Marilyn feels she needs to rest her voice the day before the opening. 'I'll only come if I feel really guilty,' she laughs to Plácido, begging *him* not to come if she does not. Next day, as Marilyn rests and Plácido goes out of town to a football match, the others all turn up and run through the piece one more time.

'*Zarzuela*' means a little thorn bush. There are not many in the Calle de Jovellanos, but an awful lot in the vicinity of the traditional home of the Kings of Spain—not the massive Palacio Real in Madrid proper but the smaller Palacio de las Zarzuelas tucked away discreetly in the outskirts. So many, indeed, that the word became associated with the musical entertainments commissioned by the eighteenth-century monarchs. The short journey from the Palacio of the little thorn bushes to the Teatro of the same name has often been travelled in recent years by Queen Sofia of Spain, a tall, beautiful Greek blonde of Habsburg lineage; she is the music-lover in the family. On this particular evening, the first night of *La Fanciulla del West*, she is said to be coming with her husband.

King Juan Carlos has been a controversial character. It was Franco who ousted and then reinstated the monarchy, Franco who pulled this young prince out of relative obscurity and then placed him, at the time little more than a puppet king, back on the vacant throne of

Spain. When Franco died, the young King was soon seen to have a mind of his own and appeared genuinely to believe in a democratic, constitutional form of government. His beliefs and his independence of mind were put sharply to the test in February 1981 when the attempted military coup, carefully planned by men invoking traditional Spanish values, came close to success. With firm resolution, the King asserted his authority, ordered the entire army to reassert its loyalty to him as commander-in-chief, and had the dissident generals arrested and stripped of their powers. It is not often given to an individual to act at the very pivot of his nation's historic fortunes, but Juan Carlos found himself at such a point, made his decision, and acted on it with firmness. Thus, it is over a liberal democracy, with established government and opposition parties, that King Juan Carlos now finds himself ruling. Perhaps the next time his face is photographed for the Spanish 5,000-peseta note he will manage to look a little less anxious.

Certainly he looks relaxed and happy at the opera, almost as though he were an habitué. Everyone stands and applauds the King and Queen, even those wealthy and aristocratic members of the first-night audience who possibly regret the failure of the 1981 coup over the road at the Cortes. The National Anthem is played and somehow its jaunty rhythms set the tone for what shows every promise of being an exceptionally good-natured evening. The King applauds the first act heartily and then he and Queen Sofia meet the cast over a drink in the office of the theatre's director. Juan Carlos chats amiably with Domingo and his wife and parents, talks in excellent English to Marilyn Zschau, and tells foreign visitors what a wonderful friend of Spain as well as a great artist Plácido has always proved to be.

It is a good evening of theatre though there are the usual crop of first-night mishaps. Marilyn cracks her finger when running into Ettore in Act II. The sun rises too rapidly in Act III, while the rock supporting the tree from which Johnson is to be hanged lurches unsteadily beneath the weight of the goldminers who clamber over it. Emerson Buckley does not always manage to persuade the orchestra and chorus to adopt the same tempi, while some of his players are perturbed to find polystyrene snow sprinkling over them in the second act. Still, flakes of snow are better than bits of jagged glass, and the première has much to commend it. Emilio Sagi and his team have accomplished miracles with a production that, a few days ago, seemed incapable of coming together in time. The three principals are in splendid form, Marilyn's cracked finger seeming to have no effect upon a superbly healthy larynx. She positively skips off the stage with delight after the great ovation she receives at the end of the evening. Domingo's big moments—the 'vergogna' outburst in Act II and 'Ch'ella mi creda' in Act III—are magnificent. He sings with great sensitivity, too, in some of the quieter moments, achieving wonders of legato phrasing, for example, as he takes his tender leave of Minnie just before the Act I curtain. At the end of the evening, after the applause for the cast and then for the King and Queen and after a further rendition of the National Anthem, the royal party wave and leave—and the applause for the cast bursts out all over again.

The Teatro de la Zarzuela is one of the smallest in which Plácido Domingo sings these days, and even though the backstage crush is steamy and relentless he can work his way through such a crowd in a mere hour or so. Thus, at about 1 a.m., after the royal couple and the rest of the audience and all the cast and stage crew have left, there are three people still at the theatre: Plácido, his friend Achilles, and his secretary Paul Garner. A few opera houses provide transport for their stars; at most Plácido hires a car ahead of time or drives himself. Tonight, however, it is Paul's job to go out into the streets of Madrid and scout around for a taxi to take Plácido and Achilles on to supper with friends and family. What would Paul do if no taxi materialized on one of these occasions? He has no idea. The unthinkable has never happened. Yet.

Filming *Carmen*

When did Plácido Domingo last spend three whole months in his native Spain? His brow darkens and he pauses for a moment, not because he does not know the answer but because he does and on reflection is a little shocked. 'Not since I was seven,' he says slowly.

But he is a Spaniard, travels on a Spanish passport, has for much of his adult life kept a principal home in Spain, and has made a point of returning to Spain, to spend time with his family and to perform opera there, as often as he can. Most years the visits to Spain have been all too brief—a few weeks in the early summer, a matter of days around Christmas or New Year. Friends joke that, like the rain in Spain, these visits are often spent mainly in the plane. But this year, 1983, is different. Once Plácido's operatic commitments in Barcelona and Madrid are over, he and Marta move south to the beautiful Andalusian town of Ronda in and around which for the next two months, except for a brief foray to Vienna, he will be working on a film of Bizet's opera *Carmen*.

In these days of advanced audio and video technology there are several ways of making a visual record of an opera. You can film a live performance in the opera house, as Britain's National Video Corporation have done, for example; make a studio version complete with artificial sets, as in the BBC's *Macbeth* or *Flying Dutchman*, or Hans Jürgen Syberberg's *Parsifal*; or you can shoot an opera on location. The new *Carmen*, produced by Gaumont International, the company that produced Joseph Losey's *Don Giovanni*, was initially the brain-child of the young and energetic Gaumont boss Daniel Toscan du Plantier. As with *Don Giovanni*, the idea was to assemble a cast of first-class singer-actors, get them to pre-record the entire opera under Lorin Maazel, as with the earlier film, and then, months later on location, act to the sound of their own voices. Only opera singers who look good and can act as well as they can sing need apply for this sort of enterprise, and in the case of *Carmen* only those with good French.

The *Don Giovanni* film had achieved a large audience for a movie of presumably limited appeal, and the Zeffirelli *Traviata* starring Domingo as Alfredo was at this very moment doing brisk international trade. Yet for all the advantages of modern technology, opera films are still far from perfect. For one thing, few singers are paragons, and most sing perceptibly better than they act or vice versa. Then again, film, with its emphasis on movement, is impatient with immobility so that Losey, for example, has his characters moving about incessantly and sometimes distractingly in *Don Giovanni*, while Zeffirelli flashes to other times and other places whenever one of the *Traviata* characters has any extended solo piece to sing. Film includes everything from close-up to long shot but cinema sound tracks do not normally allow for variety of aural perspective; indeed, cinema sound is usually undifferentiatedly loud, giving none of the subtle interweaving of textures that are the very essence of live performance. Finally, most singers hate miming to pre-recorded sound. Domingo is an old hand but this does not enamour him any more of the process. If he merely mouths the words he sings, his facial expression may be too bland for the sound he is supposed to be making, while if he sings out as he acts he will drown the sound of his own pre-recorded voice and get out of sync.

For all these problems, the best opera films have undoubtedly been important artistic and popular successes. Everybody at Gaumont is determined that *Carmen* will be the finest of them all. If *Don Giovanni*, with its relatively static numbers and unrealistic story, could look and sound as good as it did and make converts to opera, think what a *Carmen* could do, with its powerful, realistic plot and universally loved music—particularly if shot with the world's finest singing actors against some of the world's most magnificent settings!

Visitors to the south of Spain usually come for one of two reasons. Most make straight for the wall of balconied matchbox hotels that line the big Costa del Sol resorts like Torremolinos and Marbella and spend their time and money trying to consume enough food, drink and seaside sun-and-fun to last, camel-like, until the next opportunity. Those with a greater sense of history seek more lasting sustenance by visiting the famous Andalusian triangle of ancient cities, Seville, Granada and Cordoba, which between them embody a rich and varied cultural history going back through the Catholic Kings, through centuries of Moorish domination, to the Visigoths, the Romans and beyond. When the surging vitality of Islam overwhelmed much that stood in its path, the major cities of Andalusia became and remained for centuries among the great repositories of a Moorish culture whose contribution to architecture, literature, mathematics and medicine achieved great distinction in a mediaeval world marked by much barbarism and warfare. Not that Moorish Spain was itself unmarked by warfare. Underlying a succession of what to our distant and detached eyes read like so many petty local squabbles between rival Moorish chieftaincies runs one struggle of epic proportions—the gradual unification of Spain under the Christian monarchs as they wrested control of the peninsula from the hands of the Moors.

It was only after the marriage of Ferdinand of Aragon and Isabella of Castille and the consequent consolidation of northern Catholic power that the Moorish hold on southern Spain was finally broken. And one of the last outposts to be conquered, in 1485, was a picturesque city built on what seemed to defenders and would-be conquerors alike to be an almost impregnable fortress perched high on a rocky bluff equi-distant to the three big cities.

Ronda is the shape of a long, narrow isosceles triangle, the somewhat straggly point to the south and the uneven base to the north. Much of Ronda, most spectacularly its long west-facing side, is built on a plateau of cliffs which rise hundreds of feet above the surrounding countryside. The bluff falls away at an angle vertiginous to those brave enough to lean over the railings that mark the precipitous city limits. Stand, if your head will take it, at the far end of the grounds of Ronda's magnificent Edwardian hotel, the Reina Victoria (built by the British as a retreat for officers from Gibraltar, though its most celebrated resident was the German poet Rilke), or down behind the eighteenth-century bullring, and you will find yourself looking out, ahead and to both left and right, over a perilously receding drop to the valley of the trickling Guadalevin River some 300 feet directly below. Perfect for would-be suicides, though even better is the narrow eighteenth-century bridge that links the larger, northern section of the city to the Moorish old town to the south. The 'New Bridge' took forty years to build, vast stone on top of vast stone, with an accompanying loss of life not recorded in the local guidebooks. What few books tell you either is that from Ronda's leafy Alameda del Tajo, hundreds met their deaths during the early stages of Spain's twentieth-century Civil War.

Stroll through the 'New Town' or 'Mercadillo' up from the New Bridge and you will find yourself in streets and connecting alleyways and the occasional broad square or plaza almost unaltered from two or three centuries ago. If you can programme your senses to ignore the noise and sight and stench of the traffic, or the graffiti and political ads that inevitably deface the walls of unoccupied buildings, you can take a walk backwards in time, along tiled and cobbled paths, past white-fronted and red-tile-roofed houses, their lower windows grilled like gaols and the upper ones balconied in the most delicately filigreed patterns. Along the streets you pass people with proud, dark faces lined by years of hard work under the fierce Andalusian sun, young girls wearing trendy short yet traditionally layered skirts, old men in black berets making their slow, bandy-legged way with the aid of a stick. At noon everyone walks, or sits over a drink, on the shaded side of the street. At four in the afternoon the streets are deserted except for the occasional eccentric tourist. But by ten or eleven at night, everyone is awake, eating, drinking, the youngsters stretching to the limits the tolerance of Ronda's basically conservative citizenry by making as much noise as they dare with their unmuffled motor-bikes, their transistor radios, and their guttural, Arabic-sounding voices.

Walk south across the New Bridge, or perhaps a little to the east along streets that begin to curve and careen uncertainly, shifting breadth and direction as they fall downwards, and you enter an even earlier era. For this is the old Moorish city or 'Ciudad'. Here, the stuccoed walls and cobblestones are more uneven, the doorways lower, the metal lattice work more curved, the fountains more embellished, the narrow roadways more sharply angled, the hills steeper than in the Mercadillo.

At one of the lower points of the Ciudad roller-coaster is an old eight-tapped drinking fountain with a waste-water trough behind. The fountain dominates one of those little plazas that add so much charm to the Moorish *barrio*. To the left of the fountain is a church and directly behind it a block of old-style modern apartments. If you happened to pass this spot in late June or early July 1983 you would have found the whole environment miraculously transformed. Some of the changes are subtle; bright new stucco on the houses down towards the fountain is rendered grey, for instance, and the stonework made to appear cracked. But the principal change is sensational. An entire new façade has appeared over the apartments and obliterated them from view, a façade of stunningly realistic-looking stonework, complete with occasional cracks, discoloration and even the odd clump of faded grass apparently growing in the cracks. Windows are few and severely barred, and the whole is dominated by a great central stone portico. For several weeks, the modern-day inhabitants of the newly concealed apartments have had to leave home as their building temporarily supports a carefully contrived replica of the Seville cigarette factory.

Past the fountain and the stone 'factory', along the little roadway to the right, you immediately cross over another of Ronda's bridges, this one smaller and older than the more famous one up the hill, but its views to right and left (and the stench of sewage from far below) memorable none the less. Then up a steep cobbled hill, through a stone gateway dating from Moorish times, and then the narrow roadway doubles almost 180 degrees back upon itself and the gradient increases sharply. If you or your car are capable of climbing further, and you can see why mules and donkeys are still a popular form of transport hereabouts, you will see that your road is about to branch into two, one rising steeply and the other very steeply. The latter is Calle Santo Domingo. Immediately adjacent and marginally the easier to climb, is a street named not after a saint but merely a local noble, the Marquès de Salvatierra. But there is a nice symmetry in the fact that the street of the Marquès contains the temporary home of El Tenor Domingo.

And not only of El Tenor himself, but of his wife Marta, their Philippine cook, Yoly, a maid who comes with the rented house, the Domingo boys once they can all get away, and at any one time anything up to six or eight further relatives and friends. From the front the house does not look as though it will comfortably accommodate more than four or five, but it opens up, fan-shaped, into a great airy, spacious house with a large garden culminating in what for Spain is a welcome rarity, a swimming pool. Downstairs, a crate of Coca-Cola is delivered by a tough little boy dwarfed by what he carries, Paul Garner talks with unflappable politeness on the phone, and incessant sounds of summer merriment echo across the hallway from the garden or the front lounge as a large extended family

mingles over drinks and jokes. Sometimes Plácido is among them, in
swimming trunks, tennis shorts or casual slacks, his large feet bare or
in canvas shoes. Much of the merriment he has to miss, however,
partly because he is struggling to master the score of his next major
new role, that of Aeneas in Berlioz' *Les Troyens* in which he is to star
at the opening night of the Met's Centennial season in September,
partly because even here he has interviews to give and phone calls to
make and answer, but chiefly because fully six days out of every seven
have to be spent working on the project that brought him here in the
first place.

A casual visitor to Ronda might be forgiven for not knowing that the
Carmen show was in town. There are clues for the observant,
however. That 'cigarette factory', for instance. You might not notice
that its façade was a fake. But if you kept a careful watch you would
observe the same group of people entering each day and then, a
couple of hours later, another group, this time dressed in nineteenth-
century dress, leaving. One of the apartments inside this very block
has been rented by Gaumont for their soloists' costumes and make-
up. The rooms inside are small, the lighting inadequate, the air
musty. The toilet works, but only if 'no paper of any kind' is flushed.
On the walls are prints of nineteenth-century Andalusian peasant
girls, townsfolk and so on, and it is with these in front of them that
Gaumont's make-up artists do their intricate work. From this
unlikely location Carmen, José, Micaela and the rest emerge into the
fierce sunlight every morning, and to here they return eight or ten
hours later, to be transformed back into weary denizens of the
twentieth century.

There are other clues too. If you scan the local paper carefully you
may notice that volunteers are invited to help form the crowd in the
bullfight scene soon to be filmed in Ronda's Plaza de Toros. And
when filming switches to the mountain location outside Ronda, little
cut-out arrows sprout on gateposts and trees along the stony roadway,
rather as though 'CARMEN' were the codeword in a cross-country
treasure hunt.

In a way it is, for to get to the location you have to undertake quite a
lengthy cross-country trek, but the spot once reached is unforgettably

beautiful, particularly at night when most of the mountain scenes are shot. For two weeks in July, Carmen and her friends spend much of the day trying to sleep, most of the night awake. Shift work can be a bore if you are a security guard or factory worker, and even film stars have been known to complain about the odd hours they are sometimes required to work. But not the *Carmen* cast.

Have you ever stood still in the middle of an isolated countryside location at night as the rest of the world sleeps, in a spot remote enough to give no hint whatsoever of civilization? No distant sound or smell of traffic, no red haze from city lights, no roadway, no sound at all, indeed, but the buzz of distant crickets and the occasional flap of nocturnal wings or the bark of a restless dog, and nothing above but a brilliantly clear, starlit sky seemingly almost within reach? Add the overwhelming smell of pure mountain air, the rich flora pouring out their intoxicating perfumes and no men and few beasts to inhale or pollute them. Such a spot is that chosen for the mountain scenes in *Carmen*. Such, indeed, was doubtless the spot chosen as a temporary encampment by all those authentic nineteenth-century Andalusian gypsies who came up from the coast laden with contraband.

During those two weeks of July 1983, these hills are once again filled with smugglers, and to the wonderful countryside sights and sounds and smells are added others less intoxicating, perhaps, but scarcely less exotic. For the hills are alive with the sound of operatic music, and of men with loud hailers calling 'PRONTI!' and 'AZIONE!' to colleagues a mountain and a valley away; with the sight of nineteenth-century gypsies, twentieth-century electric cables, and ageless mules carrying crates full of sandwiches or lighting equipment; and with smells of everything from dollops of manure to the occasional puff of incense.

Nothing worthwhile in this world is achieved easily and that includes access to this mountain location. You drive south over the New Bridge and straight on down beyond the city walls out of Ronda, then a short way along the road towards Algeciras and Gibraltar. Soon you make a right turn—unmarked normally but right now there is a discreet treasure-hunt 'CARMEN' arrow nailed up on a post. If your car will take the punishment you drive along a twisting uneven stony pathway for perhaps two or three kilometres; only those not driving dare look at the olive groves to left and right by which the stony roadway is encompassed. The path gets ever more bumpy and uneven until at last you reach a little plateau to your right. Here are parked the big trucks that form a temporary lifeline to all who venture further. For from these trucks is dispensed everything from the electricity that powers the location lighting to the food and drink that sustain the stranded cast and crew. From this last base camp few cars will venture and those that do can go only a few hundred metres more. From then on you are on your own. You climb down a treacherous, rocky path, the ground slipping away from you at every step. Your track then turns upwards and if you have a good head for heights you will have a spectacular view down to your right of a ravine far below. It is a river valley, but as so often in these parts it is not the river itself but the gorge that has been carved out over many centuries that is most memorable. This particular river is completely obliterated by an exuberant jungle of oleander bushes that has grown along its course, in the early evening light a positively evanescent river of flowers. If you trust yourself, glance upwards to your left. Towering above, right overhead it sometimes seems, is sheer cliff face. Look up at the sky and the cliff will surely appear to be falling towards you; turn back to the river of flowers in the ravine below and your sense of motion will hardly be stilled. Nor is your giddiness 'all in the head'. The cliffs above and below are pock-marked with evidence of continuing erosion. One evening Gaumont's make-up team are narrowly missed by a small avalanche of falling rocks caused by a pair of cinephobic mountain goats.

One more curve in the mountain path and there before you, looking like the interior of a great mother-of-pearl seashell, is a spectacular grotto hollowed out from under the side of one of the hills. In front of it is a narrow grassy pathway, and beneath this is a continuation of the ravine we have been skirting all the while. On the other side of this narrow valley a huge perpendicular block of sheer rock juts ominously forward near its summit as though trying to reach across to refill the grotto.

As the Andalusian summer sun begins to retreat behind the hills, the shadows lengthen and the sweet smell of eucalyptus trees comes to predominate over all others. Up there on the sloping grassy verge just below the grotto and just above the edge of the precipice down to the ravine are people, perhaps a hundred of them, sitting, standing or squatting, immobile like penguins on an antarctic ice cap. It is a surreal tableau, a composite picture of nineteenth-century gypsies and smugglers with their contraband and their horses alongside a small army of twentieth-century technicians, cameramen, make-up artists, sound engineers, the occasional armed security officer, plus many others whose contribution to the work in hand is doubtless more real than immediately apparent. The tableau is rendered more remarkable for the fabulous setting, by the emergence of superbly placed spotlighting in place of the rapidly fading sunlight, and by the extraordinary stillness of the scene. Movies move, but movie-making involves an accumulation of what must amount to several weeks of doing nothing by most participants. Only a fraction of the army can have anything to do at any one time.

As you approach the scene, parts slowly unfreeze. Look at that short, balding man of sixty-odd with green-tinted glasses and his right arm in a sling, sitting on a rickety canvas chair near an inconspicuous camera. He is, on closer inspection, in fact pretty animated, turning this way and that, calling instructions and asking questions in a high-pitched voice that speaks perfect Italian, good French, and when necessary occasional Spanish or English too. This is director Francesco Rosi, a man who served his apprenticeship in movies as assistant to Luchino Visconti and has been responsible for some of the great classics of Italian cinema—*Salvatore Giuliano*, *The Mattei Affair*, *Lucky Luciano*, *Christ Stopped at Eboli* and *Three Brothers*. Rosi's work has achieved the highest critical acclaim and has been particularly hailed for its subtle mixture of great visual beauty with the most unflinching insights into some of the more emotion-laden aspects of contemporary Italian life. Why has Rosi taken on the filming of an opera placed in nineteenth-century Spain? Because *Carmen*, he insists, is perhaps the most realistic of all operas, one that lends itself better than any other to filming with authentic faces in authentic locations. Rosi's *Carmen* will certainly look superb, shot as it is in such beautiful and evocative spots in southern Spain. But it will also look like a realistic story fought out by and between real men and women, the kind of drama that could build up in the life of any powerful, headstrong woman today. Rosi has seriously injured his right arm and is threatened, unless he goes straight into hospital for ten days or so, with the possibly permanent loss of part of its strength. But to Rosi this film is more important, and he constantly waves and points and gesticulates with his injured arm almost as though trying to squeeze whatever power he can from it while the going is good.

A few yards up from Rosi is another cluster of canvas chairs, most of them occupied by figures in dark brown costumes. Here too the tableau unfreezes as you approach. Three of the figures are women. In a chair misleadingly marked 'JULIA MIGENES' sits a dark-haired Andalusian beauty with radiant blue eyes who turns out to be Lillian Watson, one of the loveliest light sopranos to come out of England in recent years. Having come out Lillian all too rarely returns, for since becoming recognized on the international operatic circuit she has been performing all over Europe. Right now she is Carmen's friend Frasquita, but Lillian and her architect husband and their children, who are in Ronda with her, soon have to go on to Salzburg where she is to sing Marzelline in *Fidelio* under Maazel. A British singer heard even less frequently in Britain nowadays is playing Carmen's other friend, Mercédès. This is mezzo-soprano Susan Daniel. Susan has been a leading singer at the Bavarian State Opera in Munich with occasional guest appearances in places like Paris and Berlin, while important future engagements include a season at the Vienna State Opera. In addition to all their other accomplishments, both Lillian and Susan are first-class French-speakers.

In another chair sits the woman who is to play Carmen, Julia Migenes Johnson. Born in New York of Greek and Puerto Rican parents, Julia is that rarest of birds—an operatic performer who can really act and dance as well as sing. Indeed, she is not primarily an opera singer at all but an exceptionally versatile performer who, among other things, sings opera. The other things have included starring roles on Broadway (*West Side Story*, *Fiddler on the Roof*) and hosting television shows. Her operatic repertoire is not large but Met appearances, for instance, have already included the title-role in *Lulu*, Jenny in *Mahagonny* and Musetta to Domingo's Rodolfo in the Zeffirelli production of *Bohème*. Julia's voice is lighter than that of most who sing Carmen. 'I doubt if I could do the role successfully on stage, certainly not in a large house,' she acknowledges. 'And I had to work very hard at getting the chesty lower register the part requires.' But she enjoyed recording the role last December and is obviously getting a kick out of filming the part. Julia is irrepressible. Watch her dancing, on or off the film set, or listen to her telling a slightly off-colour joke with her hearty New York accent and voluptuous laugh, and you get an idea why she was cast as Carmen over a number of better known operatic exponents of the role. Her elder child, nine-year-old Martina, a bright girl who has inherited her mother's wide smile, spends much time on the set and becomes something of a *Carmen* mascot.

And Plácido Domingo? He was here a moment ago, dressed in his brown Don José outfit, sitting in the 'FRANCESCO ROSI' chair. But he can never remain still for long. At one moment he is clambering down over the uneven stony surface to chat to Gaumont boss Daniel Toscan du Plantier who has shown up on the set, or else to producer Patrice Ledoux, a slim, undemonstrative character whose thin face, thick lips and large glasses give him the air of a careworn student. Plácido sees Isabelle sitting idle. She is a young French architect and theatrical designer currently working for Gaumont looking after the artists. Domingo goes over to talk to her about transport for tomorrow night. Then to Francesco Rosi for a quick word, back past the make-up people who give his short growth of beard a quick touch-up to make it paler, a wave to script-girl Ariane, a joke here and an embrace there, until finally he is back among his more sedentary lady colleagues.

Not for long. Plácido's leg begins to twitch, a sure sign, like the rod of a water diviner, that it must soon be time for action. 'Suzanne, Liliane, Yolande!' Yolande is Julia. Yesterday the assistant director called her Sylvia. Variations on a theme. Julia enjoys the joke and gives as good as she gets. The three women, splendid in their gypsy dresses and shawls, amble down to where horses and horsemen await them. It is the scene early in Act III where the smugglers arrive at their mountain retreat. What Rosi and his Director of Photography Pasqualino De Santis have to orchestrate is a long procession of men and women, horses and donkeys, coming rapidly around the twisting mountain pathway and then deciding to put up for the night.

Carmen, Frasquita and Mercédès each sit side-saddle behind one of the men, and when the little posse comes to a halt just near the grotto the women help each other to dismount. The whole thing will take perhaps fifteen seconds in the final film. But as the sun sets and the arc lights come up, as Rosi fusses about the distance between the various horses as they round the bend and become visible and about the correct amount of smoke that should be seen to linger around the hills, a couple of hours at least will clearly be necessary before the scene is safely in the can.

Riding a horse on this sort of terrain is a risky business even if, like the agile Susan Daniel, you are an experienced equestrienne. The other day, Jean-Philippe Laffont, playing Dancaïre, had an accident and is now in what feels to him like semi-permanent pain and plaster. At one session, Lillian's horse was backing perilously close to the edge of the ravine, its hooves shovelling away at the loose earth, before someone spotted the danger and came to the rescue. A few nights later, Ruggero Raimondi, playing Escamillo, had a painful tumble among the bushes and stones. Still, the show must go on and this particular evening Lillian, Jean-Philippe and the rest make their entrance around the mountain pathway again and again for Rosi and his cameras. Julia's horse positively canters in each time. 'Great for getting a broad backside!' she jokes, though her actual phraseology is rather more colourful.

Domingo admires the devotion to duty displayed by his colleagues but does not relish the thought of an accident. He too has his share of problems, however, as later in the filming he cracks a bone in his wrist during an over-energetic brawl in the tavern scene. He will ride his horse during the less precarious scenes and those that require greater camera intimacy. But for a distant view of the whole posse rounding the mountainside they can as easily use a stand-in. Plácido himself is not, strictly speaking, required.

Which is just as well since he has committed himself at this very time to being somewhere else. In the Cinema Merced back in Ronda, to be precise, at a gathering of young musicians. A week or two ago he agreed to judge the finals of their Festival of Song. Nine o'clock seemed a safe enough promise at the time. Now, however, Rosi is filming at night and Domingo is expected to be permanently on call even if Rosi is not actually using him at the moment. Can he go off for just an hour or so, he wonders, and his absence go unnoticed?

Domingo is famous for his apparent capacity to be in two places at once. Tonight as he slips away from the mountains he has pangs of guilt. He jokes to Isabelle, his accomplice in crime, that he already hears Francesco's voice crying, *'Dov'è Plácido?'* Anxiously, he keeps asking Isabelle the time. When you are dressed as Don José you do not wear your Rolex watch. Once safely out of earshot of the film company, as he walks along the mountain ledge above the river of flowers, he lets out a whoop of delight. Plácido Domingo's whoops of delight are different from most people's. They have an operatic ring to them, a sort of tenor equivalent of Brünnhilde's 'Ho-yo-to-ho!' He knows he cannot stay long at the cinema tonight, certainly not long enough to do any judging, so he will have to sing something, if only to be allowed to leave. If you are going to sing in public you have to vocalize, and if you are going to vocalize you might as well do so in the spirit of your mood. With the security of hearing that the voice is there, exhilaration takes over completely, there is no more talk of time, and Domingo's voice breaks, literally, into a series of yodels. Real mountains, Spanish ones as opposed to Swiss ones at any rate, do not cause much echo, and it is safe to assume that while the yodels reach the oleander bushes below and the goats far above they do not reach the ears of the *Carmen* people. It is they who are the poorer.

On this particular evening there is no lingering to admire the scenery. A taxi is waiting up at base camp. It is Antonio. Antonio and Rafael are the only Ronda taxi drivers prepared to come out this far. Antonio's car radio is playing flamenco music and Domingo cringes, not because he does not normally like flamenco but because now, as he tries to warm up his own voice after several days without singing, he feels physically pained by the cracked vocal technique this music requires. He drowns it out with animated talk to Antonio and Isabelle—and a few ear-splitting scales and arpeggios.

Antonio gets to the Cinema Merced in record time. Domingo is ushered in the back way, through a darkened boiler room full of invisible irregular steps, and stands breathless backstage. Does he need anything? *'Agua, por favor,'* and a big plastic bottle of cold mineral water is produced. Immediately the master of ceremonies is apprised of Domingo's arrival the proceedings are interrupted and Plácido's presence announced. The place erupts with a roar such as only a thousand exuberant teenagers can make and Plácido in his dusty Don José outfit, sweat beading his brow and filtering through his artificial chin stubble, marches out on to the stage. Behind him, though he does not notice it, is a huge black-and-white line drawing someone has done of him. He goes over to the MC's microphone, hands raised, and gets instant silence. He plays this excited audience like a musical instrument, talks directly to them. He shouldn't really be here, he explains with a guilty grin, but is supposed to be filming out in the mountains. But to tell the truth he is very happy to have been able to make it. Massive applause. He can't stay as long as he had originally hoped (groans and long faces) . . . but (yes?) . . . perhaps people wouldn't mind if instead of judging the competition as he had intended he might just sing a song himself . . . This is a completely unexpected bonus and a thousand throats shout themselves silly with excitement.

There are times when Plácido Domingo looks every inch one of the world's great elegant artists. This, however, with his brown, dusty riding clothes, his hair tousled, his face and body sweaty, is not one of them. The kids do not mind. On the contrary, the obvious sincerity of the man and his patent delight in their happiness at seeing him creates a bond of joy that is almost tangible. Never can Domingo have had a more responsive audience than in this provincial Spanish cinema tonight. He slouches over the rickety upright piano in the corner looking like a character out of a John Ford Western, sits himself down on the stool, and bangs out the accompaniment to 'Jurame'. He knows he will have to give an encore. That is why he said he would sing 'a' song. If he had said he was going to sing two songs his audience would have felt cheated if he had not sung three. The applause after 'Jurame' cracks out like gunfire. Plácido gets up, his spurs get tangled in electric wiring, and he trips his way back to the microphone and addresses his audience again. He signals to the wings for another drink of *agua* and knocks it back like any bar pianist. OK, an encore (roars of approval), but I really shouldn't. Then back to his corner for a tremendous rendition of 'Granada'. His hands try to beat some sense into, or out of, the honky-tonk piano—shaming it, it almost seems, by the persistent beauty of his own singing into producing an adequate accompaniment. He plays with panache, a pair of elegant turns here, a dramatic back-hand upward scale there, and fortissimo octave tremolo chords as he holds his final high note. There is almost a stampede. The youngsters are ecstatic and feel that they have received double bounty, two songs from their hero when they had expected none. The whole thing has taken less than fifteen minutes and immediately it is over Plácido is speeding, courtesy of the waiting Antonio, back out of town and towards the darkened sierras. As he clambers back up to the film location exactly one hour after slipping off, he chuckles to himself.

Had they missed him? No, of course not. They are still shooting the arrival of the *contrebandiers*, Plácido's saddle still filled by his patient stand-in. As a matter of fact if his departure was well timed so is his reappearance, for it anticipates by just a few minutes the moment Rosi lets everyone break for their evening meal.

What are film stars given for dinner? Thick, dry rolls each containing a single thin sliver of cheese or ham, some fresh local fruit, and water or wine to wash it down. Plus mouthfuls of flies and mosquitoes which temporarily desert the donkey dung as they are attracted in their droves by the arc light that illuminates the table at which the movie principals sit. Better to be one of the extras munching away in the obscurity of the nearby rocks; fewer flies get into your food and you cannot in any case see those that do.

'That's what I like!' says Plácido as he approaches Julia, Susan and Lillian at the table. 'All my ladies enjoying themselves over a good meal!' He joins them, expatiates on the virtues of Andalusian ham and the advantages of *not* eating dry Andalusian rolls, and swigs down a couple of plastic cups' worth of bottled water. Not much wine is consumed—though you would scarcely guess this from the Rabelaisian hilarity that soon emanates from the principals' table. Ruggero Raimondi emerges from the shadows. He is Escamillo in this movie and had the title-role in *Don Giovanni*. A man of good looks and great presence, he so enjoys acting for movie cameras that he is launching a parallel career for himself as a film actor alongside his existing one as an opera singer. Ruggero is not needed tonight, but you never know. In any case, there is not much to do back in Ronda when all your friends are out in the mountains working. He produces a little statistical guide to matters gastronomical and earnestly instructs Plácido on the complex calorific implications of adding mosquitoes to one's diet: 'And I thought you were trying to lose weight!' Faith Esham turns up too. Last night she spent hours miming Micaela's aria to the reverberant recording of her own voice. Tonight she thought she would come along to the set 'just to make sure you're all working properly!' Faith sits down and joins the eating-a-cherry-with-no-hands-from-the-stalk-up-with-your-head-forwards competition. Susan is the champion. She sits in uncharacteristic silence, hands on lap, while all around stare at her. Susan tries not to laugh as she concentrates on the advanced feat of eating her cherry, handless, while leaving the pip and stalk attached. 'Quite a tongue artist!' Dirty joke time is clearly just around the corner. So is a little rectangular tent that is presumably supposed to serve as the toilet for the entire company. Julia announces her intention of paying it a visit—and comes running back like Donna Elvira after seeing the walking statue in *Don Giovanni*. 'There's something inside there,' she announces aghast. All troop off to investigate and find a tiny, crouching field toilet. Doubtless it works wonders as it cleans as it rinses as it flushes; Gaumont would not provide anything less than the best. Except that in the half-light it looks like a malevolent beast with two large, dark eyes. 'Don't be afraid,' laughs Plácido, reassuringly taking the situation firmly in hand. 'It's only R2D2.' Nothing to panic about after all. Except that Plácido has now, to everybody's uncontrollable amusement, unintentionally rendered the toilet even harder to use than it was before.

Most shooting sessions are much like this—hours of alternating hard work and immobility interspersed with relaxing sessions of jokes and laughter around the food and drink table. At most sessions, the performers are miming to the sound of their own voices blaring back at them, though there is a lot of 'straight' acting and some specially written French-language dialogue as well. On stage a singer can enter his or her character more or less for the duration and give a carefully paced performance. On a film set there can be no sense of continuity and the performers are hard put to act the tiny snippets they are required to shoot and re-shoot with any real sense of sustained intensity. During all the various mountain scenes on horseback there are lengthy delays between takes as one restless horse is given a pat and a piece of sugar and another has its blanket smoothed down. At one session, after two or three takes, it transpired that Plácido's horse was carrying the blanket that Dancïare's wore the day before when they shot what would be the immediately succeeding scene. Panic as several blankets are re-allocated in a game of musical horses; you cannot have Mercédès sitting behind her man on a blanket of one colour as her horse rounds a bend in the mountains, and have her arriving in the next shot sitting on the blanket just now belonging to Frasquita.

I have an abiding memory of one of the mountain scenes where the women were required to help each other dismount from their horses and gather up their long skirts into their belts like knickerbockers and walk off camera. When you are wearing long heavy skirts you need help every time you mount your horse, and when it is two in the morning and you are asked to get on your horse yet again for a scene that you long since thought was successfully completed, the effort can almost defeat you. Jumping down gracefully on to uncertain, sloping ground is no easy matter either. And then having to rustle around between your legs for the back of your skirt and pull it up in front of you to tuck into your waistband . . . A tiny, trivial scene in the final film but immensely hard work at the time. 'Suzanne, Liliane, Julia, please!' By now Julia is Julia. Wearily the three women return to their horses, their men offering them hands and knees to help them mount. One horse will not stand still and has to be mollified. Another disgraces himself and a man with a shovel immediately appears. 'Ready?' asks Rosi at length. Apparently so. '*Silenzio!*' shouts a man with a megaphone, and silence gradually descends. '*Pronti!*' The fellow with the clapper-board performs his recurrent ritual before the camera and the megaphone man shouts '*Azione!*' The horses approach, Susan slips down with agility to the ground and helps Julia and Lillian, and the three move forward and hitch up their skirts as though for work. 'Halt!' Everyone relaxes and the women, so tough and earnest on camera a moment ago, break out into weary smiles. 'It's so funny, this skirt business,' they say, one of them pretending to hunt around in all the copious folds as though for a missing needle or worse . . . Hunt, hunt, hunt. 'It's gone!' she exclaims in mock alarm, rummaging around suggestively; 'I could have sworn it was here when I came!' 'L'ho perduto' sings a beautiful tenor voice from up above, quoting Mozart. It is Plácido, watching from his horse and thoroughly enjoying the mock discomfiture of the ladies. Of course Rosi wants yet one more take, and of course they do it with complete professionalism.

Each day is much the same as the next and as the days lengthen into weeks and then filming enters its second month Domingo's life develops a sense of settled routine. Despite the long hours of work he enjoys filming and finds it relaxing. Not physically, perhaps, but mentally. With no performances to worry about for the time being (though there is always Les Troyens looming up) he can clear his head of immediate anxieties. There is a steady and welcome stream of friends and relatives to Ronda. Plácido's cousin Jaime and his family from Madrid come to stay for a few days. So do Marta's sister Perla and her husband and daughters. They live in Barcelona. Plácido loves to have a house full of people and patently enjoys his role of paterfamilias. Marta is in her element here too as she keeps a sharp eye on everyone and everything, supervises the kitchen, decides who should sit next to whom at table, and in general protects the environment of her husband. Tense and alert, her dark Mexican eyes flashing brightly through her thick, oval-shaped glasses, Marta is a captivating woman of firm views and tastes, intensely proud of Plácido, jealous of those who want more of his time and attention than they deserve. It has not always been easy being Mrs Plácido Domingo. Marta often says she would have been perfectly happy had Plácido been destined to lead a more private, less starry existence. But she willingly gave up her own promising career as a singer many years ago in order to raise his children, and here in Ronda, after twenty-one years of marriage, Marta continues to preside over a happy household and to fulfil her various roles with total devotion.

Visitors continue to arrive. Milt and Rosemary Okun turn up in Ronda for a while. Prince Alfonso von Hohenlohe is frequently present too; a wealthy Austro-Spanish aristocrat with an insatiable entrepreneurial drive, Alfonso owns the exclusive Marbella Club and is full of ideas for developing the prosperity of southern Spain—and attracting his friend Plácido to spend more time there. José Luis Rubio from the Madrid journal *Cambio* comes to Ronda for a few days. One day Plácido has a conference with people from Deutsche Grammophon about a new disc they wish to issue; on another he is interviewed by French radio. And it is not quite true that he has no performances to think about. During the first couple of weeks of filming he was commuting back and forth to Madrid where he still had three performances of *Fanciulla* to give. Then there were a pair of *Bohème*s in Vienna. Originally Domingo was contracted for three but the filming schedule was so tight that Rosi begged him to excuse himself from the first. Fortunately, the boss of the Vienna State Opera also happened to be the conductor of the sound-track record-ing of *Carmen*, Lorin Maazel, so the awkward disengagement was effected relatively painlessly. And what triumphs the remaining two performances were! After the second, Domingo and his Mimì, Mirella Freni, achieved what must be a record of some sort by receiving no less than eighty-three curtain calls over a period of one and a quarter hours after the final curtain. The rest of the night was spent at a champagne party thrown by Alfonso von Hohenlohe who flew back to Spain with Plácido the next day.

These are good times for Domingo. Back in Ronda he catches one of his rare colds, and thoroughly enjoys the luxury of being able to sneeze his head off without it mattering in the slightest. 'Listen how low I can sing!' he regales anyone within hearing range as he emerges late one morning and lets out a bottom G flat worthy of a Chaliapin. He beams as he watches his sons showing off their linguistic and athletic skills, and plays *ad hoc* piano duets with seventeen-year-old Placi. When he was that age he was playing the piano in night clubs in Mexico City to help earn enough to pay for his musical studies and support his first son, José. Domingo still enjoys vamping at the piano; one evening in Ronda he turns in what amounts to a very creditable cabaret act as he plays 'E lucevan le stelle' as a tango, ad libs 'La donna è mobile' in a witty sequence of painfully adjacent keys, and shifts the first movement of the Moonlight Sonata imperceptibly into 'Night and Day You Are the One'. And just when you think his piano playing is still no more than that of a talented amateur, he accompanies his youngest son Alvaro, who starts singing 'Bésame Mucho' from sheet music, and has to transpose the piano part down a minor third as he goes—and then breaks into an almost symphonic amalgam of chordal sequences from half a dozen Puccini works.

Domingo needs a period like this, a time without performances, without pressure, with plenty of physical demands but few mental ones. Upstairs, it is true, often late at night, he goes slowly through his Berlioz score, marking his part in yellow pencil, worrying how he will deal with Aeneas's first entry, listening on earphones to Jon Vickers in the part. One morning he has a slight *frisson* as the postman delivers the official Met invitation to the first night of the Centennial season and he sees his name there in the cast list. But in general this is a period with much happiness, free of serious worry. 'You know,' he says impulsively, 'I really think I might one day decide to clear my diary for a whole year and just accept engagements I feel like doing at fairly short notice.' It is a recurrent fantasy, one on which he is never really likely to act. This very summer there was to have been a family holiday during the latter half of August, but that period is now booked for a television programme in Los Angeles with Carol Burnett. Perhaps, after all, *this* is his holiday, the nearest at any rate that Domingo is likely to get to one—a period of two more or less uninterrupted months in one delightful part of the world, with good food, good company, and virtually no singing to do. El Domingo really is at home in Spain. It is true he has to work for six days out of every seven. But Domingo is no good at having nothing to do. Even on holiday. Even in Spain.

ENTR'ACTE

A New Golden Age?

Things are said to be not what they used to be. They never are. Harold Rosenthal, long-time editor of *Opera* magazine and encyclopaedic expert on operatic casts of all times and places, tells how his mother took him to a performance of *La Traviata* in the early 1930s. When he got home his father asked him who was singing. 'Rosa Ponselle and Dino Borgioli,' the lad replied. 'My boy,' pontificated Rosenthal senior, 'you should have heard Melba and Caruso.' To which the precocious young Harold gave the riposte: 'I suppose *your* father told you that you should have heard Patti and de Reszke.'

It seems there is a deep-felt human tendency to believe that giants once stalked the land which is now populated by pygmies; just as we cannot easily imagine our great-grandfathers as other than venerable old men so we find it hard to picture Caruso, say, or Patti as a youngster having vocal insecurities or off-nights. Singing is, in fact, one of the most intriguing examples of this Giants-of-the-Past tendency. It is not just that our elders and betters brought us up to believe that in their day there were *real* singers. The special point of interest is that we can begin to test that hypothesis, for the principal singers of our great-grandfathers' day lived at the time of the invention of the gramophone and were therefore the first to have been recorded. My father's memories of Martinelli and his father's of Melba are to some extent testable by the legacy of the gramophone.

People talk of a 'Golden Age' of singing, a sobriquet that has become almost officially accepted, like the 'Dark Ages' or 'Renaissance', though like them, nobody seems quite sure when it began or ended. That giants walked the boards of the opera houses at the end of the nineteenth century is undoubtedly true—Lilli Lehmann, Sembrich, Patti, Nordica, Eames, Calvé, Melba, among the ladies; the de Reszke brothers, Santley, Plançon, Maurel, Tamagno, among the men. But it is tempting to attribute at least part of the Golden Age legend to the fact that its singers happened to flourish at the dawn of recording history. If the gramophone had been invented in the 1830s or 1840s we would probably consider the era of Malibran, Pasta, Tamburini, Lablache, Rubini, Grisi, Nourrit and Mario as the Golden Age of singing.

One of the implications of Golden Agery is that the phrase can tend to devalue what immediately preceded and succeeded it. The voices of the 1880s are not recapturable and we can only guess what Patti, Lilli Lehmann or Tamagno, who made records late in their careers, sounded like in their prime, much less the voices of people who lived in the pre-recording era. But we do have an idea of what post-Golden Age singers sounded like. The most famous opera singer of all, Enrico Caruso, was also the first of the major recording singers and there is almost something perverse in *not* referring to the era in which Caruso, Bonci, Farrar, Tetrazzini, Scotti, Destinn, Amato and Chaliapin were all in their prime as a Golden Age. Perhaps the term may be extended to cover the period just after, as well as that just before, the turn of the century.

Once one is in the inter-war years, however, some feel that standards of singing began to decline. To a discriminating connoisseur like John Steane, for example, author of *The Grand Tradition*, the general inter-war standard was distinctly less impressive than that of the immediately preceding decades. In particular, he has suggested, singers in the 1920s and 1930s often seemed less capable than their predecessors of singing a really smooth legato line or of singing fast, florid music accurately. Or, rather, neither of these skills, so essential to the Golden Age singer, was as highly valued between the wars as before. The inter-war years saw some outstanding individual achievements, particularly in Wagner, and singers such as Melchior and Schorr, Ponselle, Jeritza and Rethberg, Gigli and

Martinelli, Leider, Lotte Lehmann and Flagstad, touched heights of glory. In addition, the development of new electric recording techniques in the mid-1920s meant that these singers' voices have reached us with much greater resonance and authenticity than those of their predecessors. For all this, Steane and others* argue that overall standards in singing were probably lower between the wars than earlier.

If this is so, there are a number of possible reasons. The twenty-one years that elapsed between the world wars saw such political and social disruption in most countries that little planned development of operatic life or anything else could easily take place. In continental Europe, many opera house administrators, producers, singing teachers and coaches found their job tenure and income precarious. People were hired and fired for reasons unconnected with music. Many went to America only to find their fame and fortune jeopardized by the Depression.

But there were also some reasons more rooted in musical history. Virtually all the standard operatic works were written between the 1780s and the 1920s—some two-thirds of them in the half-century 1850–1900, including all the mature works of Wagner and Verdi (both born in 1813) plus *Faust, Carmen, Boris, Cavalleria Rusticana, I Pagliacci, Bohème* and *Tosca*. By the early 1900s much of the steam had gone out of the composition of opera as composers struggled to find an individuality in the wake of Wagner and Verdi. The outstanding creative musicians of the early twentieth century, people like Stravinsky and Debussy, were primarily instrumental composers to whom the voice was really just a part of their overall sound texture. Their genius is not in doubt. Nor is the fact that their early lead, developed by Schoenberg and his followers, led to the composition of operas in which the singing was subtly integrated into the musical and dramatic conception as a whole. The trend had been coming for a long time. But whereas outstanding singing was overwhelmingly the primary prerequisite of a good performance of an early nineteenth-century work like Rossini's *Barbiere* or Bellini's *Sonnambula*, there was no way that *bel canto* singing alone could

* See, for instance, Michael Scott, *The Record of Singing*, vol. 2.

sustain a performance of a later work like *Carmen* or *Tosca*, let alone the integrated music dramas of Wagner. As for the major operatic works of the twentieth century, excellent performances of *Pelléas*, *Wozzeck*, *Moses und Aron*, *The Rake's Progress* or *Peter Grimes* can be achieved by singers whose musical and dramatic intelligence exceeds their purely vocal attainments.

This shift in the requirements of composers became increasingly perceptible after World War I, and singers had to make the first stab at a decision that is by now virtually endemic to the profession: whether to concentrate on the earlier, more ingratiating repertoire, or whether—possibly at serious vocal cost—to try and master the more complex music of their own times. Some dauntless pioneers there were, but most opera singers preferred to sing the standard and proved classics than to venture into unknown and difficult territory. Thus the standard operatic repertoire, instead of receiving regular transfusions of new blood as it had done for a century and a half, began to stagnate to a certain extent.

Alongside these changes came an alteration in the status of the singer. The great stars of the Golden Age had lived and travelled in opulence, often with a great retinue, and were lionized everywhere and paid fabulous fees. By the 1920s, this sort of treatment may have been enjoyed by the stars of the new Hollywood-based movie industry but it was no longer quite the same with opera singers. Some—Grace Moore, Lawrence Tibbett—tried to bridge the two professions and a handful of top singers, notably Gigli, continued to surround themselves with the appurtenances of celebrity. Most, however, took to heart Toscanini's famous reproof to Geraldine Farrar who, complaining that she was a star and not accustomed to being pushed around, was told roundly that the only stars he knew were the ones in heaven and she had better do what she was told. A singer was simply a singer—the *'umile ancella'* or humble ancillary worker of Cilèa's *Adriana Lecouvreur*—whose job was to contribute as best he or she could to the work in hand.

During this period, performance styles appear to have shifted in various subtle ways and it may not be too fanciful to relate some of the vocalism of the inter-war years to the changes in composition styles and the related shift in the musical and social status of the singer.

There is no single cause and effect at work here. Nevertheless, just as the singer was being relegated to the role of ancillary by the composers of the day, and just as partly by consequence mainstream opera singers for the first time found themselves retreating into the music of the past, their vocal pyrotechnics sometimes took on a degree of extra-musical mannerism less common among their 'Golden Age' predecessors.

What of modern times? Most of the factors that might have helped contribute to this vocal decline continued to apply, many in strengthened form, in the years after World War II. If the 1920s and 1930s were a period of political, social and economic disruption, the modern era has not exactly been one of universal peace and stability. And if singers and other musicians moved around the frontiers of Europe and the Americas a great deal in the inter-war years, and some tried to develop careers that regularly straddled both sides of the Atlantic, their mobility was nothing compared with that made possible later by the jet plane, when leading artists would buzz around the continents like bees around a clump of flower beds, alighting briefly here, then there, then moving on to the next place.

If these factors are bound to have had some impact upon the lives and careers of modern singers, so has the modern history of opera composition and recording. With the possible exception of Benjamin Britten, no new composer emerged in the post-World War II decades to contribute to the regular operatic repertoire and the period of maximum operatic creativity receded further into the mists of musical history. New operas still continued to be written* and produced, but no new works of Tippett or Poulenc, Barber or Henze, Shostakovich or Stockhausen really ignited the opera-going public. If there were stage musicals that did, they tended to be by people like Rodgers and Hammerstein, Lerner and Loewe and others—successors rather of Johann Strauss and Franz Léhar than of Verdi and Wagner, though Leonard Bernstein's *West Side Story* succeeded in integrating aspects of both traditions as well as a lot else besides.

Since 1945 the frontiers of popular music have gradually shifted

---

* One major prospect is an opera on the life of the Spanish painter Goya being composed specifically for Domingo by Gian Carlo Menotti.

further from their classical roots and incorporated not only elements of jazz—sliding *portamenti*, strong unvarying rhythms and so on—but also new sounds made possible by electronic synthesizers and by multi-track recording and mixing techniques. As much popular music became tougher, rougher, louder, more electronic, more anarchistic, with a more pervasive beat, singers were required to perform in an idiom for which no traditional vocal training could prepare them. Instead of the ability to read music, sing in tune and in time, control one's breath and phrasing, adjust volume to that of one's fellows, and focus the sound so that it would carry in a large auditorium, the new singer of the rock age was often required to gyrate physically and vocally close to a powerful microphone and to sing with no vocal subtlety of any traditional sort but with an abundance of animal energy. Modern recording techniques, furthermore, meant that many of the most popular performances were not performances—or even performable—at all, but complex studio confections produced by controlling and then mixing a number of effects unreproducible in 'real' time.

As the frontiers of popular music became increasingly distant from the singing of the classical tradition, it became harder for anyone seriously to consider trying to perform successfully in both. Occasionally a singer from the world of popular music would enter that of opera, a tiny handful of them, René Kollo, for instance, with distinction, and Domingo is not the only classical singer to perform middle-of-the-road pop. But the real frontiers of pop and classical music are now a universe apart and almost unbridgeable. If Domingo would have difficulty performing the work of most serious contemporary operatic composers—Stockhausen, say, or even a fundamentally melodic writer like Henze—there is probably no way he could sing punk rock except by a total repudiation of his entire art and training.

Thus, the opera singer of the post-World War II decades has been increasingly isolated from many of the principal musical tendencies of his day. Most of his staple artistic fare is the product of an era which nobody living can remember, while the frontiers of neither the 'high' nor the 'popular' trends of his time have taken much notice of his skills. He is in some ways like the performers in the Moscow Arts

239

Theatre or the D'Oyly Carte Company, repeatedly turning out performances of the same handful of hundred-year-old classics according to production formulae that by the very passage of time are increasingly dated.

As the guardians of an essentially museum culture, opera singers have tended to play safe, to retreat behind the firing line, to perform everything correctly and do nothing actually wrong. The results are often astonishingly accomplished, not a note out of place, not a *piano* or a *sforzando* missed or overdone, not a breath in the wrong spot, every *rallentando* carefully observed. But the impact can sometimes be largely cerebral and the rendering therefore a little arid. Even some of the most outstanding singers of the post-war decades— Schwarzkopf, Fischer-Dieskau, Björling, Katia Ricciarelli, Norman Bailey, Joan Sutherland, Kiri Te Kanawa—have sometimes seemed to lack, not interpretation exactly, but a sense of personal commitment to the passions they are trying to communicate.

Much of this was unavoidable. Opera singers have been constantly expected to re-present and re-package products of a past age in an art lacking sufficient infusions of new creative blood. They can hardly be expected always to approach their art with the freshness of those amongst whom some of the major creators of new works were still flourishing. When Caruso learnt *Bohème* or *Tosca*, or for that matter *Iris* or *Fedora*, it was with the open-mindedness of one who knew that what he was approaching might prove to be an enduring masterpiece. One might misjudge and over-prepare a work that did not warrant it or else underrate a score that in time proved greater than one had realized at first acquaintance. But rather like the film star in the 1930s or the pop star in the 1960s, the Golden Age singer was at the hub of a busy and creative profession and knew that much that would pass through his hands and vocal cords would prove genuinely popular. Eighty years later, top opera singers still occasionally go through the motions of performing new works, but these exercises are generally regarded as a worthy chore akin to, but far more onerous than, giving an occasional free concert for charity. The real business of an opera singer in the modern era is to perform as well as possible the tested and tried masterpieces in the tested and tried ways.

If the continued stagnation of opera-writing has played its part in contributing to shifting styles of singing, so has the history of recording. From the beginning of this century, recordings of opera had an important reciprocal relationship with the development of the art. The young Enrico Caruso was said to have been hired by the Metropolitan Opera partly on the strength of a batch of recordings the young man had made which the manager-designate Heinrich Con-ried was able to play to his directors in New York. By the time the new electrical broadcasting microphone was introduced into the recording studio in 1925, every singer of note was making records and any singer who did not was almost by definition of the second level.

The big technological breakthrough came in the early 1950s when the long-playing record became available. Instead of three or four minutes of music, twenty-five or thirty could henceforth be con-tained on a single side of an unbreakable disc. And as the engineers came to use magnetic tape instead of clumsy and uneditable wax discs, they were able to develop greatly improved new ways of recording, editing and reproducing monaural and later stereophonic sound.

All this had its effect upon performers. In the new LP era they could perform 'takes' of ten minutes at a time rather than the old three or four, could re-record shorter passages several times if they wished, and could relax in the confident knowledge that the top note in the first take could probably be edited into the otherwise preferable third or fourth. At recording sessions, they would hear their own perform-ances played back through massively sensitive speakers at high volume. Any fault, however tiny, would be noticeable in the listening cubicle and out they could go again to get it right.

Every performer is of course interested in obtaining the best recording possible and everyone knows that the music will flow best when it is permitted to do so. Nobody likes to chop up works of art into snippets to feed into the recording sausage machine, to record out of sequence, to re-do tiny passages in isolation. Yet—against everybody's deepest musical instincts—the logic of the situation demands this type of activity. After all, the technology permits errors to be rectified, so it would surely be foolhardy *not* to try and rectify them.

Thus, the development of recording technology has seemed to conspire with the history of opera composition to emphasize the importance of correct or 'perfect' performance, even sometimes at the expense of inspired music-making. The aim is to provide, literally, a record—something, that is, that will stand as a kind of historical document of 'the way it was'. And when you play or sing something 'for the record' you are naturally more careful than in live performance to make sure that everything is technically correct. 'It was my aim,' said the great record producer Walter Legge, 'to make records that would set the standards by which public performances and the artists of the future would be judged.'

If the technology of the modern recording studio has had a profound impact upon the nature of the performances issued on record, there has surely also been something of a knock-on effect upon the nature of live performance itself. Every performance, after all, except those of works outside the nowadays very large repertoire, will have the shadow of various recordings pressing down upon it as a standard of comparison. It is not every artist who, like Domingo, has himself recorded most of what he performs, but most singers are familiar with recordings, by others if not themselves, of the works they perform in public. And in the age of the ubiquitous record player any performance that fluctuates too widely from the accepted studio norm will probably be disliked by many listeners. Tamagno or Paderewski or Ysaÿe could be—we know they were—somewhat cavalier about note values or tempi, but their successors today cannot be.

On the face of it, then, opera has become by the 1980s to a very large extent a museum art, and the role of the singer is largely to re-package and re-present as correctly and authentically as he can a product of a rapidly receding historical past. All of this might be expected to inject a great deal of caution and even insecurity into the profession, while much of the technological gadgetry that surrounds the modern singer's life and career—recording techniques, the temptation to jet around from one engagement to the next—would also appear to lead towards a standard of all-purpose vocal proficiency rather than real re-creative artistry.

And yet the experience of one's eyes and ears belies much of this.

For all the factors that may militate against, for all the blandness of many performances of old works and the aridity of most new ones, for all the economic belt-tightening the modern world has had to undergo, it is difficult to resist the unexpected verdict that we are living through a renaissance of operatic singing and of performance quality in general that would stand proudly alongside the highest achievements of earlier generations. When one thinks of the dazzling yet powerful coloratura of Sutherland or Horne, the heart-breaking desperation of Vickers in, say, *Tristan* or *Grimes*, the nobility of Domingo in *Otello*, the elegance of Bergonzi or Pavarotti, the passion of Carreras, the plangent sensitivity of such mezzos as Janet Baker, Teresa Berganza or Frederica von Stade, the sonorous authority of a Martti Talvela or a Ghiaurov or the rich, creamy tones of a Margaret Price or a Kiri Te Kanawa, and the sizzlingly responsive conducting of a Riccardo Muti or a Carlos Kleiber, it becomes patently absurd to think of opera in our day as 'merely' a museum art guarded by over-cautious curators.

As Covent Garden approaches its 500th performance of *Carmen* and the Met its 600th *Bohème*, Paris and La Scala their *n*th *Faust* or *Aida*, there can be no doubt that the staple fare at all the world's major opera houses is the re-playing of popular masterpieces from the past. It is rather as though the legitimate theatre all over the world relied for over ninety per cent of its productions on a repertoire limited to the major works of Shakespeare, seventeenth-century French drama, the Scandinavian tragedies and a smattering of other classics, entire seasons going by with nothing by a living writer performed. In addition, many aspects of operatic performing style undeniably lie encrusted in the long-dead past—the traditional cuts, interpolations, flourishes, sustained high notes, the often rudimentary acting, even in many cases the type of scenery and costumes. But nevertheless, for all this, there is no doubt that the quality of operatic performance nowadays is often astonishingly high, that performers do not resemble the tired antiquarians our previous analysis might lead one to expect, and that the popular appetite for good opera, far from atrophying, has been growing in many countries in recent years. It would not be going too far, indeed, to talk about an operatic renaissance in the post-war decades. Possibly even of a second

Golden Age. How, in the light of all we have been saying, can that be true?

Take, first, the question of repertoire. It is true that most of it is honoured by age, that in the 1980s, unlike the 1880s, most opera houses perform works on average a century old and include very few in their repertoire by composers still alive. However, things in the past were often different only in degree. Giulio Gatti-Casazza, who ran La Scala from 1898–1908 and the New York Metropolitan Opera from 1908–35, tells plaintively in his memoirs how hard he always tried to persuade composers to write new works for him and his board to agree to new works being mounted. After the great success of *Pelléas* Debussy repeatedly promised Gatti that the Met could have his next two operas but they never materialized. Boito took thirty years over his *Nerone* but died with the work incomplete. The Paris Opéra, anxious to encourage Charpentier after the success of *Louise*, eagerly produced his *Julien*, but it turned out to be a damp squib rather as the later works of Mascagni and Leoncavallo proved to be. Certainly, any new work by the mature Meyerbeer, Verdi or Puccini would be sure of an early airing, while Wagner, like Britten, would in his later years supervise performances of his own works under his own auspices. But we should not be misled by the genius of Wagner or Verdi into thinking that at the time they were turning out their towering masterpieces other composers of stature were also producing major works every year or two. A glance through the repertoire of most opera houses a century ago confirms that then as now most opera managements tended to put on familiar works by major composers rather than risk public displeasure by mounting new ones by composers less well known. At no time was the proportion of hits to misses very high among new works, and most performances most of the time were of operas that had already established themselves.

If the repertoire in the nineteenth century was not always growing quite as lustily as is sometimes supposed, the modern additions to it may be greater than they appear to be at first sight. Some new works take immediate hold: with others it takes time, and only future generations will know, as we ourselves cannot, whether *The Bassarids* or *Susannah* or *King Priam* will eventually establish themselves. Furthermore, in an era of stringent economies and of increasing emphasis on local self-help in the arts, there has been a growth of chamber-scale opera, and the works to which chamber opera producers turn are almost invariably recent compositions by modern composers such as Britten or Malcolm Williamson or Richard Rodney Bennett. Some would go further and argue that the best works for the musical stage by essentially popular composers are akin to opera; if the English National Opera can put on *Kiss Me Kate* and the New York City Opera Bernstein's *Candide*, then an era that has seen the flowering of the American musical, not to mention the runaway successes of Andrew Lloyd Webber, can scarcely be said to be deficient.

There is a further respect in which the repertoire has been growing in our own times: the rediscovery and reinstatement of older works often ignored by earlier generations. The finding (and losing) of older works is a continuous process; the mid-nineteenth century did not listen to Mozart's *Così* and the mid-twentieth does not listen to much Meyerbeer. Who can say what today's core repertoire will look like a century hence? By the standards of any earlier period, our age has been remarkably eclectic in the breadth of its tastes. There have been notable revivals of interest in the operas of Monteverdi and his contemporaries and of Handel, and singers of the quality of Callas, Sutherland, Horne, Sills and Caballé have widened the *bel canto* repertoire enormously and discovered gold (musically and financially) in relatively unfamiliar works by Rossini, Donizetti, Bellini and others. If audiences a century ago heard a lot of Meyerbeer, as well as recent works by Pacini, Franco Faccio, Halévy, Ambroise Thomas, Cornelius or Anton Rubinstein, we are probably more likely to hear, and sometimes see, *Il Pirata*, *Medea*, *Roberto Devereux*, *Maria Stuarda* and *Il Turco in Italia*. A museum art? Possibly, but the material on display has been greatly enriched in recent times.

In one way, opera is less a museum art than some would like it to be. We have had occasion to speak of outstanding singers and conductors as particularly instrumental in bringing a wider repertoire before the public and reintroducing works of merit too long forgotten. But to many the modern age is not primarily that of the singer or the conductor; it is the age of the producer. Just as people talked with awe about Patti or Melba Nights or of performances with Toscanini or Bruno Walter or Beecham in the pit, people today talk of Wieland Wagner's, or Patrice Chéreau's, or Peter Hall's *Ring*, Zeffirelli's *Tosca* or *Traviata*, Ponnelle's *Figaro* or *Barber*, Peter Hall's *Così* or *Don Giovanni*, Jonathan Miller's *Rigoletto*. Nothing is so calculated to set operatic tongues a-wagging as an attack on, or defence of, the opera producer. For every person who thinks the producer has expropriated the role of the composer, directed a particular scene 'against the music' or imposed an inappropriate modern interpretation upon a work, another will get up and assert that the composer would have wanted it this way and that, in any case, all great works of art must be reinterpreted by each generation.

Victor Gollancz attributed what he saw as the decline in singing directly to the ascendancy of the producer, and plenty of singers will complain about the heavy costumes and headpieces they have to wear, the precipices they have to ascend, the awkward positions they have to assume while singing and the mistakes of characterization they find themselves called upon to adopt. There have been neo-gay Otellos and Iagos, nineteenth- and twentieth-century Rigolettos, Flying Dutchmen who are all figments of their Senta's fevered imagination, *Parsifals* that set out to deride Christianity and *Fidelios* and *Forzas* to apostrophize the working class. But it is also true that production as we know it today—an attempt to plan and to integrate all the visual, dramatic and musical aspects of performance—is in general far more advanced than in earlier periods.

The advance is partly a matter of technology: we now have revolving stages and sophisticated computer-based lighting systems; also jet planes and direct-dial international telephones which enable producers, set designers, singers and conductors to keep in touch long ahead of a production on which they will be working together. But the chief reason why production is taken seriously nowadays, by those who admire and those who decry, is that there have been an impressive crop of strong-minded producers, including many eager to move from the straight theatre or films into the world of opera.

In a poor production, opera can be routine and dull, the mere re-enactment of old masterpieces in a way that has become not time-honoured but rusty and musty with age. But given adventurous and imaginative production, a conductor who can approach a familiar work with freshness and vigour, and singers who have not only excellent solo voices but also proficiency and intelligence as actors and as ensemble players, the results can be magical, a true merging of several art forms to create a rounded aesthetic experience. Doubtless, this has always been the case. The greatest practitioners in the past were always those who took the art seriously and cared about all its elements. A Toscanini or a Mahler, like Klemperer or Karajan in more recent times, cared deeply about details of stage production, as did every one of the major opera composers. In modern times, a Gobbi or a Callas or a Domingo among singers, a Haitink, a Muti or a Levine among conductors, will become deeply involved in the production details of any work they are performing. And the best producers, for all the opprobrium heaped upon their more perverse brethren, always illuminate rather than obfuscate the dramatic implications of the music. Gone are the days when some great star would be invited to come and do 'his' Don Giovanni or 'her' Aida at such-and-such a house, when a Patti or a Pons could send an emissary to the stage rehearsal (if there was one) to report back on the set and the moves. Eva Turner recalled to me how she used to be expected to travel round with her Turandot and Aida and Leonore costumes from one production to another rather like a violinist or cellist with his instrument. Not so today, when Hamburg's Desdemona or Elsa or whatever has to fit into an entirely different production and costume from that of Cologne or Milan or Chicago.

Opera today is, then, a multi-media entertainment that at its best aspires to producing an all-embracing artistic experience without parallel. Caruso may not be alive today, nor Mozart or Verdi; there are no Wagnerian tenors or sopranos currently to compare with several who flourished earlier. But we have singers who are far more musically literate than many of their forebears, men and women who have a reasonable idea of what their colleagues are singing, what the orchestra is playing, what the producer expects of them and why; designers with ears as well as eyes; conductors and producers who work together towards a common goal. It is true that the temptations offered by the jet plane, the blandishments of recording and film companies, and the financial and artistic invitations emanating from opera houses from one end of the world to the other may all have conspired to prevent many of the performers most in demand from remaining as members of a single company for any length of time in the way many of their predecessors did. Many of the world's most prestigious houses, therefore, lack what might be called a house style. But if more people in more countries have a chance of hearing some of the best practitioners of some of opera's most popular roles, what is wrong with that? So why not use the jet plane, the long-distance telephone, closed-circuit television, computer lighting and anything else modern technology has to offer, if these enable the best people to come together from round the world to create high standards of opera together? Many fall by the wayside, singers who cannot deal with the physical or psychological demands of opera-making in the modern world, producers seduced by the technology into mounting opinion-ated travesties of works they supposedly intend to serve. But the opportunities available today to those capable of using them intelligently are surely greater than ever before. If they are artistically talented, personally sensitive and physically robust, there are few limits to their potential achievements other than those of time and space.

Things are not what they used to be, people still say, and they are right. In many ways we must conclude that things are better. Caruso was probably seen in performance by about one and a half million people during his career; Domingo can be heard by millions whenever any of his performances are broadcast, while entire pro-ductions are nowadays captured in both sound and vision for future generations to enjoy.

We may have no Verdi or Wagner alive today, but we can enjoy their music (which Mozart could not) and Puccini's (which they could not) and hear and gradually get to see several generations of singers performing it. A new 'Golden Age' of singing? It is rash to impose such labels upon an era, impossible, really, to compare the overall operatic achievements of one period with another. What we can say is that in our own time there are singers, particularly in the Italian repertoire, to compare with the finest of earlier generations, and that good opera well performed is accessible to more people, 'live' or in increasingly sophisticated forms of reproduction, than ever before. Perhaps if our great-grandfathers had known what delights the Age of Domingo was to hold in store, they might not have harked back quite so insistently to the Age of Caruso . . .

ACT V

The Star

'Le Grand Echiquier'

Like all great cities, Paris is constantly changing. When Plácido Domingo first came to sing here in 1973, most of the trains in the metro still clattered along on noisy metal wheels, and if you and a train approached a platform at the same time the chances were that you would be excluded by a large automatic iron door. Today the trains run with twice the speed and a quarter the noise on rubber wheels, and the authorities leave it to the good sense of their patrons not to kill themselves in the rush for an arriving train. There are fewer graffiti in Paris now than there used to be. 'Yankees' are still periodically invited to go home, but no longer from Vietnam. This particular week, at the end of October 1983, it is from a little Caribbean island scarcely anybody in France had heard of a week earlier, called in French 'Grenade'.

Domingo used to be a frequent visitor to Paris, appearing regularly at the great ornate Théâtre National de l'Opéra, the Garnier 'Palace' as the place is appropriately called after its mid-nineteenth-century architect when it was run by Rolf Liebermann in the middle and late 1970s. There was a superb *Forza* in 1975, a restrained, lyrical *Otello* in 1976 (repeated two years later), memorable *Bohèmes* and *Carmens*. Liebermann chalked up a number of triumphs, and if most seemed primarily due to the regular presence of non-French artists (Domingo, Solti, John Dexter—not to mention the Swiss-born Liebermann himself, for years Intendant of the Hamburg opera), the Paris opera-going public did not seem to object.

French officialdom was another matter, however, and Lieber-

mann felt he lacked the support he needed if his policy of 'nothing but
the best' was to continue. It was not a matter of funds exactly, though
then Prime Minister Chirac made threatening noises in this direction, nor did anybody in government tell Liebermann in so many
words what operas or casts to present. But that he was under attack he
had no doubt, and he let it be known that he would not be available
once his present contract ran out in 1980. Liebermann's successor,
former Aix-en-Provence Festival director Bernard Lefort, soon set
about the task of 'Frenchifying' the Opéra. As Domingo puts it,
Lefort did invite him to appear, but in roles he knew Domingo would
not be able to accept. Bernard Lefort did not last long, however, and
his successor, Massimo Bogianckino, is a lively Italian opera administrator, his spurs principally won as the successful director of the
Teatro Comunale and the Maggio Musicale in Florence. Bogianckino took over the Opéra in 1982 and his imaginative stamp is already
evident. This very week, for example, you can see, if you can beg,
borrow or steal a ticket, Rossini's rarely performed *Moïse* with
Samuel Ramey and Shirley Verrett, and both Puccini's original and
revised versions of *Madama Butterfly*. Will Domingo be back at the
Opéra? Bogianckino has been keen to get him and Domingo to say
yes. Plans are to be discussed and refined within the next few days for
possible future appearances as Domingo arrives in Paris to make a T V
programme: Jacques Chancel's 'Le Grand Echiquier' on French
television's cultural network, Antenne 2.

Chancel, a former war correspondent in Indo-China but now well
into his fifties, greying and suave, is by repute one of the best, perhaps
the smoothest, interviewer on French television. Since 1972 he has
carved a special niche for himself by hosting a regular series of live,
evening-long shows around the life and work of a major figure in the
world of art or entertainment. The format is simple. The featured
'Grand Echiquier' and a number of other more or less appropriate
celebrities all take turns performing for the cameras and the invited
audience, while between acts, as it were, Chancel engages his star
and principal guests in ostensibly relaxed but often very revealing
conversation. The whole operation is a marvel of controlled television production, the more so since the shows are normally
transmitted live. While Chancel and guests have their periodic three

or four minutes of chat, armies of cameramen and others set up another corner of the vast studio in preparation for the next piece of action. If the show were recorded a fastidious producer would doubtless keep everybody on set for a week.

Most of Chancel's 'Great Chess Players' have been French and have included such celebrities as François Truffaut, Yves Montand and Jean-Louis Barrault. Foreigners have included Karajan, Rubinstein and Menuhin. Now it is the turn of Plácido Domingo. Domingo is a law unto himself and everybody else's rules have periodically to be bent to accommodate him. As Chancel tells the studio audience the night of the show, this is the first time 'Le Grand Echiquier' is not to be broadcast live. The reason, quite simply, is that although he had been negotiating for Domingo for a couple of years or more, Plácido's diary was so booked up that this was the only time he could do the show before the late 1980s. But tonight's programme, Chancel goes on, will be broadcast in three weeks' time exactly as it takes place this evening—no tricks, no edits, no retakes, nothing added or cut. The broadcast will be 'as live'.

This is not to say that it has not been carefully prepared. It has; or at least some of its constituent parts have been. Earlier in the week Domingo rehearsed and taped two or three items which, along with a few clips of opera films, will be played into the programme, thus giving everyone in the studio a few minutes' respite from the glare and tension. And on the afternoon of the show itself Domingo spends three hours rehearsing, *inter alia*, a delicate, unfamiliar song by Fauré, 'Après un Rêve', and a tricky Dvořák piano duet with the visually spiky but audibly mellifluous Alexis Weissenberg, and taking the Orchestre National de France (the ONF) through various pieces in which he is to conduct them tonight.

The rehearsals have all been just a little lacklustre and this final one is no exception. The studio, one of several each the size of a plane hangar in a vast windowless barn in the Buttes de Chaumont district of Paris, is too hot and noisy for comfort, and most of the musical numbers are just that bit too easy for either Domingo or the ONF to be really on their toes. The ONF is, with Barenboim's Orchestre de Paris, one of the élite orchestras of France. The last time they saw Domingo was when, under Lorin Maazel's direction, they recorded the sound-track of *Carmen*, with Domingo as Don José, for the Gaumont film. How could Plácido Domingo really tell an orchestra of this quality how to play Verdi's *Forza del Destino* overture or the slow movements of the Mozart piano concerto no. 9 (with Weissenberg again at the piano) or the Mendelssohn violin concerto? The Mendelssohn run-through is particularly lacking in electricity since it has to be done in the absence of the young soloist Pierre Amoyal, but memorable none the less for the fact that much of the time the violin solo part is sung in the inimitable if subdued voice of tonight's conductor. On the rostrum Domingo tends to give a somewhat generalized lead: a clear, two-armed upward beat with little attention to particular sections of the orchestra. But everyone knows that the occasion will not be one for finely calibrated playing nor is Domingo's conducting to be put under the critical microscope tonight. All that is really required during the afternoon run-through is for professional musicians to reassure themselves and each other that they will be able to do the pieces properly when the time comes, and this much at least the rehearsals achieve.

The afternoon rehearsal runs overtime. 'Where are the two hours' rest Plácido was supposed to have?' asks his French agent Michel Glotz, eyes rolling up to heaven as cigarette butt turns down towards the floor. Throughout the long afternoon, as always at rehearsals, most people spend most of the time sitting around doing nothing. The handsome, stocky man with a thick shock of hair, for example, who watches particularly avidly as Domingo takes the orchestra through the *Forza* overture. This is conductor Garcia Navarro, who earlier displayed his own skills in a spirited run-through of the various Spanish pieces he will conduct tonight. And that beguiling girl in the tight black leather skirt, sitting decoratively on the bleachers along one wall of the studio—she is a star of the Folies Bergère and despite being called Norma Duval is in fact Spanish. It is a matter for regret that when her turn eventually comes to rehearse it is merely as a singer. 'She has no bottom register,' comments one shocked bystander as Norma clutches her microphone ever closer as though for support. 'Oh, but she does!' grins a companion, his eye fixed on the shiny black skirt. It is a matter for even greater regret that when Norma's turn comes to perform in the show itself she has a momentary lapse of memory at the pivotal moment in that most famous of all French songs, 'La Vie en Rose'. 'Never mind,' smiles the world's greatest opera singer reassuringly to his crestfallen compatriot, 'we all forget words in songs from time to time!'

A few feet away from La Norma at the afternoon rehearsal sits a beauty of an altogether different genre, a woman with the sculpted profile of a Nefertiti and the elegance of the models who parade outside the Domingos' Ritz Hotel in the Place Vendôme. This is the opera world's favourite French language coach, Janine Reiss. Janine too will not be without mishap in tonight's proceedings. When she is invited to show how she coaches a singer like Domingo in an unfamiliar opera (they work on a passage from Ambroise Thomas's *Mignon*) her microphone lets her down and much of her gentle but authoritative prodding at Plácido's imperfect French is inaudible except to its immediate recipient. *'Dieu te consolera'* Plácido sings tenderly, as though meaning it. *'Consolera, pas consolera, pas consolerra!'* corrects Janine firmly. Microphones are it seems as indispensable to television as cameras, though when you have a voice with the projection of Plácido Domingo you may be forgiven for wondering why. When towards the end of a long evening Domingo launches into 'My Life for a Song' he is stopped by Chancel, who calls out that he must hold a mike. 'What's the matter?' Plácido shoots back. 'You think that after midnight I have no more voice left?'

The evening is indeed a long one, longer even than Chancel had planned. At 8.30, Plácido entered the studio, smartly attired in white tie and tails, and, accompanied by Garcia Navarro and the ONF, gave one of his roof-raising accounts of 'Recondita armonia'. Fully four hours and forty-odd items later, Plácido, now dressed in a lounge suit, is cheered to the echo by a happy crowd as Chancel finally winds up what must have been one of the longer uninterrupted television variety programmes on record.

Marta Domingo has been sitting just behind her husband all evening and beams with pride as Plácido tells people how ('apart perhaps from my voice') he owes everything to her. It has been a wonderful occasion for her. Another lady who has had a great evening is Mireille Mathieu. Still young enough to look like a little girl in a party frock yet at the same time the natural successor to the tough, permanently shop-worn Piaf, Mireille set her stamp upon the evening early in the proceedings with a resolute performance, in almost guttural, Piafesque French, of 'La Paloma'. She tells people she thought she was dreaming when invited to sing with Plácido Domingo—a specially written and far from easy duet, appropriately perhaps entitled 'Tous Mes Rêves', by Michel Legrand. Legrand himself was in the studio this evening, resembling a shambling, bespectacled provincial professor rather than the doyen of French popular music and composer of some sixty film scores. His various contributions to the evening culminated in a stunning display of pianistic virtuosity as he improvised upon his own 'Moulins de mon Coeur,' accompanied by the light orchestra of Jean Claudric, complete with slinkily-clad 'ba-ba-doo' girls, two to a mike. Redhead Régine, queen of the Paris night-clubs, did well for her friend Plácido tonight, too, and so did a young pianist named Michael Rudy who gave a shudderingly beautiful performance of a Chopin nocturne. And as for Charles Aznavour, he proved that, at nearly sixty, he is still the very epitome of the French *chansonnier*. Aznavour, son of Turkish Armenian immigrants, a man whose lined face and tiny body suggest the suffering that his songs express so eloquently, poured out so much passionate despair in 'La Salle et la Terrasse' that Chancel's audience was at first almost too stunned to applaud. 'Tremendous!' says an admirer afterwards as Aznavour leaves the studio with his manager, Lèvon Sayan, who also manages Domingo's publicity in France. 'Thanks,' responds Aznavour with a wan smile, adding that he couldn't stop his legs trembling with tension as he sang but hoped it didn't show.

And the latest Grand Echiquier himself? He performed well tonight too. In all senses. His singing, whether of opera, *zarzuela* or the music of Michel Legrand, was stupendous. He managed to manoeuvre with grace and wit the hoops Chancel laid before him and left his audience with the impression of a man whose warmth of personality matched his genius as a musician. And if he too stumbled on occasion—the Fauré song for instance was clearly not his métier, and the inadequately rehearsed Dvořák piano duet fell to pieces in the middle—none of this mattered. If anything, it merely served to show a sympathetic audience that Domingo, too, was a vulnerable human being like themselves. Now, at the end of the evening, Domingo is all smiles—of happiness and, doubtless, some relief that it is all over. 'This was the hardest thing I think I have ever done,' Plácido confides to friends. He often says things like that. But on this particular night, after all those hours under hot TV lights during which he was required to sing, in effect, a full-length concert, conduct three orchestral pieces, play the piano, and between times participate in a dozen separate French language interviews before what will the following month become a nationwide audience, he may just possibly be right.

The Maestro

A problem child can often be the most lovable in the family and so it is to many opera goers with Johann Strauss's *Die Fledermaus*. *Fledermaus* is a problem because quite simply it is not an opera. Operetta, certainly, and a leader in the category that includes the finest works of Offenbach, Gilbert and Sullivan, Léhar and perhaps Richard Rodgers or Lerner and Loewe. But with its improbable story and characters and its succession of light musical numbers linked by lengthy dialogue, *Fledermaus* is scarcely the same genre as *Figaro*, *Falstaff* or *Rosenkavalier*. On the other hand, *Die Fledermaus* contains some of the most delicious music ever written for the stage, a feast of solo and ensemble singing and of orchestral writing overflowing with sentiment and sparkle. And the plot? A high-living scion of Old Vienna is persuaded by a scheming friend to defer a gaol sentence for a few hours and go instead to a fashionable party where every imaginable adventure befalls him, his wife, his maid and the prison governor, none of whom is quite sure who all the others are—this is the stuff that stage directors' dreams are made of. *Fledermaus* is, in short, a work few opera lovers—or opera managements—have been able to resist. Throughout its history, indeed, as if to compensate for its problem status, this greatest of all Viennese operettas has frequently been mounted in the most lavish productions of which the world's great opera houses are capable.

ACT V · THE STAR

By tradition *Die Fledermaus* is especially ideal for New Year's Eve, and its central scene, at Prince Orlofsky's party, with its invariable complement of surprise guest appearances, can leave a receptive audience almost as merry as if they had been sipping the Prince's champagne themselves. It is an end-of-term piece, an evening for letting down your hair, the one event in the operatic calendar when you might catch Brünnhilde singing a pop song, Giselle waving to the conductor—or, as happened at Covent Garden at the end of 1983 to ecstatic applause, the conductor joining in the singing.

However, the wide variations of tempo and of mood, to say nothing of the problem of maintaining the musical flow despite the long interruptions for dialogue, make *Fledermaus* a difficult work to carry off with total conviction. If the audience leave either untouched by sentiment or else drunk on mere sentimentality the musical party will have failed. And the host, ultimately, is the man in the pit.

Domingo is well aware of this. Despite the work's two tenor roles* he has never sung in *Die Fledermaus* but has been familiar with the work ever since the days of his parents' musical theatre in Mexico. During his years in Israel in the early 1960s he sometimes played the piano for singers doing a turn in the party scene. Then in the late 1970s and early 1980s he conducted the opera in Frankfurt, Munich and at the Vienna State Opera. There was some scepticism, however, at Covent Garden when Domingo was announced as conductor of the December 1983 revival, particularly among the orchestra. A gimmick, some said. Lots of singers would like to try their hand at conducting, others muttered darkly, but the Covent Garden management always indulge the whims of their top stars and Domingo must have made *Fledermaus* a quid pro quo for some appearances as a singer . . . The scepticism was inevitable and predictable and Domingo was anxious from the start to allay it as far as he could and establish himself as a bona fide conductor. Ever since Julius Rudel let him direct some performances of *La Traviata* at the New York City Opera in 1973 Domingo had been seized by the serious possibility of a career as a conductor once the voice eventually begins to give way,

* Alfred and Eisenstein. In the 1977 Covent Garden production, however, Eisenstein was sung by Hermann Prey, a high baritone. Prince Orlofsky, normally a mezzo, was played by tenor Robert Tear.

and on his infrequent forays on to the podium he has been keen to establish credentials.

The run-up towards Domingo's Covent Garden directorial début was not without its stresses. In early November a friend with astrological proclivities warned him, as a glance at his schedule might equally have done, that he was in danger of running into heavy weather over the next few weeks. *Fledermaus* was not the only thing in his calendar. During November Domingo was due to sing five performances of *Otello* at Covent Garden and spend much of the time in between commuting to and from Milan to rehearse a new Zeffirelli production of *Turandot* to open the Scala season on 7 December. *Otello* is probably the most demanding work in Domingo's repertoire, one that stretches all his enormous talents to the limits. During this particular run, however, his physical and mental energies were to be divided three ways. Crazy, perhaps, but the kind of ambitious planning that Plácido Domingo has carried off successfully in the past. When you are invited once again to open the Scala season you do not refuse lightly and Domingo would not want to be accused by the Milanese of skipping rehearsals. La Scala had originally scheduled *Fanciulla*, not one of Domingo's most taxing operas, and when that fell through they considered another relatively manageable work, *Tosca*. *Turandot*, a far more demanding proposition, was only chosen a few months before the opening date and by that time Domingo's *Otello* and *Fledermaus* schedules had long since been fixed. None the less, as November approached, Domingo felt confident his complex timetabling could work. *Turandot* rehearsals were conveniently placed between *Otello* performances, and *Fledermaus* rehearsals would only get really heavily under way once *Turandot* had opened. In practice, however, the malign conjunction of the stars, or of rehearsal and performance and airline schedules and a particularly nasty fog in Milan, were to get the better of Domingo's best intentions.

When Domingo arrived in London in early November he was in fine form. As he rehearsed for a Royal Festival Hall charity concert he radiated confidence and goodwill. *Otello* opened a few days later to reviews some of which found the performance under Colin Davis disappointingly muted. With it began the stint of regular commuting to and from Milan. The Zeffirelli *Turandot* showed promise of being a superb production, Ghena Dimitrova an outstanding exponent of the title-role. But Domingo was not fully at ease. The part of Calaf is a taxing one and he was finding it difficult blending easily with Lorin Maazel's forceful direction of the orchestra. By the third week of November Domingo's health gave way. Tracheitis, the doctors announced—and this, they insisted, meant no more *Otello* and probably no *Turandot*. He should not even speak more than strictly necessary if he did not want to do his voice long-term harm. But he could possibly be permitted to whisper when he met the Covent Garden orchestra for their first *Fledermaus* rehearsal a week later . . .

Henry Wood Hall is a converted church in London's Southwark district now used as a rehearsal hall. Here Domingo is formally introduced to the Covent Garden orchestra, and he croaks his way through an initial rehearsal patently depressed at his inability to communicate properly with his voice but gratified that he seems to be doing so successfully with his baton. A couple of days later in the Covent Garden opera studio, his speaking voice now somewhat repaired, Domingo gets together with his principal singers for the first time and here too the rapport works well. The cast (save for the addition of Welsh tenor Dennis O'Neill as Alfred and of Doris Soffel as a mezzo Orlofsky) is essentially the same as opened the production six years ago: Hermann Prey and Kiri Te Kanawa as Eisenstein and his wife Rosalinde, Hildegard Heichele as Adele, Benjamin Luxon as Falke, Michael Langdon as the prison governor and Josef Meinrad as the gaoler. 'How are you? Wonderful to see you.' Plácido bestows warm hugs and handshakes and smilingly warns everyone not to get too close to him if they value their voices. The opening session is a short one, more a get-together than a rehearsal. But it is immediately apparent that Domingo intends to be the conductor in fact as well as in name and not only knows the score inside out but knows precisely what he wants to do with it.

Perhaps God in His mysterious way knew a thing or two when He laid Domingo low with tracheitis. Certainly Domingo's enforced absence from Milan during these days enables him to sit in on more of the early *Fledermaus* production rehearsals than he would otherwise have been able to attend, and the hovering presence of the conductor on these occasions always goes down well with a hard-worked cast. And if any feared Domingo would try and show them how to sing their parts, Domingo's vestigial tracheitis—not to mention his scrupulous adherence to his non-singing function in this particular production—helps put everyone at their ease.

There is great *Gemütlichkeit* when stage rehearsals are reached but lazy habits intrude, lines get dropped and here and there ensemble remains obstinately ragged. Domingo in the pit, conducting a piano rehearsal one day, an orchestral rehearsal another, tries to be alert to everything and has the constant presence of assistant conductor Robin Stapleton over his shoulder for help and advice. Resident Producer Richard Gregson runs up over the bridge on to the stage to adjust the position of the chorus, while the elegant, ever-watchful Hilde Beal, Covent Garden's German language coach, firmly but diplomatically helps Kiri Te Kanawa or Ben Luxon with details of pronunciation. Ten days or so before opening night, *Fledermaus* is at the stage that all good opera productions have to go through: the point at which nobody can see how the show can possibly be ready in time even though, deep down, everybody knows that it will.

'Chum! Chum! Chum! De-diddle-liddle-liddle-liddle lum chum chum . . . ' The overture gets off to a brisk start though one or two of the fast string passages need attention and are rehearsed at half speed. Domingo's beat is vigorous, somewhat curvilinear, more up-beat than down, perhaps held a little low for everyone's comfort, and involves more exertion of body and arms (and less of wrist) than is ideal. Watch him closely and you may detect at the great musical climaxes the same resolute toss of the head, the same clenched fists and slightly buckled knees that characterize his performances on stage as a singer. For the musical impulses emanating from Domingo are essentially the same.

Conductors Domingo has worked with pay tribute to the depth and range of his musicianship. 'It's a joy having him at the other end of the stick,' says Lorin Maazel, 'because he really knows what's happening and one can communicate through just eye signals or whatever what ordinarily would take months of rehearsals to get across.' 'A wonderful sense of musical timing,'—it is Zubin Mehta speaking. 'You always know that *he* knows where he is going in a phrase.' Conductors who have directed Domingo's operatic recordings recount how, unlike many singers, Domingo's curiosity and sensitivity in the studio extend to the technical aspects of recording, the way the balance between sections of the orchestra and between orchestra and voices can be altered not only by conductor but engineers, and also how the instrumentation might be adjusted to ease recording of a difficult bridge passage or transposition. 'He's a musician through and through, not "merely" a singer,' several emphasize.

'A certain interest in conducting is very helpful to any musician because it forces him to hear everything with orchestral ears.' This is the view of Daniel Barenboim, one of the outstanding examples in our own day of a soloist who has made the transition to conductor successfully, and a friend and colleague of Domingo since the 1960s. How good a conductor Domingo will eventually become Barenboim cannot say, nor how thoroughly he çan read a complex orchestral score. But he is impressed by the way Domingo clearly 'thinks orchestrally'; Plácido always knows not only his own singing line, Barenboim says, but also much of what his colleagues have to sing and also the colours, the textures, the harmonies. 'Plácido plays the piano well and is far more aware than most singers of all that is going on under what he sings.' He adds a note of caution, however. 'Being outstandingly musical is not enough to make you into a good conductor. When you play or sing as a soloist a large percentage of your performance depends on your own musical intuition. But when you conduct you have to persuade others to play the way you hear the music in your head and to do this you must be able to analyse and rationalize—and communicate to others—your own musical instincts.' Which is why, this former child prodigy adds, you can occasionally have a child prodigy pianist or violinist, but never a real child prodigy conductor.

Does Domingo have this capacity to analyse and communicate his musical instincts or is he, ultimately, on the podium, no more than a talented amateur? Talk to Domingo himself about his conducting and it immediately becomes apparent how seriously he takes it. He acknowledges at once that of course his singing has to take priority and that he has a long way to go before he approaches similar proficiency as a conductor. But he speaks with enthusiasm about the conducting classes he sat in on which Igor Markevitch gave at the Mexico Conservatoire, and about lessons he has learnt from such admired colleagues as Nello Santi or Carlos Kleiber, and he can become quite earnest about his own aspirations. He can also be very funny. I once asked him whether he thought conducting opera was likely to prove easier than conducting the symphonic repertoire; after all, opera was in general already more familiar to him. True, he acknowledged, but when you conduct opera you've got two sets of forces to control at once, those on stage and those in the pit (the singers 'upstairs' and the players 'downstairs' as he puts it graphically). 'It's like being a Roman gladiator,' he laughed, throwing limbs precariously in all directions, 'with one leg in one chariot pulled by a hundred horses in one direction, and the other in another chariot pulled by another hundred horses in a different direction!' The sheer co-ordination of the two hundred horses, one of the hardest technical jobs an operatic conductor is called upon to do, is indeed to prove one of Domingo's toughest assignments as he nurses his orchestra, chorus and principals day by day closer to the opening night of *Die Fledermaus*.

One morning, as Domingo works away in the pit, all his concentration on the orchestra below and the singers above, a squat, darkly handsome figure marches straight across to him from behind, seizes him by the shoulders, and interrupts the proceedings proclaiming loudly, 'I just wanted to see what was going on!' The music skids awkwardly to a halt. A split second's shock and consternation gives way to smiles and applause from upstairs and down as everyone recognizes Zubin Mehta, in London for a concert at the Barbican with the Vienna Philharmonic. 'You didn't think I'd miss this, did you?' Zubin asks Plácido as the two old friends embrace warmly. If Domingo is at all self-conscious at being watched by the maestro who opened this very production in 1977, and who has conducted Domingo several times in this theatre and, indeed, in Domingo's first complete opera recording, *Il Trovatore*, back in 1969, he does not show it. On the contrary, he emits a huge smile and introduces Mehta to the orchestra. 'Ladies and gentlemen, I don't know whether you know . . .' and the rest of his words are drowned out by more laughter and applause. When the rehearsal resumes, Mehta watches discreetly for a while, exchanging whispered greetings with friends in the darkened auditorium. 'Hi!' smiles Ben Luxon, 'you here to cover for Plácido?'

With just a few days to go before the first audience there is no time for many such incidents. The official opening night is still nearly a week away, but Covent Garden has decided to try the show out before an audience of schoolchildren to get some idea of whether any sections need revision. Also, Covent Garden is for the first time trying out a series of 'sur-titles'—English translations projected onto a screen above the stage—which, if successful with the school audience, might be used on future occasions and with other operas.

As the minutes and hours and days tick away, most things fall into place. The off-stage brass is too loud and has to be kept down, while the on-stage cymbalon that introduces Kiri Te Kanawa's *czardas* in Act II must be amplified and its bass register cut if it is to be clearly audible. Plácido and Kiri work out in detail the complex tempo variations the *czardas* contains and discuss precisely when and where its gypsy rhythms should be allowed to speed up or slow down. Some of the interpolations from other operas incorporated into this production require careful rehearsal—Dennis O'Neill's sudden burst of 'Di quella pira' and Hermann Prey's histrionic 'Lebwohl' from *Die Walküre*, and a snatch of *Figaro* that Domingo later decides to drop. 'When exactly do you do your laugh?' Domingo asks Hildegard Heichele. 'And do you think your next line should be over the orchestra, or would you like me to hold the orchestra back until you have finished?' Doris Soffel, a superbly epicene Prince Orlofsky with a handsome head of long blonde hair that will be covered by a bald wig once the show opens, has to toss a vodka bottle across the stage to Ben Luxon who at one rehearsal drops it. Luxon is an ex-gymnast and in Act I performs a first-rate cartwheel; not the man to drop a bottle more than once.

At most operatic rehearsals in which Domingo is involved he tends to be ubiquitous, chatting to everyone and checking on everything when not actually required himself on stage. Paradoxically, when the entire performance and not just one part of it is to be his responsibility, he is uncharacteristically tied down hour after hour in one place. It is odd seeing Domingo, stick in hand, head bobbing up and down in the pit, unable to join in as Doris Soffel and Ben Luxon relax in the stalls watching their colleagues on stage, or as Kiri Te Kanawa gives Hildegard Heichele a superb display of keep-fit exercises. In the half darkened house, Hilde Beal slips discreetly up over the bridge on to the stage for a word with Michael Langdon, and producer Richard Gregson follows her. From the stage there are periodic exchanges with the prompter and waves to the wings, while in the recesses of the auditorium are countless whispered conferences and confabs. Yet to almost none of this can Domingo afford to be a party. He has too much to do and the conductor's desk is the only place from which most of it can be done. 'Can you sign to me with your hands the way you'd like to take this passage?' Kiri Te Kanawa, perhaps not yet fully conversant with all the details of her role and anxious in any case to save her voice, is merely marking her part in quiet *mezza voce* most of the time, but Domingo needs to get an accurate idea of the tempo and sound balance he requires from his orchestra. 'Chorus,' he calls out on another occasion, this time availing himself of the microphone by the conductor's desk, 'can you please do a big *diminuendo* on that last "*stosst an*" and come right off after the third beat?' He illustrates the point: '*STOSST AN! STOSST AN! STOSST A-a-an* OFF! The soloist has to come in very low and mustn't be drowned.'

Domingo is constantly responsive to the needs of his singers. There is no sense of an orchestral virtuoso trying to whip up the instrumental textures for effect, nor of a maestro anxious to demonstrate the importance of his new role at the expense of his old. On the contrary, if some of Domingo's tempi are on the leisurely side this is often to accommodate his singers, though his instincts in this kind of music probably in any case favour lilt over brio.

The first-night audience enjoy themselves hugely. The hero of the evening is Hermann Prey, an explosive bundle of energy and infectious good humour whose combination of artistry and sheer panache helps carry the evening along at a cracking pace. Indeed, with Prey and Luxon on stage, an abundance of good music and good fun is guaranteed. Dennis O'Neill's compulsive little Italian tenor gets a well-deserved ovation as does Hildegard Heichele's irresistible Adele. Domingo himself brings the house down when the Act III comedy routine calls for the Maestro to join Meinrad in a couple of lines from *Aida*. There are opening-night nerves from some in the cast, particularly in Act I when Covent Garden's vociferous prompter more than earns his fee. But in general the show goes well and the cast have every reason to enjoy the congratulations that Prince Charles and other members of a distinguished audience shower on them at the end. The singers eventually make their way across to the new wing to change while Domingo alone climbs back up the old stairway to the conductor's room where his wife and boys and a tiny handful of special friends await him. 'Well, that was some evening, eh?' he grins as he gives Marta a huge hug.

There is an awful lot of *Fledermaus* over the next couple of weeks: seven scheduled performances, of which the one on New Year's Eve is to be shown live on television and filmed for distribution by National Video. This means the cast have two days of special TV rehearsals for BBC producer Humphrey Burton and his team, plus rehearsals on the day itself with the surprise guests who will feature in the New Year's Eve party scene. Thus, during the dark, dead days at year's end, as London sleeps off the torpor of Christmas, Domingo and his colleagues are on almost daily call.

Almost, but not quite—which enables Domingo to fulfil yet another engagement in his diary, a new recording of Puccini's *Manon Lescaut* for Deutsche Grammophon. As at Covent Garden back in May, the conductor is again to be Giuseppe Sinopoli, but Deutsche Grammophon have engaged Mirella Freni rather than Kiri Te Kanawa for the title-role. The recording is to take place in Kingsway Hall, known to the world at large as the former head-quarters of Methodism in London and of Britain's great Methodist preacher Donald Soper, but to musicians long famous as one of the locations most favoured by the recording companies.

In its day the hall was doubtless quite grand, with its gently sloping wooden floor and balcony facing a tiered stage and organ—just the place to rally the faithful. More important, all that wood helped give Kingsway a live, reverberant acoustic that few recording studios could match, while the hall's location at the end of a long corridor back away from the Kingsway traffic immured it from all extraneous noise except the occasional subterranean tube train. For some years, however, this aging hall has been threatened with demolition and every recording has been rumoured to be its last. By the end of 1983, the front entrance is boarded up and you have to enter by a semi-bolted side doorway. Inside, the place is badly in need of a coat of paint it is never likely to get, while the whole structure looks as though it might collapse like the walls of Jericho under the impact of one loud orchestral chord. Backstage facilities are crude and inadequate, though Deutsche Grammophon do their best by providing their singers with coffee and biscuits in the little, unsoundproof room they share. In this room, Domingo and Freni and Renato Bruson who sings Lescaut and Kurt Rydl who sings Geronte warm up their voices, sip coffee and chat to their producer, just as Maria Callas and Tito Gobbi did twenty-five years before. From this little room Domingo and his colleagues can hear Sinopoli outside rehearsing the orchestra, correcting it almost bar by bar to ensure the players' familiarity with every nuance.

The orchestra is the Philharmonia, of which Sinopoli will officially become Music Director halfway through these very sessions, on New Year's Day 1984. This is the orchestra originally created by the brilliant and curmudgeonly impresario and record producer Walter Legge as a standard-bearer for his own company, EMI. The strong link between EMI and the Philharmonia continued through various vicissitudes, including Legge's attempt to disband the orchestra, up to the 1980s and many of Riccardo Muti's EMI recordings. But Sinopoli has been assiduously courted by Deutsche Grammophon and it is to this company that the Philharmonia's efforts are increasingly likely to be devoted while he is their musical boss.

Sinopoli and the orchestra already know each other well and the players respond superbly to his often dramatic variations of tempo and dynamic in Puccini's passionate music. He jumps—literally off the ground at times; he crouches down for a *pianissimo*; he shakes his stick and his left arm impatiently as he awaits silence. In his high-pitched, cracking voice, Sinopoli speaks broken but rapidly improving English to the players, excellent German to Kurt Rydl and to producer Günther Breest, Italian to Domingo, Freni and Bruson. When Sinopoli feels the orchestra is ready, and this may be as much as fifty or sixty minutes into a three-hour session, he calls his soloists.

Domingo, like many singers, dislikes the process of recording and re-recording short takes over and over again. It is disconcerting, too, to have to work intensively on sections of an opera in an order unrelated to that in which they occur in the work: a death scene one day, an earlier love duet the next. Deutsche Grammophon have managed to slot Domingo's recording calls around his *Fledermaus* performances: three (or six) hours of *Manon Lescaut* on a couple of successive days, *Fledermaus* the next, then more *Manon Lescaut*. An excessive workload for the period around New Year? Not by Domingo standards. On two extraordinary days, the 28th and 29th December, Domingo commutes several times back and forth between Covent Garden, where he conducts for Humphrey Burton's television rehearsals for *Die Fledermaus*, and Kingsway for *Manon Lescaut* sessions. The really marathon TV session is the first, on the 28th. Domingo conducts piano and singers all morning and into the afternoon as Burton and his team plot every move, each camera angle, each lighting effect. Then, handing over the baton to Robin Stapleton, Domingo hastens over to Kingsway where he and Freni spend from four until seven o'clock working on the latter part of Act I of *Manon Lescaut*. Then by 7.45 p.m., as the long, wearying TV rehearsal drags through its ninth hour, Domingo slips back into the darkened Covent Garden pit. 'Hi, Placi!' waves Kiri Te Kanawa, the first to notice his presence back at the helm. He waves back.

The following day's TV rehearsal is scheduled to last a mere five hours: from 10 a.m. until three. Domingo is in the pit for the first act and back again from Kingsway (where Sinopoli records brief sections from three different acts of *Manon Lescaut*) in time to conduct most of the third. Kiri Te Kanawa has bowed out of this rehearsal and in the course of the day Rosalinde is played by a variety of substitutes. Humphrey Burton needs to see a body on stage and Rosalinde's movements are beautifully performed by Covent Garden Ballet Mistress Romayne Grigorova. Romayne sat in on the earlier rehearsals, occasionally going on stage to twirl a balletic couple this way or that in the party scene. But she has taken in every detail of the production and knows much of Kiri's dialogue by heart. She is prompted, particularly in the German lines, by Hilde Beal who is sitting in the wings, while the voice most prominent when it comes to

Rosalinde's turn to sing is the lyrical if somewhat unexpected one of *répétiteur* Gareth Morrell in the prompter's box. To this trio of Rosalindes is added a fourth: the indefatigable Hildegard Heichele who, later in the proceedings when she is offstage, stands in the wings, score in hand, sways delicately with the music, and sings Rosalinde's lines for the sheer joy of it.

The Day of the Four Rosalindes is followed by a day of well-earned rest for the *Fledermaus* cast, but not for its conductor, who has six hours of *Manon Lescaut* recording sessions. Domingo is feeling the strain. He tells people, quite justifiably, that Covent Garden is draughty and that standing in the pit hour after hour, he has been particularly vulnerable. It is, after all, only a month since he had a severe bout of tracheitis and he is understandably more concerned about the state of his vocal health than usual. At Kingsway he does much drinking of mineral water and of soup to keep his throat clear. He and Freni have the big duet at the end of Act II to record today, perhaps the most demanding few minutes for the tenor in the entire opera. Not the sort of music you can sing in full voice more than a couple of times even when in the best of health—particularly with the intensity of Sinopoli's interpretation to contend with—not to mention the sheer volume he obtains from his orchestra. Domingo wears earphones as the only way to judge clearly the quality of his own singing.

'People think that in a recording you can go over things again and again until you get them perfect,' he says, 'but that's really not true.' Certainly he and Freni pour everything they've got into the first take and it is hard to imagine them having to repeat this music many more times. As Domingo sings, his face and body take on all the suffering, the pleading, the disdain, the yearning of des Grieux, while his fingers alternately caress the air, conduct the orchestra, clench defiantly—or, when he has a free moment, pour yet more water to drink. Freni and Domingo sing not to each other, of course, but to their allotted microphones. But as they take a few bars of rest after some passionate outpouring, each steals a glance at the other. Freni cocks an eyebrow, purses her sensual lower lip, or pretends to slit her throat. She is always making amusing self-deprecatory gestures, tongue out, eyes crossed, and Domingo smiles back, gives her a reassuring little touch—or raises his eyebrows as though acknowledging his own inadequacies. 'It was a good take,' he says when they have listened to the tape—but of course they have to do it once more. They start at the end, with a long sustained high note which Sinopoli needs them to do two or three times before he is satisfied—then it is back to the beginning, des Grieux' entry with the rapidly rising lower strings and the first appearance of the 'Tea for Two' theme, and these two consummate artists give another stunning performance of the entire duet.

As with the rehearsal of an opera, recording can often involve singers in a great deal of sitting around with nothing to do, punctuated by relatively brief periods of intense activity. Unlike at rehearsals, however, the periods of activity require singing of real performance quality; each 'take' may prove to be the one finally used. One afternoon at Kingsway, Sinopoli has the Covent Garden chorus present and spends almost the entire session rehearsing and recording various choral sections of *Manon Lescaut* in which the solo interpolations are mostly brief and episodic. The most substantial is the roll-call of prostitutes in Act III and the surging chorus (with searing phrases from Manon and des Grieux) to which it leads. A great deal of time is spent—just as it was when the opera was rehearsed at Covent Garden eight months before—getting the awkward tempo changes right during the scuffle that precedes des Grieux' 'Pazzo son', though the big tenor outburst itself is not required today. Then, with just ten minutes to go before the end of the session, Sinopoli asks Domingo to sing the Act I *arietta* 'Tra voi belle', which contains staccato choral 'ha-ha-has' in the middle section. For this Domingo needs to find a bright, sunny vocal quality, quite different in mood and timbre from the sombre desperation of Act III. It is a disconcerting gear change to make, but Domingo is game, and his entire persona seems to change. His eyebrows go up, his lower lip projects forwards in a smile, the fists unclench, and the voice acquires a youthful, almost innocent sound appropriate for this early moment from the opera. He sings the little aria once, with a rich, sustained top note in the penultimate phrase, then again for luck. Three minutes to go. The choral interpolations are not quite together so Sinopoli asks for the second half of the aria again just once more. And then, in the dying seconds of the session, one *final* final time. When Domingo reaches the high note he attacks it from on top, enriches it, savours it—and then caps the aria with a perfect little final cadence. In ten minutes Domingo has had to do as much singing as in the previous 170. The Covent Garden chorus give him a burst of good-natured applause which he acknowledges with a smile. They are good friends, he and they; he has been conducting them all this week and last in *Die Fledermaus*.

New Year's Eve starts early for the opera folk; by midday Act II of *Die Fledermaus* is already set up and final rehearsals for this evening are under way. Domingo decides to drop plans to sing during tonight's party scene, but those guests who are to do a star turn need to go over their numbers and Domingo in any case wants to make sure the Covent Garden orchestra is in tip-top form. Some of the special guests—cellist Paul Tortelier and family and the musico-comic duo Hinge and Bracket—will do their own accompanying. But for Domingo's *ancien collègue* Charles Aznavour a full instrumental backing is required and Domingo patiently takes the orchestra of the Royal Opera House through 'I'll Be There' and 'She'. Aznavour looks dwarfed by the huge Covent Garden stage and his *boîte de nuit* voice needs considerable amplification if it is to fill the house. As he rehearses he complains that his voice has been raised too high so that he can no longer hear the orchestra properly. Orchestra up, Aznavour down . . .

There is a special air of tension and excitement at the opera house today. It is not every night of the season that an entire performance is to be shown live on television and everyone is anxious for things to go well. But the tension is not only artistic. During these past weeks London has lived under threat of a renewal of the terror campaign periodically mounted in the capital by the Irish Republican Army (IRA), and in one notorious incident earlier in the month a car bomb outside Harrods killed and maimed a number of innocent bystanders. Covent Garden itself has recently been the victim of several bomb scares necessitating interrupted performances. These are jittery days for Londoners, and every suspicious car or package and every threatening phone call is treated with the utmost respect and circumspection. The Royal Opera House is, even under normal circumstances, an obvious target for groups like the IRA that might wish to cause embarrassment or worse to the nation's rich and mighty. But tonight of all nights, with an audience of several million looking in on an occasion being filmed for posterity, Covent Garden could provide a dangerous magnet for malevolent political attention-seekers. Everyone working in the building has been issued with a security pass and the normally informal Stage Door staff are augmented by uniformed police officers. 'May I see your pass, please, sir?' one of them asks big, bearded Michael Langdon as he arrives with his wife. Even prison governors are not exempt.

As performance time approaches and the public begins milling around the front of the house, last minute artistic and security checks and preparations are made within. Down in the staff cafeteria, Dennis O'Neill queues up for a hot drink and waves across to Robin Stapleton at one of the tables. In the corridors outside the dressing-rooms in the new extension, make-up girls wait to be summoned by the owners of the faces on which they shortly have to work, while up in the large opera studio, amid varied evidence of *Wozzeck* rehearsals, photographer Zoë Dominic sets up her gear for a possible portrait session with Domingo.

In the main foyer it is soon time for the BBC's Richard Baker to set the scene for tonight's television viewers, while the Covent Garden staff discreetly steer the live audience towards their seats. Promptly on time the house lights dim and a roar of applause heralds the appearance of tonight's conductor. Tired? You would not think so looking at him now. Domingo arrives at the podium with a spring in his gait, acknowledges the applause with a debonair smile, and throws himself with enormous energy into the overture.

It is a long evening and things take a little while to warm up. But at the end of four hours an ecstatic audience, showered with silver confetti from the dome and with balloons and streamers from the balconies, is dispatched with a riot of happy memories: first-class singing and acting from all the principal singers, a spectacular and good-humoured *pas de deux* from Merle Park and Wayne Eagling, vintage comedy from Josef Meinrad, and real party spirit emanating from the pit. It is an evening for party-ing, and after the final curtain there is more to come for the lucky few—a happy end-of-year celebration in the Covent Garden Crush Bar at which champagne, Johann Strauss's 'King of Wines', continues to flow as liberally as it had earlier on stage.

But as the guests in the Crush Bar await their hosts, let us slip back briefly onto the stage itself, past Julia Trevelyan Oman's huge painted flats representing assorted princely ballrooms and prison walls, past an artificial potted fern from Act II, round into a darkened recess. Here, Plácido Domingo, flushed from the success of the evening into which he has just put so much work, is surrounded by friends and family who, security or no security, have found their way up to share his triumph with him. 1983 has not always been the easiest of years for him and its last few weeks have involved considerable strain. But its final hours have been carried on wings of song, and Domingo looks well set to embark on whatever challenges and opportunities 1984 holds in store.

Carmen in Vienna

'Glücklich ist, wer vergisst, was doch nicht zu ändern ist,' sing Rosalinde and Alfred in Act I of Die Fledermaus. 'Happy is the one who accepts what cannot be otherwise.' This ability to wed self-indulgence to cool realism might be taken as a motto for the city in which Fledermaus was written and first performed. The Vienna of Johann Strauss II was the brilliant, dynamic capital of a vast, multi-national empire that extended far beyond the confines of Austria. This was Vienna, indeed, until well into the early years of the twentieth century. Four decades or so later, Austria had lost its empire, been briefly and catastrophically annexed to Hitler's, and emerged blinking from the nightmare of Nazism to find itself an occupied, middle-European stateling. Yet its capital, Vienna, a head largely robbed of its body but still more or less intact, soon showed every promise of becoming, once again and against all the odds, one of the great social and cultural centres of the new Europe. Certainly the Vienna that welcomes Plácido Domingo in mid-January 1984 may not have much in common with the Vienna of Die Fledermaus which Domingo has been helping to recreate these past few weeks. Yet it is still palpably a happy city, *gemütlich*, contented with the lot history has carved out for it.

Vienna is conservative as great cities go, its cultural life more dominated by the legacy of its past than in an equally ancient but more cosmopolitan metropolis like Paris or London. 'Grüss Gott!' say the Viennese in greeting, the older men raising their hats. Hat shops, now almost a thing of the past in London, thrive still in central Europe with their displays of brimmed, feathered Tyrolean hats or, this time of year, expensive circular fur hats *à la russe*. Vienna maintains its trams, its coffee houses where you can sit for hours with the newspapers, and—if only for the tourists—its horse-drawn *fiaker*. The giant wheel at the Prater, carefully reconstructed after destruction by Allied bombing, is still a feature of Vienna, its little red cabins hanging precariously like baubles on a Christmas tree, the sole survivor of a series of such wheels designed by a British engineer in the late nineteenth century for parks in Vienna, Paris, London, Chicago and elsewhere. And the old Habsburg opera house lives on too, despite even more devastating bomb damage. On 12 March 1945 the Allies scored a direct hit, reducing to ruins much of the building except the front façade. Opera houses all over Central Europe were destroyed during the war. Some were rebuilt according to the most modern architectural principles and some were never rebuilt, but in Vienna the decision was taken to reconstruct the opera almost exactly as it had been before. Care was taken to incorporate into the new building whatever up-to-date technical and back-stage facilities it could accommodate. But the Vienna opera looks today very much as it did a century ago. If you go into the no-smoking foyer on the right of the great staircase in the interval of the opera, you will find the Viennese parading slowly in an anti-clockwise direction much as their ancestors did in imperial days. And if you stand outside the Wiener Allianz building opposite and look up at the opera house between the two winged horses, you will see, now as then, a dedication to the Emperor Franz Josef II.

A conservative city and a conservative opera house. But not parochial. Vienna may like to take succour from its past, but the history from which it seeks sustenance is not merely local. The

Austrian Empire was always far more outward looking than that. Indeed, you would not expect a city that hosts a major United Nations complex and the headquarters of OPEC and which prides itself on being a bridge between East and West to turn its back on cultures other than its own. The very week, for example, that Domingo is to open in *Carmen*, the Vienna State Opera, the Staatsoper, is presenting works by a Czech (Smetana), a Russian (Tchaikovsky), an Italian (Verdi), and a Frenchman (Bizet) as well as an Austrian (Mozart), while over at the Volksoper the big hit is an evening of Gilbert and Sullivan. At the Burgtheater there is Shakespeare and Camus. *Peter Pan* is in town. So, doing unquenchable business in Vienna as elsewhere, is Andrew Lloyd Webber's *Cats*, showing to sold-out houses night after night in the Theater an der Wien which once saw the première of *Fidelio*.

The politics of musical Vienna are legendary. Mahler, who was Director of the opera house from 1897 to 1907, was not the first, and the new director Lorin Maazel will assuredly not be the last, to become painfully enmeshed in them. It is probably in part a question of local style, tradition, temperament. The Viennese take their music seriously, and as conscientious guardians of the legacy of Haydn, Mozart, Beethoven, Schubert and Brahms, feel they have some right to snipe at anything less than the best. Since the real men and women responsible for live performances are inevitably flawed by comparison with the gods of the past, there is always good sniping to be had. Mahler was much criticized while here, though he is a god today. Karl Böhm, who guided the fortunes of the opera during the difficult mid-1940s and again when the rebuilt house opened in 1955, resigned a year later after a hail of criticism. Herbert von Karajan succeeded Böhm in 1956, stayed eight years and was controversial throughout. Nobody seriously questioned the quality of performance the house achieved under Karajan's directorship. He introduced new works, brought Vienna a widened French and Italian repertoire in the original languages, and found time not only to conduct but also, after he had appointed an assistant director, to produce a number of productions himself. In the Böhm and Karajan years, the 'Vienna style' associated with singers like Elisabeth Schwarzkopf, Irmgard Seefried, Erich Kunz, Anton Dermota and

Sena Jurinac, and later with Lucia Popp, Gundula Janowitz and Christa Ludwig, reached pinnacles of glory. But for all this, Karajan, too, aroused enmities among the Viennese opera-going community—which his imperious style did nothing to abate. Karajan fell out with his own assistant director and resigned in a huff in 1964, and it was only with the arrival of Maazel in 1982 that the Vienna opera once more had a practising musician as its director.

To some extent the politics are built into the system. The Wiener Staatsoper is historically and constitutionally a creature of government. Historically it was owned, run and funded by the Imperial Court and it is as a direct legacy of its days as the Court Opera that it is today owned, run and funded by the State. The Vienna State Opera is now one of four theatres (the others are the Volksoper and the Burg and Academie Theatres) run as a group by the Austrian Bundestheaterverband, a body directly under the aegis of the Ministry of Culture and presided over by a Ministry appointee. There are advantages to this system. The people who run the four theatres can work as a team, share and exchange theatrical expertise (scenery and costume creation, for example, or transportation and storage facilities), and can lobby the Ministry jointly when they have grievances. Budgeting is done collectively and because some cost-sharing is possible under the system the money consequently available to each theatre is considerable. Vienna is an expensive city. Labour costs are steep, and the opera pays high salaries to its chorus and orchestra and its regular roster of outstanding solo singers and, unlike many houses elsewhere, gives them contracts that include substantial pension rights.

Vienna is an opera city. This is not only to say that more people go to more opera in Vienna than in many other cities. In the scales by which these things are weighed, the Staatsoper is a more prominent presence to the Viennese than, say, Covent Garden is to most Londoners, the Met to New Yorkers, or even La Scala to the Milanese. When he took up his post, Lorin Maazel is reputed to have said that, after the President and Chancellor of Austria, the most important person in Vienna is the Director of the Staatsoper. This sort of attitude may not exactly have gone down well with Maazel's masters in the Ministry of Culture but it does contain a kernel of truth. When I asked a Viennese friend why there seemed relatively little controversy over the huge sums of money the Staatsoper received each year he answered by comparing it to the monarchy in Britain—one of those grand institutions that most felt the public purse should continue to maintain even if they had little personal experience of it themselves. A clever analogy, for just as there are few out-and-out republicans in Britain (though many would criticize aspects of the Royal Family), so there seem to be few Austrians, certainly few Viennese, who begrudge the Staatsoper its annual millions, yet many who enjoy malicious gossip about ways the money is spent. In one vital respect, however, the analogy falls down. Of all aspects of the British monarchy, the one least likely to receive serious public criticism is the person at its head, the Queen. At the Wiener Staatsoper, by contrast, it is traditionally the beleaguered Director at whose door much of the criticism is laid.

Having been appointed Director, Maazel was determined to act like one. In his first season tired old productions were retired, some controversial new ones introduced, performances clustered in 'blocks' with every production allotted proper rehearsal time—and woe betide the old hand singing his 150th or 200th performance of a part who failed to turn up for every rehearsal! None of this was calculated to bring Maazel instant affection. His private life became a topic of Vienna gossip. So did his salary, and the quality of his administrative appointments, some of them apparently made without prior consultation with his political bosses. Maazel was accused of accepting too much work outside Vienna and of not conducting enough performances in his own house—a criticism the Ministry of Culture was known to endorse. The seamy residue of Viennese antisemitism reared up once more, too. Maazel is not—well, he's not *echt* Viennese, people say with a superior and knowing look, just as they said it about Mahler eighty years before.

A year and a bit into his appointment, Maazel is, at least in public, fairly thickskinned about all this unpleasantness and takes comfort from the fact that several of his most distinguished predecessors also had to contend with the most virulent opposition. Maazel has three jobs, really: he is both artistic and managing director of the Staatsoper and he also has to conduct a share of performances —twenty-five in his first season, pushed up against his will to forty by the Ministry in his second. Nobody, he reflects, could take on all that responsibility and fail to be controversial—unless he did all three jobs in an anodyne way. Anodyne he is emphatically not. And so the critics keep their knives permanently honed, and *Carmen* has every promise of presenting a golden opportunity for the Maazel-baiters.

Excitement mounts in Vienna as *Carmen* approaches. 'CARMEN AUSVERKAUFT' say window stickers in the city's ticket agencies, though spare tickets regularly sprout up for other Staatsoper performances. Record shops make a display of 'Guests In Our City' and nobody in Vienna can fail to notice that Plácido Domingo is shortly to appear in town. If you do not look at the opera ads or the windows of the ticket agencies or record shops, your eye may catch the posters telling you that Domingo is to take part in an all-star football match down at the Kurhalle in Oberlaa on the southern edges of Vienna, or those advertising the annual Vienna Philharmonic Ball which is to be opened in the presence of the President of Austria by Domingo, who will conduct the orchestra in the overture from *Die Fledermaus*. Other prominent posters tell you where and when Domingo will be available to sign copies of his book, while yet others tell of an already 'Ausverkauft' zarzuela concert he is to give.

The musical life of a peripatetic star like Plácido Domingo is essentially a series of themes and variations in which works and opera houses and colleagues constantly reappear in shifting permutations. This Vienna *Carmen* illustrates the point. The work itself is of course extremely familiar territory. Domingo has recorded the work three times, filmed it for Gaumont, and performed the role of Don José in the major opera houses of the world more often than any other in his repertoire, with the exception of Cavaradossi in *Tosca*. Nor is Franco Zeffirelli's Vienna production new to Domingo for he starred in its opening opposite Elena Obraztsova in 1978 when it was shown on television all over Europe. Of the *Carmen* cast, the Escamillo (Ruggero Raimondi) and Micaela (Faith Esham) were colleagues in the Gaumont film. They have been engaged, after all, by Lorin Maazel, conductor of these performances, Director of the Vienna State Opera—and conductor of the Gaumont sound-track.

The one relative novelty as far as Domingo is concerned lies in the person playing the name part. Maazel has not engaged the Gaumont Carmen. Julia Migenes Johnson's voice could scarcely do full justice to Carmen's music in a large theatre, though Maazel introduced her to the Staatsoper recently in the even more taxing, but higher, name part in Berg's *Lulu*. The singer he has cast is the Greek mezzo soprano Agnes Baltsa, someone with whom Domingo has not worked much before, though some indication of the electricity they can generate together can be gauged from the video of the Covent Garden *Hoffmann*. Baltsa as Carmen, dark-haired, bright-eyed, skinny, sexy, has a tendency to overact vocally and bodily that can give rise to *frissons* of ecstasy among many and of disdain among some. As she twirls and spits, jumps, pouts or glares, as her rich mezzo breaks below the *passaggio* into a deep velvety contralto at odds with her waif-like appearance, she positively demands reaction—from her colleagues on stage, from José in particular, and from her audience. Baltsa's may not be the definitive Carmen; her interpretation is too flamboyant, some would say vulgar, for that. But it is the finest expression of one kind of Carmen. For more ladylike Carmens, go to the Spaniards, to Victoria de los Angeles or Teresa Berganza. But for sensuous passion Agnes Baltsa is the Carmen of many opera-goers' dreams.

Baltsa is a Karajan protégée, one of that distinguished band of singers and players whose talents were spotted early by Herbert von Karajan and carefully fostered and developed under his concerned guidance. A man of superabundant gifts as conductor, producer, lighting expert, film director, and assiduous perpetuator of his own legend, Karajan has always insisted upon the exercise of magisterial power and has aroused hero-worship and controversy throughout his long career. Such men can be difficult to deal with, dangerous when they make mistakes. But Herbert von Karajan does not normally make mistakes. He is not that kind of man. Certainly, he did not make a mistake when Agnes Baltsa presented herself to his attention. This, he knew, and he was right, was a singer to nurture. In January 1983 her most recent recording is the title-role of *Carmen*. Under Karajan.

Karajan is in town for a series of concerts with the Vienna Philharmonic Orchestra, though you would scarcely guess as much from the total lack of advertising. VPO concerts are not normally advertised. They do not have to be as most tickets go to those city elders lucky enough to hold inherited subscriptions. A venal system it seems to those excluded, but understandable. The Vienna Philharmonic was the first completely self-governing orchestra in the world and its 140-odd members still govern their own destinies and promote their own concerts, mostly in Vienna's ornate Grosse Musikvereinsaal, a golden jewel-box of an auditorium in Bösendorferstrasse possessed of perhaps the world's finest concert hall acoustics. If their time-honoured subscription system keeps the bank manager happy, who can blame them for not changing it? There is another VPO peculiarity, too. Most of the world's major orchestras rehearse in the day and give concerts at night. Not so the Vienna Philharmonic, whose principal concerts take place on Sunday mornings. At night its members have other things to do. For every evening, seven nights a week throughout the music season, these are the musicians who perform in the pit of the Vienna State Opera.

This particular Monday morning they are probably a bit tired as they play for the *Carmen* dress rehearsal under Maazel. They had a Tchaikovsky concert with Karajan in the Musikvereinsaal yesterday morning with rehearsals for both Karajan and Maazel the previous two days; at night they have had to perform *Cosi fan Tutte* on Friday, *Il Trovatore* on Saturday and *The Bartered Bride* last night, while Tchaikovsky's *Pique Dame* is scheduled for this evening.

The *Carmen* rehearsal is closed to anybody but those involved, but that does not stop a hundred people or more from finding their way into the darkened auditorium. Karajan is there, diminutive, white-haired, surrounded by aides and acolytes, a living legend. This house was once his. Karajan watches quietly as Lorin Maazel, casually dressed in open-neck black cardigan, undemonstratively takes his cast through Acts I and II. He directs with a flick of the wrist here, an imperious toss of the head there. He knows exactly what he wants and why. He stops once in a while to check some tricky passage, but is obviously confident that on the night after next everyone's eyes will be glued to him and all his signals will be scrupulously followed.

On stage, the plot of *Carmen* unfolds. Baltsa appears, pours out her rich, wine-red tone in Bizet's sensuous music, and hisses and slinks her way through the dialogue. Domingo, the vulnerability of his Don José complemented by pale make-up and a head and moustache of sandy fair hair, knows every detail of this production and is completely at home in Zeffirelli's staging—though Baltsa makes no secret of the fact that she thinks he ought to have turned up earlier to rehearsals. Since conducting his final *Fledermaus* at Covent Garden, Domingo has not been in Vienna but in Rome recording *Il Trovatore* with Giulini. *Trovatore* was his first complete opera on record (1969) and he had been looking forward to making this new version for a long time. How did it go, someone asks him as he comes into the auditorium during the scene change between Acts I and II of the *Carmen* rehearsal and chats to Karajan, Zeffirelli and others. 'Mission accomplished!' he answers with a smile.

Carmen is a long opera and needs a lot of rehearsal if it is to be done well. Zeffirelli, in grey flannel trousers and multi-coloured pullover and looking far less than his sixty years, has been watching from the production desk and is clearly not happy with all he sees. He too has not been in Vienna as long as some think he should have been, but then any opera house should count itself privileged if it obtains the services of the original producer for a revival and it is perhaps an indication of the prestige of this particular revival that Maazel has managed to persuade Zeffirelli to come at all.

When the statutory three hours are up, orchestra and most of the chorus are dismissed and a piano is wheeled on to the stage. Zeffirelli can work with his principals another hour or so, long enough at least to ensure that certain carefully choreographed set pieces will work successfully. Domingo and Raimondi go through their Act III fight. The stage is steeply raked and dotted with light-weight rocks, not the easiest territory for two men no longer in the first blush of athletic youth to have to enact both credibly and safely a vicious knife fight. Still, these two spent part of last summer acting out this very scene among the real rocks and rakes of Andalusia and it is not long before, puffing and smiling, they get their routine into shape. The ending of the opera needs to be done again. Baltsa, wearing her Act III red velvet jerkin and gypsy skirt, bites off her ring and spits it at José. He stabs her and she, clutching his body, slips down slowly to her death. She is asked to die again, even more slowly—and Zeffirelli brings up the shocked crowd behind José. 'Vous pouvez m'arrêter,' sings Domingo once more, in half voice, and this time Zeffirelli ensures there are soldiers close enough for him to be seen addressing. It is getting there.

As lunch-time for everyone else in Vienna comes and goes, people on stage cluster in little groups to discuss animatedly one final time this or that detail of the production. A curious, fluctuating network of linguistic contact establishes itself. The Greek Baltsa talks German to one colleague, the Italian Raimondi French to someone else, the Spaniard Domingo English to a third. Periodically a game of Musical Languages develops as a new player gets attached to one of the teams and Domingo finds himself trying out his German, Raimondi his English. At last there is no further talking that can usefully be done. Tomorrow Maazel has one more rehearsal, but without the soloists. Their job is to relax and to pace themselves for what will undoubtedly be one of the big nights in this year's operatic calendar.

The performance is due to begin early, at 6.30 p.m. *Carmen* has four acts and Zeffirelli's beautiful but complex sets require quite a while to change, especially between Acts I and II. Also, the stage staff must be free by 11 p.m. if the Staatsoper is to avoid heavy overtime costs and they must get the statutory number of hours' rest before they are required again in the morning. All through the day people mill around the theatre wondering whether there might by some miracle be a ticket available. Tonight, top price tickets cost 1,400 Austrian schillings (around £50) but rumours circulate of mid-price tickets changing hands for 5,000. As for the 500-odd standing places that even on this night the Staatsoper makes available for the regular price of 15 or 20 schillings—surely the best bargain in all opera—these could have been filled many times over, as the frantic queue of hopeless hopefuls on the freezing pavement makes evident.

Inside the house, most members of the cast arrive early. Domingo is already more or less ready to go on by 6 o'clock. He hums to himself, asks his make-up man for a little more shadow here and there, greets friends he sees in the mirror. The men's and women's dressing-rooms at the Staatsoper form the two long sides of a rectangle linked at the bottom by a room containing the only piano (a

Bösendorfer) available to the singers. Domingo wanders into the piano room, touches the keys and sings a few scales and arpeggios, up to top C and back. The voice is in excellent shape and was of course already warmed up earlier in the day. He walks up the corridor past his own dressing-room and looks in to see if Kurt Rydl, tonight's Zuniga, is around. Toreador Ruggero Raimondi is not here yet; his first appearance is not until well into Act II.

The doors on either side of the piano room close discreetly. Someone wants a few moments' private warm-up. The someone turns out to be the Vienna Boys' Choir who are taken through their little ragamuffin chorus just once more for luck:

> *Nous marchons la tête haute,*
> *Comme de petits soldats . . .*

In twenty minutes they will be singing this before the two thousand people even now settling in their seats. A few more arpeggios from Domingo, and Maazel appears for a final word of encouragement. From the room with the Bösendorfer piano comes the voice of tonight's Carmen as Agnes Baltsa runs over her opening phrases rather as you might check that your ticket and money are safely in your pocket before embarking on a journey.

> *Peut-être jamais . . . peut-être demain . . .*
> *Mais pas aujourd'hui, c'est certain!*

By now the auditorium is humming with eager anticipation. At the back just below where you might have expected to find a Royal or Presidential box, several hundred standees are crammed, the lucky ones finding a velvet-wrapped bar on which to lean. The standees have already had a long day and most would be dropping with exhaustion were they not sustained by excitement at what is to come. The great house they look out into is handsome but not extravagantly so. In many opera houses—Covent Garden or La Scala, for instance—the colour abiding most strongly in the memory is plum red. The Vienna State Opera contains its quota of red but it is the whites, yellows, golds and browns that predominate. It is a brightly lit house, the necklace-shaped chandelier (some call it a doughnut embellished with sugar crystals) bringing out the paler hues of the auditorium. The velvet curtain is a lightish brown, and the safety curtain, embossed with a representation of the Orpheus legend, largely plated gold. The proscenium arch is mostly gold too, and—unlike the pre-1945 original—unembellished. No clock or monarch's head or chastity belt here. There is an austerity about the Staatsoper auditorium that may surprise a visitor expecting 1860s' embellishment.

This is a house in which sight and sound vary considerably from one section to another, and this variation is precisely reflected in a carefully graduated price structure whereby tickets come in perhaps twenty different denominations for each performance. From the sides above the stage or the back of the side boxes the sharp horseshoe curvature means you can sometimes hardly see the action. In addition, although the Staatsoper is generally blessed with a good acoustic, there are areas where even a strong chorus can scarcely project its sound across the wide orchestra pit (one of the few with no stage overhang above) and others where string sound is almost obliterated by brass. For all this, however, the Viennese were surely right to reconstruct the house largely as it was originally built. The front staircase and side and front foyers are grand yet welcoming and from anywhere reasonably central in the house—and that includes the privileged herd of parterre standees—sight and sound are superb. Like all the greatest houses, the Wiener Staatsoper becomes a place of magic as its lights begin to go down: the doughnut at the top, then the concealed lights in the layers of boxes that encircle the auditorium. Silence. Applause.

Lorin Maazel appears, bows, and with a confident flourish transports everyone into nineteenth-century Seville. When the big brown curtains part they reveal Zeffirelli's wonderfully lazy Spanish town square. The drama unfolds slowly at first, Maazel's deliberate tempi seemingly designed to give everyone time to savour the scene before them. Few in the first-night audience notice Domingo's first entry on stage, disguised in his fair wig and moustache,* as he gives orders to the soldiers under his command and the Vienna Boys take front stage

---

* In later performances he was more recognizable, moustache-less and with his own dark hair.

with their urchins' chorus. Fifteen minutes before, one of these very ragamuffins was begging Don José for his autograph.

The drama does not really begin until Carmen herself makes what must be one of the briefest opening appearances in operatic history. She runs barefoot on to a corner of the stage, picks up a drink from a table and pours it provocatively over the men staring at her, pivots sharply around, and runs off again. The excitement generated is tremendous, and by the time she is back on stage singing her Habañera a few moments later, Baltsa's—and Zeffirelli's—stagecraft has every pulse beating that much faster.

Baltsa is tremendous, the jumping and the spitting, the vocal velvet and grit each having dramatic point. *'Bohémienne? Tu crois?'* she asks José with mock incredulity as she insinuates herself into his affections, if only to avoid going to prison. José's honesty, naïvety even, is marvellously portrayed by Domingo. As Carmen tells him seductively what it will be like at Lillas Pastia's, he looks about him, distinctly uncomfortable, puts a cigarette in his mouth, lights a match—and is so transfixed by this impossible woman singing to him that he forgets to blow it out and burns his finger.

Already as Baltsa, Domingo and Faith Esham in her blonde Micaela wig take their first bows at the end of Act I, the stage hands are demolishing the town square and setting up the ramparts of Seville and the tavern of Lillas Pastia. In his dressing-room during the interval Domingo drinks water, talks quietly to Marta who has come round from the auditorium, signs photos his patient but persistent secretary Paul Garner thrusts under his nose. Faith looks in and gets a big hug. Half her work is done for tonight, though she still has her aria to sing in Act III a nerve-wracking hour and a half later. In the corridor Domingo passes a team of BBC engineers who are in Vienna working on a television portrait of Lorin Maazel; they filmed the prelude to Act I and he asks them how they got on.

The second interval bell rings and as the audience settles back into its seats crowds of exotically dressed Spaniards, incongruously talking Viennese German to each other, assemble backstage in the darkened wings. A few wander on to the set and take up positions around the central figure of Carmen. They can all see a blurry black-and-white image of Maazel on the various backstage television monitors as he returns to his position, though it is not obvious to them how much booing Maazel has to contend with alongside the applause. Maazel raises his stick, waits for all the audience commotion to subside, and begins. As the curtains part, Baltsa is revealed sitting, eyes smouldering, on a raised table at the back of Zeffirelli's brilliantly evocative rampart inn, knee raised high under a voluminous gypsy skirt, one long, black-stockinged leg visible like a tent peg through a darkened doorway. As the musical pulse quickens Carmen is joined in song by Frasquita and Mercédès and in her movements by authentic Spanish dancers specially recruited by Zeffirelli from Madrid. The whole scene becomes a whirling mass of sensuous sound and colour, and the audience goes wild when the music and movement reach their climax. It is Raimondi's turn for the spotlight at last and he swaggers on and gives a full-throated performance of his famous song, possibly the most famous in all opera. In the wings, Carmen's friends Remendado and Dancaïre join in the last reprise of the Toreador's chorus to sing themselves in before their own entry, just as a solo violinist might play along with the orchestral fiddles at the opening of a concerto.

The main emotional thrust of this act lies in the confrontation between Carmen and José. As Domingo's voice approaches, Baltsa primps herself and removes a dark skirt to reveal a scarlet one underneath, and then prepares to sing and dance for José. 'Where are my castanets?' she shouts angrily to the wings. At rehearsal she delivered this line with such savagery that it seemed the negligent stage hands had forgotten a vital prop. But the question is part of the production, and the prop that *is* indispensable, the plate Baltsa smashes as a substitute for the missing castanets, is at hand on the edge of the table. Baltsa works her way through this scene with the total conviction of one who believes no man could resist her. As she swivels and sings up there, clinking her broken fragments of china, a pair of trumpeters line up off-stage. To the precise beat of a member of the Staatsoper music staff who watches Maazel on the TV monitor and listens to the orchestra through earphones, the trumpeters play the Retreat that Bizet interweaves so subtly with Carmen's song. Carmen, you haven't understood me, sings José, it's the Retreat—I have to return to barracks. Carmen laughs at him, mocks him, mocks the trumpets, tells him to go if going is so important to him. At last, desperate, José pulls out the flower she once threw him. This is Domingo's aria and, as Baltsa sits quite still and looking away from him, he pours out a stream of glorious, plangent tone at once rich, restrained, pleading. When this production opened and was shown on television the audience gave Domingo an ovation that lasted a full four minutes before the uproar finally died down. Today, he gets a mere two—still an absurdly long time for any singer to have to wait, head in hand, immobile and in character, before the action can resume.

Act III looks almost as much like the hills of Andalusia as the hills of Andalusia, Zeffirelli's realism augmented by the arrival of Carmen and José on a horse. Faith Esham oils her voice by joining in, from the wings, the last few bars of the smugglers' chorus and then comes on and gives a much-applauded account of her aria. The Domingo–Raimondi fight looks good from out front but does not leave either man so puffed that he cannot sing the bars of music still left to him. 'Nous nous reverrons!' José warns Carmen with murder in his eyes and voice, while offstage Raimondi belts out his jaunty Toreador song one final time.

Minutes later the hills of Andalusia have been raised and the outer walls of a bullring lowered. Act IV begins without its accustomed orchestral introduction—this is interpolated later as a dance number. Instead, a brilliantly lit stage is revealed, thronged with a festive crowd to whose exuberant singing is added the sound of pre-recorded shouts and whistles. Horses appear as part of the procession to the bullring, and then backstage are hurriedly given other riders and led on for a second appearance. They are followed each time by a man in period costume unostentatiously carrying a shovel and pan. Eventually Escamillo himself appears, and the crowd and sound effects surpass themselves. How will Zeffirelli manage the sudden gear change from huge, expectant crowd to the gentle, intimate Carmen–Escamillo duet? By the simple but brilliant expedient of bringing on altar boys and a priest who draw the crowd's attention away to a Madonna the other side of the stage.

At last the stage is almost empty except for Carmen. A menacing figure in a dark, toga-like wrap appears over the brow of Zeffirelli's raked stage. 'C'est toi!' 'C'est moi!' The final scene of the drama is about to unfold. For much of the evening Domingo has paced his performance in such a way as to complement Baltsa's and keep the emotional spotlight where it rightly belongs, on Carmen herself. But as the drama has progressed, Baltsa's Carmen has developed a greater internal intensity while Domingo has allowed José bit by bit off the emotional leash. The carefully calibrated counterpoint of these two characters reaches its climax in the final scene as Carmen displays icy resolution in the face of danger and José pleads, implores, threatens, prays and eventually kills. 'Jamais je n'ai menti; entre nous tout est fini,' sings Baltsa with frosty finality at the start of their duet, almost as though defying José to murder her. 'Mais moi, Carmen, je t'aime encore!' Domingo responds, the desperation in his voice all the more piercing for the controlled restraint of much of his singing earlier in the evening. As the screw turns ever more tightly, José finds Carmen's repeated rebuffs almost insupportable. 'Pour la dernière fois, démon, veux-tu me suivre?' The eyes are the eyes of Canio in Pagliacci, of Otello, of a man at the very frontier of homicidal jealousy. In the wings a few feet away Domingo sees the Staatsoper chorus as they sing of Escamillo's victory; as Don José he turns to them, black eyes blazing madly, and sees a crowd celebrating the victory of his woman's lover. Almost delirious, he stabs Carmen, and as her beautiful, dead body sinks slowly down his, he sings his final, heart-breaking 'Ma Carmen adorée' and then limply allows himself to be arrested. José has taken control of destiny and Carmen succumbed to it—a final reversal of roles that gives the whole evening a thrilling yet terrifying coherence.

All acting, you may say, but once the curtain has gone down and the ovation begun to erupt it takes Baltsa and Domingo several minutes to regain their customary composure. They walk slowly together towards the curtain, faces still set in tragedy, go through the gap, and acknowledge the tremendous burst of applause that greets them. Gradually, both are revived by the bright auditorium lights, the 'bravos' and the flowers, and as they return to the stage and the congratulations of friends and colleagues, each begins to smile again for the first time since the final scene of Carmen began. Already, unseen by the audience out in front, Zeffirelli's Madonna and other removable props are being carried off while in the shadow of his bullring the rest of the cast assemble. Domingo knows from previous experience that the applause in Vienna can go on for a long time. After his previous appearance here it continued for over an hour. 'It is a small city, people can get home quickly, and performances end early,' he says modestly by way of explanation. In some houses, once the initial curtain calls have come and gone it is largely up to the principals themselves to decide if and when to go out again. Not so in Vienna. 'Meester Tomingo and Tseffirelli, please,' intones the assistant stage manager by the curtain. Domingo is embracing Marta, Zeffirelli doing a twirl on his own raked stage and posing for a photo. But when you are called you go. 'OK. Tutti frutti, please!' This time the whole cast is wanted. The applause goes on and on, and on both sides of the curtain there are smiles, waves, embraces and bouquets. Someone on stage peeps through the tiny spy-hole in the lower corner of the curtain. Hundreds of people are standing, some because they are on the verge of leaving, most as a sign of appreciation for a wonderful evening. At the sides and near the front are the seasoned bouquet-throwers. Further back, the few who insist on booing when Maazel appears. Do they know—does *he* know—that a bare two months later the Ministry of Culture will announce that his contract with the Staatsoper is not to be renewed?

Outside the winter winds bite fiercely, but not so fiercely as to prevent two or three hundred people waiting a further hour or more outside for autographs: Maazel's, short, almost calligraphic, Zeffirelli's, long, curvy—and legible. Agnes Baltsa appears, sits at a desk just inside (Domingo will do this next time), and works her way through the crowds who are let in to the presence in threes and fours. Faith Esham emerges with a group of friends, carrying an enormous bouquet of flowers. Nobody recognizes her in her own hair. Faith's friends give her a final hug of congratulation and bundle her into a taxi. Back to the hotel? No. She is on her way to the Spanish Embassy, for tonight's festivities are to end with a dinner given by the Spanish Ambassador in honour of Plácido Domingo.

Vienna was a happy time for Domingo. Friends and relatives came over from Spain and elsewhere to see him perform, and not only in *Carmen*. There was the Vienna Philharmonic Ball in the Musikverein, one of the top social events of the Viennese year. As the hour of the Ball's ceremonial inauguration approached, far more people than the Musikverein's architects can ever have anticipated crowded into the boxes and galleries of the Grosse Saal, the men impeccably attired in evening dress, some with decorations and ribbons, the women in the most sumptuous ball gowns. From whatever perch they could achieve, the galleries groaning under the unaccustomed weight, the *eleganti* of Vienna peered over each other's shoulders down towards the great hall, temporarily emptied of seating, as the distinguished guests arrived to a prolonged fanfare of trumpets. The last to enter were the President of the Austrian Republic Rudolf Kirshchläger and, looking resplendent in white tie and tails, Plácido Domingo. Domingo conducted the Vienna Philharmonic in a rousing and idiomatic performance of the *Fledermaus* overture, warmly applauded by an audience looking like guests from Prince Orlofsky's party. 'What a wonderful orchestra!' Domingo had said earlier after a brief rehearsal with the VPO. He had tried out one or two nuances which he had not done in London, and the orchestra had responded instantly. That night, once the dancing begins, Domingo is in the thick of it and soon loses himself in a mass of whirling figures.

Next day hundreds of people patiently form a shivery queue outside the offices of the Friends of the Vienna State Opera in the Goethegasse opposite the Hofburg Park. The line stretches along the Goethegasse and all the way down the Hanuschgasse to the Albertina Platz. Inside, Domingo, in suit and tie, sits at a table and patiently works his way through the crowd like a sympathetic doctor in his surgery and eventually signs over 800 books, records and pictures.

And for those to whom Domingo dressed as Don José and in white tie and tails and lounge suit are not enough, there is always Domingo in football togs. Accompanied by several of his operatic colleagues, his sons Placi and Alvaro, and several of Vienna's better known actors and journalists, Domingo celebrated his forty-third birthday playing soccer in a large indoor stadium in the southern suburb of Oberlaa. It is probably fair to say that the spectators on this occasion were not for the most part stalwarts of Vienna's sports-loving public, if only because most of those were probably at home glued to their television sets that particular afternoon watching the 'Kitzbühel '84', one of the major international skiing events of the year. Mind you, any genuine sports fans who *were* at the Oberlaa Kurhalle that day would have had the bonus of seeing Austria's brilliant centre forward, Hans Krankl, in action.

As the crowds filled up the layers of seats, the hall echoed to the sound of Domingo's latest pop album—Moon River, Bésame Mucho, I Couldn't Live Without You—though even Domingo's much-amplified voice was drowned by applause when the teams appeared. After renditions of 'Happy Birthday' and the presentation of a golden 'Perhaps Love' disc and sundry birthday cakes, including one shaped and coloured like a football and made of marzipan, and a 'welcome-to-my-world' football boot from Krankl, the serious business of the afternoon got under way with a ceremonial kick-off from long-limbed soprano Patricia Wise. In his scarlet Adidas shirt and shorts Domingo made it his chief aim to place himself near his opponents' goal in position to receive the uncannily accurate passes Krankl regularly placed at his feet. At Domingo's first goal the crowd went into ecstasies and Domingo himself, in a hilarious parody of Latin-American footballing styles, raced over to where Marta was sitting, knelt to the ground, and cast his eyes and fists repeatedly up to heaven.

Not surprisingly, with so much talent available, Domingo's team always looked like winning. There was Placi haring down after even the most unreachable ball, and Alvaro, who takes his athletics very seriously, playing perhaps a more strategic and less tactical game. There was Kurt Rydl, his reverberant bass voice unmistakable whenever he called out for a pass; of all the operatic footballers Rydl seemed to have the most staying power—just as well for a man who sings roles like Gurnemantz in *Parsifal*. Above all there was the world-beating partnership of Hans Krankl and Plácido Domingo—Krankl everywhere, dribbling the ball as though it was attached to him by a piece of taut elastic and then dropping it onto Domingo's feet right in front of the goal. At the final whistle, Domingo's team had won by 18 goals to 8, and the Birthday Boy had scored seven of them.

One night after a performance of *Carmen*, Domingo and some forty-five of his friends assembled in Vienna's Astoria Hotel for a supper party given in his honour by CBS. Or, to be precise, Domingo's friends assembled there but he himself was delayed for an hour or more signing autographs. Eventually, around midnight, everybody moved towards the huge dining table, shaped like an 'H' with a long middle bar, Marta and Plácido helping to supervise people into linguistic clusters—the Spanish speakers, including the Spanish Ambassador, melting into a German-speaking group, with a predominantly Anglophone cluster beyond. Just as the wine and conversation were beginning to flow, a massive pink-and-scarlet shape materialized through the doorway, a thousand carnations on legs. The legs bearing this sumptuous gift proved to be those of Prince Alfonso von Hohenlohe; Alfonso had had the carnations specially flown in from Spain. Plácido was visibly overwhelmed. He draped himself in the Spanish red and yellow ribbon in which the carnations had been wrapped and presented every one of his guests with a bunch from Alfonso's floral cornucopia, taking time to talk to everyone around the big 'H' as he went. It was nearly three o'clock before people began to take their leave, and once again Marta and Plácido managed to talk to everyone individually before the grand dining room was finally empty. Empty, that is, except for bunches of carnations scattered here and there which the guests simply could not carry with them.

I didn't get to bed until four that night. At eight I was up again, dry-throated and bleary-eyed; I had to get to the airport for a flight back to London. Shortly after ten, a welcome mug of coffee inside me though still heavy-eyed and unshaven, I was in line to check my baggage when I spotted a familiar figure walking towards me in the airport lobby, wearing a peaked cap and dark coat and carrying a carefully-packed suit as hand luggage. It was Plácido, looking as sprightly as I have ever seen him. He was with his uncle Pedro and a Spanish friend and his daughter. Plácido came over and we had a brief chat. He was off to Madrid for a day; there was a dinner that evening at which Prime Minister Felipe González would be present. He waved a cheery goodbye, and bounced off.

CHRONOLOGY

June 1981	*Tosca* in Central Park, New York Completion of 'Perhaps Love' album in New York
July 1981	*Otello* in Bregenz, Austria
August 1982	'My Life for a Song' recorded in London (completed in November)
November 1982	'Call Me Kiri' for BBC-TV *Fanciulla* at Covent Garden Ceremony at Royal College of Music
December 1982	*Ernani* at La Scala, Milan *Carmen* recorded in Paris
February–March 1983	Metropolitan Opera, New York
May 1983	*Manon Lescaut* at Covent Garden 'Always in My Heart' (Lecuona songs) recorded in London *Tosca* at Liceo, Barcelona
June 1983	*Fanciulla* in Madrid
June–August 1983	Filming *Carmen* in southern Spain
October 1983	'Le Grand Echiquier' in Paris
November 1983–January 1984	Conducting *Die Fledermaus* at Covent Garden
December 1983–January 1984	Recording *Manon Lescaut* in London
January 1984	*Carmen* in Vienna

Titles of operas are listed according to
the version and language used in the text

INDEX

INDEX

INDEX